STEPHEN GIRARD

STEPHEN GIRARD

America's Colonial Olympian, 1750–1831

James J. Raciti, PhD

SUNSTONE
PRESS

SANTA FE

Sunstone books may be purchased for educational, business, or sales promotional use.
For information please write: Special Markets Department, Sunstone Press,
P.O. Box 2321, Santa Fe, New Mexico 87504-2321.

Book and cover design › Vicki Ahl
Body typeface › Goudy Old Style
Printed on acid-free paper
∞
eBook 978-1-61139-385-9

Library of Congress Cataloging-in-Publication Data

Raciti, James J., 1933-
Stephen Girard : America's colonial olympian, 1750-1831 / by James J. Raciti.
     pages cm
Includes bibliographical references and index.
Summary: "Biography of a Colonial/Revolutionary-era American patriot, philanthropist, and founder of
Girard College in Philadelphia, Pennsylvania, who, by the early eighteen hundreds, had become the richest
man in America"-- Provided by publisher.
  ISBN 978-1-63293-070-5 (softcover : alkaline paper)
 1. Girard, Stephen, 1750-1831. 2. Philadelphia (Pa.)--Biography.
3. Bankers--United States--Biography. 4. Merchants--United States--Biography.
5. Philanthropists--Pennsylvania--Philadelphia--Biography. 6. Girard College for Orphans. I. Title.
 F158.4.R33 2015
 974.8'03092--dc23
 [B]
                          2015017624

Sunstone Press is committed to minimizing our environmental impact on the planet. The paper used in this book is from
responsibly managed forests. Our printer has received Chain of Custody (CoC) certification from: The Forest Stewardship Council™
(FSC®), Programme for the Endorsement of Forest Certification™ (PEFC™), and The Sustainable Forestry Initiative® (SFI®).

The FSC® Council is a non-profit organization, promoting the environmentally appropriate, socially beneficial and economically
viable management of the world's forests. FSC® certification is recognized internationally as a rigorous environmental and social
standard for responsible forest management.

WWW.SUNSTONEPRESS.COM
SUNSTONE PRESS / POST OFFICE BOX 2321 / SANTA FE, NM 87504-2321 /USA
(505) 988-4418 / ORDERS ONLY (800) 243-5644 / FAX (505) 988-1025

To Girardians
Past, Present and Those
Yet to Become

Olympus was notable in Ancient Greek Mythology
as the Home of the Twelve Olympians.
In Colonial America, Stephen Girard held such a distinction.

Stephen Girard, 1750–1831. Posthumous portrait by Bass Otis.
Gift of Henry A Ingram to US Treasury Department.
From the Treasury Department Collection.
Courtesy of the Treasury Department.

Acknowledgments

From concept to review to completion to publication, my wife, Maryhelen Raciti-Jones has been the shepherd of this book. Without her support and hard work, we would not have reached this culmination.

I would also like to thank the administrative staff of the Centre D'études Supérieurs for facilitating microfiche support for documents, certificates and personal letters of Stephen Girard.

Contents

List of Illustrations

Frontispiece: Stephen Girard, 1750–1831

Significant Dates—Life of Stephen Girard

1750—Birth of Stephen Girard

1762—Stephen Girard's mother dies

1764—Girard's first experience at sea

1767—Pierre Girard remarries

1772—John Girard becomes ill with Yellow Fever

1774—Girard visits California / Fails at his first trading effort in San Domingo
In July, Girard Meets Thomas Randall

1775—Merchant Trade New York to New Orleans

1776—Girard's ship driven by British Navy into Port of Philadelphia / Stephen meets and marries Mary Lum

1778—Girard becomes citizen of Pennsylvania

1787—Mary Lum is declared insane
Girard takes a mistress, Sally Bickham / Girard begins global trade

1788—United States Constitution ratified / Pierre dies

1789—French Revolution begins

1790—Colonies become the United States of America / Mary Lum committed

1791—Slave uprising in West Indies

1793—Philadelphia has yellow fever epidemic

1794—Five ships of Girard's fleet seized by Great Britain and France

1796—Girard occupies house on Water Street

1797—Another yellow fever outbreak

1798—Congress passes Sedition Bill

1800—Girard wins Republican Select Council seat

1801—Thomas Jefferson becomes President of the United States

1802—Public Education begins in France

1803—John Girard dies

1805—Battle of Trafalgar is fought

1807—Girard purchases Market and Chestnut Streets properties

1810—First United States Bank opens

1811—Girard purchases stocks in expired bank lease

1812—War with Great Britain / Girard rescues US Treasury

1813—British frigate captures *Montesquieu*

1815—Real estate purchase surge

1816—Girard urges US Government to establish Second US Bank

1822—Girard loses two vessels in shipwreck, *Voltaire* and *Montesquieu*

1825—Danville & Pottsville Railroad built

1830—Auction of First US Bank

1831—Stephen Girard dies at age 81 of pneumonia

Introduction

November 19, 2014

Dear Mr. Girard:

Please forgive the formality of this salutation. It is not a usual way for a son to address his foster father. I am, however, only one of many thousands of foster sons you have provided for through your kindness and foresight. From the date of this letter, one hundred and sixty years have passed since your orphanage which is now known as Girard College first opened its doors. I cannot speak for the many fatherless boys that have passed through the gates of the college. I shall speak only for myself.

I entered the college in 1940 at the age of six. My older brother Charles was admitted the year before. We lost our father in August 1938 from a major heart failure. My mother with her two aging parents and two small boys remained the sole wage earner. No two children could have been more fortunate in being admitted to your beautiful campus. Where you once saw rolling green pastures in the eighteen twenties, today we see a busy metropolis. South Philadelphia in your day was mostly farm land. By the nineteen thirties, it was inhabited mostly by recent immigrants from Southern Europe.

As a six-year-old newby, I did not understand the financial burden my mother faced. I only wanted to know why she was giving me away, probably not a unique sentiment among the children. In 1940, Girard College had reached a significant enrollment size, just about 1700 students.

The boys were poor, white orphans more in need of assistance at this particular time because of the effects of The Great Depression and gathering menace of war in Europe. The number seventeen hundred was to be a high mark in enrollment which we didn't realize at the time. That's a far cry from the three buildings which would house about three hundred boys that was anticipated in your will. At this writing, the college makes no distinction of race or sex. The black slaves that you saw commonly serving their white masters were emancipated by the sixteenth President of the United States, Abraham Lincoln. All slaves were freed just as you freed your Hannah and provided her with support for the rest of her life. You admired Benjamin Franklin and his desire that education should be available to all young men regardless of their ability to pay. Also on the campus of Girard, we now see young girls as students. In your day it was not considered proper to educate girls beyond the necessary skills of keeping a home and being wives and mothers.

But I digress. We were speaking of Girard College in 1940. The west end of the campus was reserved for the House Group. If my memory serves me, there were six sections A through F. Each section had a governess and consisted of about thirty of the youngest boys living in an atmosphere most resembling an ideal American home. The buildings were constructed in white marble and formed a semicircle which surrounded the playground area. At the far end of the playground, there were two cement pools which I had the pleasure of splashing in during the summer of 1941. We had no knowledge or care of how the world was falling apart across the sea. Our minds were filled only with the memories of our recent vacation at the Girard College Camp in the Poconos.

The overall layout of the House Group was well planned and pleasant. A senior housemaster oversaw the Group. There were two entrances into each section—one main entrance into the dayroom area and another into the service area where a seamstress worked to repair and organize the laundry for the boys. At the far end of the dayroom was the dining room where the boys had their three meals daily. I remember that there were three long tables and a single round table for the governess and guests.

From the dayroom one could go up to the dormitory, washroom and showers. The boys quickly learned the daily routine so that a simple ringing of a bell would indicate that a line was to be formed for meals, for going outside to play or for going upstairs to shower and prepare for bed. During the winter months there was little urging necessary to get the boys up to bed at eight o'clock. During Daylight Saving Time, however, it was another matter. Nobody wanted to go upstairs to bed while the summer sun was still shining. Our free time in the dayroom allowed us to do our homework or play games. The organized dayroom time usually meant that the governess would read to the boys until it was time to go up to bed. On Sundays the governess would read from the Holy Bible. This again was your plan to have no professional church people enter Girard but rather have the Bible read by lay people.

One disadvantage to being in the House Group was that classes were held in the Junior School. It was about a fifteen minute walk for little legs going up the Main Road past the Mechanical School on the left and the Baseball Playing Field on the right. The Mechanical School consisted of a shop for drafting, sheet metal work, foundry work, printing, patternmaking and automotive training—today motorized vehicles called "automobiles" have replace horses and carriages.

Once in high school, the boys would be rotated through the various shops in order to teach them the basics of all the trades. This Mr. Girard was the direct result of your insistence that the boys' education be well rounded to include academic subjects as well as trade experience.

The Junior School building, for older boys, was rather large and included two wings divided in the middle by the dining room services and other services for support of the dish washing and laundry. If my memory serves me, there were four sections in each wing. The West Wing included sections 9-12; the East Wing included sections 5-8. After spending only one year in the House Group, I was moved with my class to Junior School. I was assigned to section 10 along with about forty boys. The Junior School was also constructed in white marble that met with your wishes for buildings made of permanent materials. The Junior School playground was much larger than the one we had in the House Group. There were two areas for sand lots. The larger of the two had swings, a jungle gym (climbing bars) and seesaws. Often the more courageous boys would climb to the top of the jungle gym and jump down onto a pile of sand, daring others to do the same. It's a wonder no one broke a leg.

Other boys would find different ways to spend their time. One such pastime was to create a small amusement park where marbles could be shot into various holes in the sand. Missing a hole meant forfeiture of the marble; hitting the hole meant receiving another marble from the "owner" of that particular establishment. In the height of its popularity, one could see a row of marble games all along the length of the sandlot. There was also a game called "Chew the Peg" which involved a contest between two boys to throw a sharp sick into the ground (knives were not permitted). If a stick failed to penetrate the soil the thrower would have his peg pounded into the ground until it could barely be seen. The loser then had to pull out the peg with his teeth. No sooner had we boys invented a game than the housemaster would evaluate its worth and invariably outlaw it.

Across from the playground of the Junior School was the playground of the Middle School. West of that playground was the Armory. Here, during my high school days, classmates and I would take part in military drills of our battalion. We learned how to march, carry our rifles and prepare for parades. A retired army colonel had the responsibility of supervising the drills. Students could study the manuals to be promoted to officer ranks within the battalion. I was surprised to learn, in later years that the battalion had been eliminated.

Across the street from The Junior School and a bit farther to the east was the building "Good Friends," named after your valued relationship with the Quakers of Philadelphia. Not only was a building named Good Friends but it was the name of one of your finest ships. Next to Good Friends was the building "Lafayette," named after General Lafayette who served with General Washington against the British during the War of Independence. These two buildings, residences for teenage students, were very old and had to be torn down. On the same side of the street a bit farther east was our magnificent new chapel.

Across from the chapel were several buildings that no longer exist as I remember them—the infirmary and dental clinic. I spent eight months of my first year at Girard in the infirmary. I was admitted on December 13, 1940 for whooping cough. I was given my first pair of glasses in the third grade when my teacher asked me if I had trouble seeing the blackboard. I had the pleasure of having a molar drilled and filled—sans Novocain at the dental clinic when I was in the fourth grade. My only medical intervention which involved cutting was a below the belt procedure—not one of my fondest memories.

The eleven years I spent at Girard were years of change. The Ginny (gingerbread cookie) baked in our own bakery was outsourced to a bakery shop off campus. It was not the same. How I wish I had put one aside as a souvenir. The strict dress code of my younger years included a cap, a tweed jacket, a shirt and tie, tweed knickers, long stockings held up with an elastic band and the marvelous brogues—high top shoes great for kicking a soccer ball. As I reached middle school we were all yearning to wear long pants. The first ones went to the tallest boys in the class. I was not in that group.

Eventually we were all given long pants. The next on our agenda for change was to convince the authorities that we needed colorful sports jackets. They agreed. In high school, we petitioned to spend Saturdays and Sundays at our homes within the city limits. This was a hard nut to crack because our attendance at chapel services on Sunday mornings was required. How could we not use such a beautiful chapel? In time this was also approved.

The only resident building, aside from those in the House Group, which I did not live in was Banker Hall. When our class arrived in high school, half of the class went to Banker Hall and the other half went to Merchant Hall. We all went to Mariner Hall in our junior year and to Allen Hall in our senior year. The only buildings that I did not mention were the Library, The Dining and Services Building (D&S) and Founder's Hall.

The D&S Building was a place for dining rooms, rooms for sewing and ironing and related administrative and cleaning functions.

An hour each week was scheduled for the classes to use the library. This was a free hour except for those who had to prepare papers for their teachers. I was surprised by the appearance of the library on my last visit there. I didn't see any books. It must have been in transition.

Founder's Hall was referred to as the "Main Building" in your will. It was a building dedicated to you, Mr. Girard. At the main entrance are your statue and sarcophagus. We gather there on special occasions to further honor your memory, especially your birthday—May 20, 1750. Behind Founder's Hall there is a playing field, mostly used for our soccer and our track teams. A contest that I entered in my sophomore year was to have students suggest ways they would improve activities at Girard College. I was fortunate enough to win second prize. One suggestion I made was accepted—to use the second floor of Founder's Hall for something that the students had been requesting—a break room and candy store. We were all pleased when this was accomplished.

Founder's Hall had been used for various purposes. Aside from housing many of your records and business papers, there were pieces of furniture and other household items from your own home. The junior and senior classes had been given permission to use a downstairs room for end-of-year dances. Also in your collection, there is a light weight carriage called a "gig." This gig, we learned, was for a single horse which you used to go out to your farm. There is also a portrait by Nicholas Vincent Boudet of Sally Bickham, your first housekeeper and companion.

I am now at the age you were when you invested in coal mines and the railroads that made them accessible. I cannot help but speculate that it would have taken generations of Stephen Girards to make your financial legacy function to your liking. Administrators, some good and others not so good handled your monies as best they could while juggling their careers, their personal ambitions, political leanings and their families. They didn't have your laser beam of analysis, preparation, insight and dedication. With diminishing funds, the college can afford fewer expenditures each year. Would you have done better leaving your will to be administered by your family? You knew your siblings and their offspring and you decided not to entertain that idea. And while we are speculating, what if you had had a son or daughter of your own? Although this would have created a profit motive or impetus, it might also have engendered greed and internal squabbles. Your Girard College has run for more than one hundred fifty years.

Although many of your conditions, outlined in the will, have been set aside, the college still educates young people in need. In your lifetime, you would often sell off property that no longer met your rigid standards. What would you do with Girard College today? Would you have found a more challenging goal for yourself in education, where many more would benefit at a less demanding per capita cost? Like Montesquieu, Rousseau, Helvetius and others that you admired who had lost a parent, you felt a need to help the poor male orphan. But you, Mr. Girard lost both parents—your mother to death and your father to his self-absorbed lifestyle. No funds for education or support did he ever provide for you. From your writings, I have concluded that a young man who has been nurtured simply but well and given an education to prepare him for the demands of his world has all he needs to succeed. The Girardian does not inherit a fortune but is prepared to make one of his own, if he has the ability and the desire. Like you and many others, I received nothing material from my family, but what I received from Girard College has been enormous and I shall be always grateful. My philosophy has been to pay it forward, even before I knew the meaning of the term. I hope that my donations to causes that I feel close to have some positive effect—not on a grand scale like yours but I believe that paralyzed soldiers and hospitalized children need assistance at a more fundamental level. If you were alive today, I think you would not necessarily want us to pay back to help support the college but to find our own ways of helping the disadvantaged of our society.

With warm affection and gratitude,

James J. Raciti
Class of 1951

Note to the Reader

The following will give you an idea of the events, times, places and influences of Stephen's early years.

While the infant Stephen Girard was involved with those occupations of a newborn, his country—France was once again in conflict with England. This time in North America with the British imperial officials when frontier tensions had exploded in what was named The French and Indian Wars. The war began in 1754 and ended with the Treaty of Paris in 1763. The war pitted France, French colonists and their native allies against Great Britain, the Anglo-American colonists and the Iroquois Confederacy which controlled most of upstate New York and parts of northern Pennsylvania.

In Williamsburg Virginia, a young man of seventeen, schooled in mathematics had been made surveyor of the new County of Culpeper. He presented his credentials from the College of William and Mary to the court and was directed to take four oaths of office. The first oath was to the King; the second oath was to not support the issue of James II; the third oath was to disbelieve in the principle of transubstantiation and the fourth oath was to his new profession—that of a surveyor. George Washington who was later to command armies and become the first President of the United States had heard of the bravery of the French-born Philadelphian who almost single-handedly fought off the yellow fever epidemics while most of the well-to-do patrons of the city fled for their lives.

While Stephen Girard was still a young child in France, far away in his later-to-be adoptive city of Philadelphia, Benjamin Franklin flew his kite in a thunderstorm to experiment how lightning was the same force as electricity. It was June 1752.

Young Stephen would later learn that the border between French and British possessions was not well defined, and one disputed territory was the upper Ohio River Valley. The French had constructed a number of forts in this region in an attempt to strengthen their claim on the territory. British colonial forces, led by Lieutenant Colonel George Washington, attempted to expel the French in 1754, but were outnumbered and defeated by the French. When news of Washington's failure reached British Prime Minister Thomas Pelham-Holles,

Duke of Newcastle, he called for a quick undeclared retaliatory strike. However, his adversaries in the Cabinet outmaneuvered him by making the plans public, thus alerting the French Government and escalating a distant frontier skirmish into a full-scale war.

It was a time of great intellectual movement in France. Not far from the university town of Grenoble, across the Swiss border in Geneva a young man drew the attention of the French court by making his philosophical beliefs known to the literary world. At the time of Stephen Girard's birth, Jean-Jacques Rousseau was thirty-eight years old. Jean-Jacques was to lose his mother while she gave birth to him, a fact that was to resonate with Stephen whose mother died when he was still a young boy. Jean-Jacques was born of French Protestants. His father Isaac Rousseau was a clock maker. He had little time for his son and was unaware of the lad's voracious appetite for reading. Of the many contributions that Rousseau made in music, theater, education and philosophical thought, the work that influenced Girard the most was *The Discourse on the Origin of Inequality* written in 1753. Could it be that Girard, this little man, deformed from youth, a target of hateful pranks, armored his heart against pain and thought that his only recourse in life to balance the scales was to amass such a fortune that could not be ignored—a fortune that would make him respected, if not loved, feared if not followed?

Preface

Bordeaux, like many French cities, especially those close to the sea has had inhabitants as early as 300 BCE. They were Celtic tribes living along the Garonne River. Although their history there is much older, the inhabitants have left very little in their wake from ancient times. We know that the Romans ruled the area in 60 BC and that the settlement became the capital of Roman Aquitaine. In the 16th century, it was a slave distribution center. It was in Bordeaux that Michel de Montaigne retired to his country estate, at the age of thirty-seven to write his personal essays. Those of us today who enjoy the variety of wines from Bordeaux have the Romans to thank for the rich Medoc, Saint-Emilion and Pomerol to mention only a few. The 18th century represented its Golden Age with considerable town construction and trade development. To a family of merchant mariners came a young man to make a significant mark as a humanitarian who would touch the lives of thousands of students.

Material for the story of the life of Girard as mariner, merchant and banker is abundant. The Girard manuscripts number more than 50,000 pieces. Of these, 14,000 are contained in his office letter books and represent his side of a voluminous correspondence.

Stephen Simpson who knew Girard very well and had worked for him wrote the following in his preface to *Biography of Stephen Girard* which was written in 1832. "I am aware that in the following pages, I shall neither gratify his friends, who thought him infallible or satisfy his enemies who believed him to be everything that was frail. The truth will be found to lie between the two extremes. As to his genius, there can be but one opinion." It was indeed an unusual preface for Stephen Girard's first biographer to write.

I have consulted many sources for the information I've gathered. I have found some factual discrepancies in their biographies but have made no attempt to resolve them. Wherever possible I have cited secondary sources which highlight the Girardian authors who have more directly benefitted from a life within the walls of the college.

And finally, to answer the question: Why did I select the question and answer format to introduce Stephen Girard to prospective readers? I believe this Socratic style focuses on the essentials of the material, providing small portions of information at a time, with planned review passages that reemphasize salient facts.

Such key points can be more easily referenced and readily accessed. The questions are not numbered and may be read sequentially or not. Just as Girard would dip in and out of his feelings for his father and his siblings over the years, so can the reader open the book, during a short subway ride for example, and read whatever page comes into view. As with any description of life, events overlap and rarely stand alone in isolation.

1

Childhood

Chartrons, France
1750–1764

Who is Stephen Girard?

Stephen Girard first and foremost was a philanthropist and a visionary whose life has remained over the years a model and inspiration for generations of Americans.

Was Stephen Girard an American by birth?

No. Stephen was born May 20, 1750, near Bordeaux France, the largest seaport in the country. Stephen was the second of ten children. Pierre and Anne Odette Lafargue Girard's first child was a girl who lived only a few days. Girard was baptized Etienne at St. Seurin, a Roman Catholic Church in Bordeaux. He was named in honor of his godfather Etienne Souisse, an important citizen in Bordeaux. The Girard family had owned ships since 1642. Stephen's great, great grandfather left the inland city of Perigueux to live on the coast in Bordeaux.[1]

How many children were born to Pierre and Odette?

There were ten children born to this couple: Jeanne, born March 4, 1748; Etienne always known as Stephen, born May 20, 1750; Jean (John) born August 12, 1751; Madeleine, born February 2, 1753; Pierre Arnaud, born June 18, 1754; Anne Félicité, born September 26, 1755, died in infancy; Etienne II, born April 24, 1757; Anne Victoire, born August 31, 1758, feeble-minded epileptic; Marie Sophie, born July 17, 1760 and Louis Alexander, born August 26, 1761.

Who was Pierre Girard?

Stephen's father Pierre was a sea captain and merchant who had acquired a substantial fortune trading with the West Indies. Louis XV bestowed on Pierre Girard, the Royal and Military Order of Saint Louis for bravery during the 1744 conflict between France and England. From such fragmentary records as have come down to us it appears that Pierre Girard in his day was a man of force, a merchant of some importance and a citizen of distinction.[2]

Was there any possibility that Pierre might have been given a knighthood for his act of bravery?

The rules of the Order of Knighthood state that only a naval officer is permitted to be conferred after an act of bravery.

What was the reason he was serving in the naval services at that time?

It was the custom in those days to require would-be shipmasters to serve two years in the French navy before receiving their licenses to command merchant ships. In 1744, while Pierre Girard was serving his time, the war of the Austrian Succession began. He also became a pensioner of the French monarch. He was awarded the title of Burgess of the city of Bordeaux in 1767. Pierre was strong-willed and domineering and terrified his young bride as he was to do the children she was to have. Stephen was born in a tiny house at no. 2 Rue Ramonet. The entire ground floor was used by Pierre for his trading business. The small rooms on the second and third floor were the family's living area.[3]

Some biographers have written that Stephen Girard was born in the town of Chartrons. Who is right?

Both are correct. The town of Chartrons was a separate town in 1750. It was later integrated into Bordeaux.

Was Stephen Girard born to a privileged family?

The family was not privileged but comfortable. His father Pierre was strict about money and expected his children to make their own way in life. Girard was the oldest of the children and his father was eager to have his son follow in his footsteps. Stephen had natural intelligence but little education. When he was old enough, his father took him aboard ship and taught him the life of a sailor. By any standard, Pierre bullied Stephen, making the boy do all the chores that Pierre was too lazy to do himself.

Why wasn't Stephen given an education as a child?

He was tutored as a child by his mother and other tutors. He had no formal education. He was able to read and do math calculations. It must be remembered that public education was not available when Girard was a child. The governmental supervision overseeing public education was first created in France in 1802.

Were the schools established after the French Revolution coeducational?

No. It was the tradition throughout Europe that only male children would go to school. Girls would stay at home and learn household duties that would prepare them for being wives and mothers.

Did this education include religious training?

Yes. Girard's parents were devout Roman Catholics and brought up their children in the teachings of the Church. Stephen was baptized on the day after his birth.

Being the oldest child, did Stephen gravitate towards his father wanting to be like him?

Stephen did want to grow up to be like his father but because of his walleye, he relied very much on the warmth and compassion of his mother. Many have supposed that Girard had lost his eye entirely and that it was closed up but this is not the fact. The eye was entire though deformed and sightless. Simpson also states that Girard's eye was seen by a doctor who told him that a simple cutting of the film over the eye would restore his sight but according to his first biographer, Girard refused.[4]

How does biographer Henry Atlee Ingram explain the loss of Girard's sight of his right eye?

"At eight years old, as a result of throwing wet oyster shells upon a bonfire, the heat of which splintering the shells, a fragment entered Stephen's right eye at once destroying the sight in it beyond the hope of restoration."[5]

What were the main criticisms leveled at the writings of Ingram on Stephen Girard?

It is generally considered that Ingram relied too heavily on William Wagner's account on Girard and that Ingram gave too much importance to the life of John Girard in Stephen's affairs.[6]

Was there a reason that Ingram accentuated John's role?

Lawyer Henry Ingram was the grandson of Antoinette Girard Hemphill. His great grandfather was John Girard.[7]

To what extent was Stephen's childhood stressful?

Unfortunately, we know little of his boyhood. His biographers tell us that he was ridiculed because of his wall-eye. We also learned that he grew up shrinking from other children and living in a world of his thoughts. One could ask under what conditions did he leave his home in France? Details are few as to why he left home. One biographer states that Girard, at the age of ten or twelve, signed on a ship as a cabin-boy. Never had any boy a smaller capital on which to build a fortune.

Where did Pierre do his trading in San Domingo?

As a merchant Pierre Girard traded with the ports in the French part of the island of San Domingo. It was to Port-au-Prince, therefore, that Stephen went in 1764, on his first voyage as cabin boy in a vessel in which his father had taken a venture.

How did Stephen manage to go to San Domingo?

According to Elbert Hubbard, a Girard biographer, Girard intended to go aboard a ship as a stowaway. At about two o'clock in the morning, he said goodbye to his little sisters and walked down to the dock which was about a quarter of a mile from his home. He was well hidden while he watched the loading of the vessel. Just as soon as he stepped out of the darkness, planning to sneak aboard a man approached him. It was the captain who wanted to know if the lad could serve as cabin boy. Stephen jumped for joy and the Captain invited him aboard for coffee and a biscuit.[8]

Voltaire (1694–1778).
From the Portrait Gallery,
Perry-Castañeda Library,
University of Texas at Austin.
Courtesy of the University of
Texas Libraries, The University
of Texas at Austin.

Jean Jacques Rousseau
(1712–1778). Painting by
Allan Ramsay, 1766. Gallery:
Chateau de Coppet, Paris
France. [Public Domain].

Do we know if Stephen had time to read during his first voyage?

According to his biographers, he worked twice as hard as the other mariners. His strong arms and nimble feet had him climbing and running all day. He could see better with one eye than others could with two. In his spare time he did come into possession of a book lent to him by the first mate. It was a copy of Voltaire's *Philosophical Dictionary*. Stephen read it with great interest. His reading of Voltaire—seventy volumes—began from recommendations of his friend Baldesqui. Later he was to become acquainted with another French philosopher and educator Jean-Jacques Rousseau for whom he held great respect. Girard had held a membership in the Library Company of Philadelphia from 1790 until he died. His books were constantly overdue for which he paid all dues on time.[9]

How does Harry Wildes, one of Stephen Girard's biographers, describe Joseph Baldesqui?

"Baldesqui, a partner of Stephen's for a short time, was not wholly devoted to his work; the dashing Polish cavalryman lived in a dream world which had as its total population the fair ladies whom he sought to captivate."[10]

What became of Girard's friend and partner after their partnership ended?

Baldesqui retired in Germantown, now part of Philadelphia, where he set up a hair-powder factory.

How did the death of his mother affect Stephen?

Stephen was devastated as was the whole family by her death. Stephen at eleven probably felt it the most. Gone was his safety net; gone was the warmth and protective love he needed so badly in his life. His mother died at the age of thirty-six. Her death was probably brought on by birthing so many children and the difficulty of her life.[11]

How was Stephen described as a boy before the death of his mother?

Henry Ingram wrote: "He possesses precocious dignity and grave self-assurance coupled with a passionate and domineering temper."[12]

How did Pierre Girard plan to keep a large family with no mother for the children?

Pierre couldn't return to sea without providing a caretaker for the children. He managed to have his wife's half- sister, Anne Marie Lafargue, move into the house to serve as housekeeper and stepmother. She was Stephen's godmother and became the mother of the children. Pierre and Anne Odette Girard had been aware of Stephen's growing love for a life at sea and were keenly attentive as their young son outlined his dreams to them, dreams that would soon take him across the seas and, eventually, to a new home. Stephen's early childhood was not a happy one. He would serve as office boy for his father, was constantly blamed when things went wrong, was responsible for the welfare of the younger children, and was the object of his father's quick temper. His father was always stern with the boy and never played with him. In his eighty-one years of life, Stephen had never learned the meaning of carefree relaxation.[13]

How did Girard learn about his new step-mother?

In 1767, Girard was returning from San Domingo and learned that his father had remarried. She was Marie-Jeanne, a widow. Girard was sixteen at the time. By this wife, according to the record of baptisms in St. Seurin, Pierre had four children.

In 1760, when Stephen was ten years old, what was happening in France?

On September 8, 1760, Governor General Pierre, Marquis de Vaudreuil-Cavagnal, surrendered the French colony known as Canada. Britain assured the 60,000 to 70,000 Francophone inhabitants freedom from deportation and from confiscation of property, freedom of religion, the right to migrate to France, and equal treatment in the fur trade (backbone of the local economy). The Treaty of Paris made the northern portion of New France (including Canada and some additional lands to the south and west) officially a British colony. The Quebec Act of 1774 confirmed the previous agreement.

What voyage gave Girard his first feeling of independence from his family?

His first voyage was to the West Indies and this proved to be the starting point of his independence. He went from an unhappy home, ignorant, without funds and sadly unfriended and unknown to rise to the rank of merchant prince. This is surely one of the marvels of human history.

What does Ingram say about the breakup between Stephen and his father?

He speaks about an outburst at dinner when Stephen's stepmother scolded him. His father intervened against him saying that Stephen should learn to get along with the family or go out and live somewhere else. Stephen answered that he would go at once if his father would provide him with a place on board a ship leaving Bordeaux for the West Indies.[14]

How old was Stephen when he owned his own trading vessel?

Stephen Girard was sailing his own sloop, *L'Amiable Louise*, at the age of twenty-four. As a ship captain, he had the authority to trade, buy and sell. His first trip took him around Sandy Hook and up New York Bay.

In 1770, when Girard was twenty years old, what was occurring in France?

At Versailles, Louis, the French dauphin, married Marie Antoinette, the daughter of Austrian Archduchess Maria Theresa and Holy Roman Emperor Francis I. France hoped their marriage would strengthen its alliance with Austria, its long-time enemy. In 1774, with the death of King Louis XV, Louis and Marie were crowned king and queen of France.

Port of Bordeaux, France, 1770. Engraving by Darshan after an original painting by Clause Joseph Vernet. Europeana.eu/portal/record/9200365/.

How did Stephen manage to move up so quickly as a mariner? How would his good conduct and industriousness help the young man?

As a consequence of his good work, Captain Randall promoted Stephen at every opportunity. And in a few years, he was given the command of a small vessel and sent on trading voyages. It was not achieved through smiles or making compliments or social maneuvers. Stephen worked harder that anyone on board and would volunteer for any job that was available.

Had Stephen been to America before he settled in Philadelphia?

He had gone there with his father years before. This voyage, during which he was captain, took Girard westward, arriving in New York in July 1774. In short order, he became acquainted with ship owners and merchants in the teeming city. During a series of voyages to New Orleans on vessels owned by Thomas Randall, Girard managed a highly profitable business association for both of them. Stephen Girard began to develop an appreciation for the potential of the American market, buying sugar and coffee in the West Indies to sell in the new nation, while in return shipping American goods to the West Indies. This arrangement allowed him to quickly accumulate considerable capital.[15]

Father and son traveled together to New York several times. In 1764, when only 14 years old, Stephen, followed in his father's footsteps, went to sea. Girard was signed on as a Pilotin. Pierre arranged this appointment on his ship *Pélerin*, bound for Saint-Domingo in the French West Indies. Girard was glad that the sea had offered him a release from his father's tyranny.[16]

The ship's roster listed Stephen as an apprentice pilot (he proved himself to be a quick learner). He was grateful for the start his father had given him and in this capacity he began his study of navigation. When asked how he felt about going to sea so young, he said: "I have made my way alone with the means gained from my nurse, the sea."[17]

In what way did the merchants in Bordeaux take advantage of Girard's inexperience in purchasing cargo?

Among the items Girard had bought and hoped to sell were: twenty snuff boxes for ladies, fourteen dozen silver cords, a Solomon violin, beaver hats, velvet saddle cloths, gloves, lace, ribbons etc. It did not take Girard long to recover from his losses. In 1774, he was broke and a year later, after being employed by Thomas Randall, Girard had put aside 17,000 francs and not a sou would go to paying the swindling merchants in Bordeaux.

How did Girard get back at these unscrupulous merchants?

He took his revenge by not paying the merchants and allowed them to go for years without seeing the debt cleared.[18]

What important lessons did Girard learn from this disastrous trading experience?

He learned that San Domingo did not need trinkets but food. He resolved to sell American beef and flour in exchange for sugar, coffee and cacao.

2

Young Business Man

1764–1774

How did the inexperienced businessman Stephen Girard learn about extending credit?

Girard trusted a young Dutchman who owed him money and promised to pay him at once. Then Girard saw this man boarding a ship for the West Indies. Girard called the police and had the Dutchman arrested. Again Girard agreed to let the man out of jail and get on a ship for Holland where he would get the money to send to Girard. The man wrote a mocking letter to Girard which taught him a valuable lesson about granting credit.

Why did Girard take a cargo to New York in 1774?

July, 1774, Girard sailed for New York, taking with him sugar and coffee purchased with the proceeds of the sale of his Bordeaux goods. At New York he probably sought employment by some merchant who traded with San Domingo.

Was Thomas Randall fully sure of his young apprentice?

It is not to be supposed that Captain Randall would esteem him so highly without being careful to instruct him in the nautical knowledge of the day. A genius like Girard would learn quickly and well.[1]

The position of a pilotin is that of an apprentice merchant sailor. In most cases the pilotin reported to the captain. When Girard's father sailed with a small crew, he served as both owner and captain and Girard reported to his father. The pilotin had to learn how to sail the vessel. He had to learn the rudiments of buying and selling cargoes. He had to be prepared for any emergency aboard ship. He had to know all the functions of the sailors and at the same time know the responsibilities of the officers.

What was Girard's first impression of San Domingo in 1764?

It was an area a little more than ten thousand square miles. There were seven hundred thousand African slaves overseen by fewer that thirty-eight thousand French slave owners. He saw it as a difficult situation to say the least, seething with unrest.

What were the principal products for export by these West Indies islands?

Sugar and coffee were the most important.

How long did it generally take to sail from Bordeaux to the West Indies?

Girard noted in his journal that it would typically take between 57 and 65 days each way, depending on good sailing weather.

What was the attraction for merchants to go to San Domingo?

Of all the West Indian colonies, the fairest, the richest, and the most prosperous was French San Domingo (La Partie Francaise de Saint-Domingue). It comprised the western end of the island Columbus had called "Hispaniola," and was divided into three provinces—the North, the West, and the South.[2]

What were the locations important to maritime merchants?

In the North Province were the towns of Cape Francais, commonly called Le Cap, Fort Dauphin, Port de Paix, and Cap Saint Nicholas. Le Cap, with a population of twenty thousand, lay at the foot of a high mountain called Le Morne du Cap. To the east, stretching away for fifty miles was a great plain devoted solely to cultivation of sugar. Port-au-Prince in the Western Province, the metropolis of the French Colony, numbered some six hundred houses. In the Southern Province were no safe harbors, and but three towns of importance, Jeremie, Les Cayes and Jacmel.

Is there any truth to the story that Girard cheated Toussaint L'Ouverture?

There has been some controversy concerning the origin of certain funds Girard attained in San Domingo. It has been claimed that Toussaint L'Ouverture gave money to Girard to purchase arms. These arms were to be used against the slave owners during the slave uprisings in 1789–1802. A myth persists that the foundation of Girard's wealth involved two million dollars he supposedly swindled from Toussaint L'Ouverture.

The originator of the myth, perpetuated by people claiming that Girard was a racist said that Toussaint gave Girard the money which became the foundation of Girard's wealth. Although Le Cap, the major port in San Domingo was among Girard's frequent trading ports, the swindle story is totally without fact and logically impossible.[3]

How was this claim disproved?

It was shown that Girard had never met Toussaint much less made a pact with him. It was also shown that Girard had ceased travel to the West Indies before this agreement was to have been made.

Did Girard ever have the occasion to buy back a vessel that had been captured from him?

The brig *Kitty* had been captured from him in 1793. Girard learned that it was on the market and despite the fact that it needed repairs; he bought it back and returned it to service.

How did Girard focus his trading interests after the 1791 uprising in San Domingo?

Girard turned his efforts toward Europe in 1793, just when France became a Republic and waged war on Great Britain and brought on the great war of 1793–1815. Girard suffered, as did other American merchants, from the plundering French Decrees and British Orders in Council. One after another his ships and his cargoes were seized by the French, by the British, by the Swedes and the Danes. During this period of loss, Girard redoubled his boldness and courage.[4]

How did his agents show their gratitude for the business Girard provided them?

So pleased were the agents with the profits they were making that they began sending Girard delicacies as presents with his cargoes. One letter to Girard in 1792 ended with this postscript: "I will try to send you pineapples and oranges, but scarce since slave insurrection. I have ordered some turtles for you as Mr. Heraud says you are fond of them."[5]

After the trouble had run its course in San Domingo, why did John not want to return?

John told Stephen that he hated "the criminal and low class of mulattoes who occupy a social position on a level or above that of my own."[6]

Did Stephen and John enter into a formal partnership that John had been requesting?

The brothers entered into a formal partnership in 1789.

What were some of the points of contention between Stephen and John that led to their business breakup?

There were many points of friction. Stephen said that John was pigheaded and careless with funds, that John's wife Eleanor urged him to take money out of the business for her household expenses. John accused his brother of being money mad, never satisfied with profits, of being too intense. Stephen disapproved of John's wife Eleanor. He blamed her illogically for the death of John's first two children. Ingram treats the relationship of the brothers more positively. "Their friendship forms the brightest thread in the whole fabric of the elder brother's life."

After the breakup of the two brothers, how did John hope to get even with Stephen?

John hoped to get their father to change his will and name him administrator and sole heir of Pierre's interests. John even managed to have his father advance him 10,000 livres to purchase slaves and horses.[7]

Were John's attempts to become friends with everyone in Pierre's second family transparent?

Yes. He was awkward in his dealings and was considered a "fortune-hunting swindler." John's remarks to Stephen on the matter were: "These Bordeaux people are not worth the devil."

Although Girard did not permit portraits made of him during his lifetime, subsequent paintings show one eye to be oddly different from the other. Was this an attempt to show his right eye condition?

Girard's early life was difficult. Whether or not he was born without vision in his right eye is unknown. What is certain is that the eye was not only sightless, but it became a repulsive-looking abnormality that brought young Girard ridicule and, later, unwarranted social isolation. His eye bulged out and looked grotesque. The children called him "fish eye." The cruelty of those with whom Girard associated in business and in casual social activity as they observed his affliction with obvious distaste, forced him into seclusion at times, and brought with it a stigma that labeled him as shy and withdrawn.[8]

How is it that a portrait of Stephen Girard exists, if he did not want to allow such a portrait to be made in his lifetime?

The portrait painter Bass Otis painted the face of the dead Girard and completed the portrait in one week.

Did Girard ever comment publicly about his sightless eye?

Biographers have noted several occasions. When Girard was nearly eighty years old, he wrote to an oculist in Paris. "I do not remember when I lost sight in that eye, indeed if it is since I was born and I must have been very young."

Did Girard ever consider wearing a patch to cover his eye?

We have found nothing in the literature to indicate that Girard wore or contemplated wearing a patch, but this is not surprising. His whole philosophy was to face the world openly and honestly and this he did without hiding behind a patch.

What was Stephen's first partnership?

On recommendation of his friend Mr. Robert Ramsey, Girard was introduced to Isaac Hazelhurst who took Girard into a partnership in 1771 for commerce to San Domingo. Girard took two brigs but unfortunately the brigs were captured and the partnership was dissolved. Girard probably learned more from this experience than he did with his father. [9]

Did Stephen Girard ever become licensed in his own right?

Yes. He became a licensed captain at the age of twenty-three in 1773.

When did Girard begin to earn his living as a trading merchant?

With the help of a New York associate, he began sailing to New Orleans and Port au Prince in 1775.

When did Girard become half owner of *La Jeune Bébé*?

By the middle of April, 1776, Girard was at Cap Francais and a month later sailed from St. Pierre, Miquelon, as master and half owner of the bateau *La Jeune Bébé*.[10]

How did Girard handle the problem of the lack of drinking water on his voyage to New York in 1776?

Knowing that his crew would not survive with only one hogshead of water, Girard turned the ship into the port of Philadelphia. He was perhaps naïve and certainly still inexperienced to think complete strangers would drop everything and come to his aid. Girard put into the port with little money and less ability to communicate in English. He was determined to get water for his men.

3

A New Nation

1774–1776

What was Philadelphia like to the eyes of a young man from France?

In 1776, Philadelphia was America's largest city and the second largest English-speaking city in the world—London being the largest. The population of Philadelphia that year was about 35,000. It would remain the largest American city until 1830 when it was surpassed by New York. Philadelphia seemed to Girard a city of churches and Girard over the years helped enhance that image by donating to their continued construction.

Was Girard particularly concerned with the uprising in the British colonies at first?

As a Frenchman trading with the West Indies he was not concerned in the rebellion of the British colonies. Ships, commerce, the accumulation of a fortune alone occupied his thoughts. Nevertheless his arrival, though he didn't know it, marked an epoch in his life, for, from that day till his death fifty-five years later, Philadelphia was his home.

What were the living and working areas of Philadelphia in 1776?

The confines of the city were the Schuylkill and Delaware Rivers, Vine Street on the north and Cedar or South Street on the south. According to Wildes, in 1778, Philadelphia huddled close in the seven blocks between the Delaware River and the farmlands.[1]

What did Girard learn about the history of the city?

He learned that William Penn was the founder of the city and that Quakers had been a dominant force there since its founding in 1682. George Wilson writes: "Penn, a strict Quaker himself, had known about religious intolerance from his life in England and was to make sure that the Quakers in the City of Brotherly Love would support religious freedom." As the Quaker founders of the colonies changed, so did the demands of their god. He became less forbidding. The founding Quakers had their old-time religion; the revolutionaries had their newer brand.

Philadelphia Waterfront, [177–]. Engraving by Balthazar Friedrich Leizelt. LC-DIG-pppms-ca-31798. Library of Congress Prints and Photographs Division, Washington, DC.

It has been noted that Philadelphia has not treated its prominent citizens well.

It is true, with the exception of Benjamin Franklin who was highly regarded. William Penn was scarcely noted at all with only a statue at the top of City Hall that can't even be properly viewed.

How much land was William Penn given in the new continent?

Penn's province, by calculation of the area within the charter boundaries, contained in excess of 35 million acres. The final adjustment of these boundaries with the adjoining states of Maryland, New York, and Virginia took place years later, as did the ownership of the Delaware River—including its lands—by a compromise with the state of New Jersey.

William Penn (1644–1718). Artist unknown. Wikimedia Commons [Public Domain].

Where in the city did Girard go to get information on repairs for his ship and for information on cargo sales?

He was given directions for going to The London Coffee House which was a meeting place for tradesmen and mariners. There he could get tea as well as coffee with any variety of spirits—whiskey, rum and various kinds of ale. Just about anything could be bought or sold there including slaves and indentured servants.

How was news posted in The London Coffee House?

A book was kept for ship captains to enter information about their voyages, about cargo requested and vessels for hire.[2]

How many newspapers were published in Philadelphia the year Girard arrived?

Philadelphia had five newspapers: *Gazette, Journal, Ledger, Evening Post* and *Packet.*

London Coffee House, Philadelphia, 1845. Engraving by Thomas Howland Mumford.
LC-USZ62-106832. Library of Congress Prints and Photographs Division, Washington, DC.

What information did these newspapers generally carry?

Ship sailing dates, goods for sale, rewards for runaway slaves, debates in Parliament copied from London newspapers, businesses for sale or lease etc.

Did Girard ever use his ships to transport slaves?

Girard, the Frenchman, was rapidly embracing the standards of his adopted American society. It was acceptable practice for wealthy and prominent citizens to acquire slaves as a commodity. Girard was no different in that regard; he felt no stigma in owning slaves. But while he had slaves in his household, he did not carry slaves on any of his ships. Biographer George Wilson said that Girard was emphatic about not allowing his ships to be used for the purpose of buying, selling or transporting slaves.

Did Girard ever meet Betsy Ross in Philadelphia?

Yes. They lived several blocks from each other. Girard bought flags from her from time to time.

How long had Girard been in Philadelphia when he heard the first reading of The Declaration of Independence?

Girard had been in Philadelphia less than five weeks. He realized that his remaining in America was problematic but he had options. He could request a return to France or to San Domingo but he was excited by the fervor of independence and chose to support the colonies against the British. He decided to stay. Girard decided to throw his newly developed business influence, tenuous though it might have been in those first months, on the side of the Americans. As a Frenchman, he had no great love for the British, and saw an opportunity to help the fledgling nation in its bold determination to gain independence, not in any combative way for him, but in the profitable business of supply.[3]

Did he ever think about taking up arms in the Continental Army?

There is no evidence that he did but he would prove time and time again his patriotism in many ways.

What would have been the risk for him to continue moving his vessels under cover of night around the British blockade?

He risked a great deal. He could have been considered an enemy of the Crown and hanged.

Did Girard's arrival in Philadelphia come about by chance?

Biographer James Parton describes it in this way: "It was lucky for Girard that he got into Philadelphia just when he did, with all his possessions with him. He had the narrowest escape from capture. On his way from New Orleans to a Canadian port, he had become lost in a fog at the entrance of Delaware Bay, swarming then with British cruisers, of whose presence Captain Girard had heard nothing. His flag of distress brought alongside an American captain, who told him where he was, and assured him that, if he ventured out to sea, he would never reach port except as a British prize. "Mon Dieu!" exclaimed Girard in great panic, "what shall I do?" "You have no chance but to push right up to Philadelphia," replied the captain. "How am I to get there?" said Girard; "I have no pilot, and I don't know the way." A pilot was found, who, however, demanded a preliminary payment of five dollars, which Girard had not on board. In great distress, he implored the captain to be his security for the sum. He consented, a pilot took charge of the sloop, the anchor was heaved, and the vessel sped on her way. Girard arrived safely at Philadelphia on one of the early days of May, 1776. Thus it was a mere chance of war that gave Girard to the Quaker City." If Girard had not been able to borrow the five dollars he might very well have been captured by the British man-of-war and made prisoner of the Crown.

What was Girard's reaction to the Quakers?

In the whole world he could not have found a more congenial abode, for the Quakers were the only religious sect with which he ever had the slightest sympathy. He liked the Quakers and held them in high esteem, partly because they had no priests, partly because they disregarded ornaments of faith and reduced life to its simplest and most obvious utilities, partly because some of their opinions were in accord with his own. He had grown up during the time when Voltaire was sovereign lord of the opinions of Continental Europe. Girard was never affiliated with the Quakers of Pennsylvania, although he clearly admired their philosophy. Also, any interest he might have had in becoming a Mason, would not have been possible because he would not have been eligible to join them due to the blindness in his right eye.[4]

How did the beginning of the American Revolution affect Girard's business?

After being forced in May of 1776 by the British fleet into the port of Philadelphia, he decided to stay but he was fearful for his business because he had a full load of merchandise on board his vessel. He needed a place to unload it.

What decision did he make to accommodate his cargo?

He rented a house and store on North Water Street and was able to leave his cargo. With this store he was able to sell and demand retail prices for his wares. Still a young man, Stephen opened a thrifty but thriving trade. In his shop he became engaged in bottling cider and claret. When the British army occupied Philadelphia, he moved his bottling business to Mount Holly, New Jersey and continued his business there until the end of the war. In 1779, Girard returned once again to Philadelphia to occupy a range of frame stores on the east side of Water Street. His stores were filled with old cordage, sails, blocks and other materials for ship building.[5]

What was the cost of his Water Street rental?

Girard rented the house and store for "80 pounds hard money."

We know that Girard rebounded financially after the Revolutionary War. Was he able to resume his merchant voyages?

As soon as the war ended and peace was declared, Girard loaded his two ships with grain and cotton and dispatched them to Bordeaux. They returned in six months having sold all the cargo. They returned with silk, wine and tea which brought a profit of just under a hundred thousand dollars.

4

Marriage

1776–1777

How did Stephen meet Miss Lum who was to become his future wife?

Although details differ on how Stephen met the attractive servant-girl, we know for sure that the meeting took place on Water Street in front of Stephen's shop. The water pump would attract many people who would stop for a drink. Whether it was fate or just by chance that, a beautiful brunette in her teens arrived skipping along in bare feet. Biographer Patton tells us she was sixteen and flirtatious as are most young girls, sure of their own beauty. Stephen was captivated. She had what Stephen could never claim for himself—physical attractiveness. He had what she could never attain—a brilliant mind. Something clicked between them and they began seeing each other, despite the difference in their ages.

"One might ask what thoughts might Mary Lum have had after receiving a proposal of marriage. The temptation of an offer of marriage to a young servant girl by a captain and merchant who even then was supposed to be a favored votary of fortune was certainly too great to permit her to question or scrutinize the emotions of her heart. What might have been the destiny of Stephen Girard had his marriage been crowned with offspring?"[1]

When did Stephen become betrothed?

It was in 1776 that Girard became engaged to Mary Lum, a native of Philadelphia. Mary or "Polly" was almost a decade younger than Stephen but they married within the year.

What was Girard's main disappointment in his marriage?

Girard lamented most of all that his wife did not become pregnant. For some reason she was unable to have children with her Stephen. He was all the more upset because he came from a family of many children. The men in the family were virile and the women were fertile.

How could a young attractive girl be drawn to a man ten years older than she who was not physically appealing with an eye deformity?

Mary's desire was to marry a man of wealth and have children. Girard had everything she did not have: drive, intelligence and money. Polly had youth and beauty. He was perhaps flattered that she would want him. A year before meeting Mary Lum, Girard had met a beautiful woman in New Orleans by the name of Bébé Duplessis. She was French which pleased Girard but he found her to be too light and nimble a wit. In conversation, he was unable to match her repartee.[2]

When did Stephen and Mary get married?

The marriage took place on June 6th, 1777.

Where did the newlyweds stay immediately after they were married?

They immediately stayed in a little room above the store.

Did they have a honeymoon?

The only honeymoon they had was to stay on board his boat while it was still anchored in the harbor—only a couple of days.

What attributes did Mary bring to the marriage?

Not many at all. She had no education; she couldn't cook, was not good with figures, and could not be counted on to tend to the store.

Were any of Stephen Girard's biographers negative about Stephen and Mary getting married?

Biographer Parton wrote: "Of all miserable marriages this was one of the most miserable. Here was a young, beautiful, and ignorant girl united to a close, ungracious, eager man of business, devoid of sentiment, with a violent temper and an unyielding will. She was an American, he a Frenchman; and that alone was an immense incompatibility. She was seventeen, he twenty-seven. She was a woman; he was a man without imagination, intolerant of foibles. She was a beauty, with the natural vanities of a beauty; he not merely had no taste for decoration, he disapproved it on principle. These points of difference would alone have sufficed to endanger their domestic peace; but time developed something that was fatal to it." William Wagner described the union of Stephen and Mary differently. "She (Mary) possessed a quick intelligence...and a ready appreciation of knowledge in others that went far to render her a most agreeable companion."

5

Mount Holly

Happiness and Turmoil for Newlyweds
1777–1778

Why did Girard decide to move to New Jersey?

When the British troops had occupied Philadelphia, Girard wanted to get away from the noise and confusion.

When did he buy a house in Mount Holly, New Jersey?

He bought the house on July 22, 1777 from Isaac Hazlehurst, paying 528 pounds and nineteen shillings Pennsylvania currency.

With the British troops occupying Philadelphia, did Girard benefit in any way from their presence?

He made considerable money selling claret to the British officers who came to his house in Mount Holly, New Jersey. On returning to Philadelphia, these officers turned a profit by reselling the claret to the troops. Girard, however, did not spend all his time in Mount Holly. He would take trips by way of the Rancoras River to Philadelphia where he kept a watchful eye on his property which was in the hands of the British.

Did Girard ever go back to Cap-Français after he got married?

After the trip which brought him unexpectedly into the Port of Philadelphia in 1776, he was not to return again to San Domingo.[1]

What news did a letter in 1776 from Mr. Thomas Randall to Girard contain?

This letter said: "The sloop *Sally* whereof you are now master, being complete for sea, it is our desire that you proceed to the Cape (Le Cap) with all possible expedition and dispose of your cargo to the very best advantage." Due to his marriage, Girard never took this venture. Biographer Cheesman Herrick reports that the ship Girard owned with Thomas Randall was named *L'Aimable Louise*.[2]

During several voyages Girard had previously taken to New York, he became acquainted with ship owners and merchants in the teeming city.

Was the family of Mary Lum in maritime trade as well?

No. John Lum, Mary's father was a shipbuilder but not a very successful one. He owned very little property and his savings were meager. Unfortunately, he died three months before his daughter's wedding. Biographer Herrick reports that John Lum built a small vessel for Stephen for local trading trips and that Girard named the vessel *Water Witch*.[3]

Do we know why this vessel was named the *Water Witch*?

According to Hubbard, Girard bought one brand new boat and named it *Water-Witch*, for this was the name he had for Mary Lum when she used to come with her jug to the pump in front of his store.

When did Girard build his first ship?

Girard built his first ship in 1789. Historians disagree on its name. Some claim it was the *Water Witch*. Harry E. Wilde claims there is no record of a ship called *Water Witch*. McMaster, who spent several years reviewing the Girard Papers, claims that the *Water Witch* was the first ship and since the British captured it in its first year of operation, no records exist in the Girard Papers. Harry Schad, Girard College Class of 1920, reporting in the December 1963 *Steel & Garnet* states: "In his lifetime he (Girard) owned a total of twenty-four ships, but never more than six at once. Regularly he supplemented his fleet by chartering the vessels of others."

Who was Henry W. Arey?

He was secretary of Girard College. His book *Girard College and Its Founder*, written in 1852, emphasizes the origin and growth of the college. He relied heavily on Simpson's *Biography* although he did not repeat Simpson's criticism of Stephen Girard.[4]

How did Professor Wagner speak about the Simpson biography of Girard?

"Any one," says Professor Wagner in his first lecture upon Girard, "who will read this biography of Mr. Girard, which I thus publicly pronounce a tissue of lies, sticking out on every page, will perceive that the whole account is embittered and venomous, and that the author has tortured his imagination to find an opportunity to falsify and pervert. Now, before dilating upon it, let us inquire for a moment who this biographer was. When the charter of the old Bank of the United States expired and Mr. Girard purchased the building, establishing in it his own Bank, he appointed George Simpson, the cashier of the former institution, to the same position in his new concern. Stephen Simpson was the son of this latter, and, with Mr. Girard's consent, was appointed by his father to the situation of clerk in the Bank, in which position he continued until the death of his father. Stephen Simpson then aspired to the cashier ship that his father had held, but, unfortunately for him, Joseph Roberts, the first teller, stood between him and the coveted office. Mr. Girard had confidence in Roberts, but very little in Simpson, the result being that the former received the appointment, and the latter became thereupon the uncompromising enemy of Mr. Girard."

Which of Girard's biographers did Professor Wagner favor?

Wagner made a notable exception among Girard's biographers referred to above for Henry W. Arey, formerly secretary of Girard College, who, having free access to the papers stored at the college, impliedly protests against the false inferences drawn by Simpson, and presents in his own sketch a fair picture of Girard as he actually appeared to his fellows. To this sketch the present writer has great pleasure in acknowledging his indebtedness; and though the possession of certain documents and evidence not at that biographer's disposal compels him to differ from several of the latter's conclusions, he recognizes everywhere the author's endeavor to present his facts with the strictest impartiality. But, unfortunately, having depended mainly upon a journal kept by Girard, commencing in the year 1774, this author, like the others, has relied for information as to Girard's origin upon common report.

How does biographer Henry W. Arey speak about the relationship between Stephen and Jean?

An early intimacy between the two brothers being thus commenced that lasted, with but one interruption, during the long period that stretched to the death of the younger. This friendship forms the brightest thread in the whole fabric of the elder brother's life, and was of equal warmth on the part of both brothers, a happy result of the patient care with which their mother had sought to render her family a unit, and one the more worthy of remark when it is remembered that to all other persons the elder showed an exceedingly undemonstrative disposition. His reserve of character was no doubt rendered somewhat morbid by the comparative isolation to which his proud and sensitive temper had relegated him, and it is curious to consider the influence such a trivial and childish circumstance as his playmates' ridicule had in the after-development of his life, for it is doubtless to this event may be fundamentally traced that distrust of, and semi-contempt for so many of his fellows which he later displayed; and the disposition whose most salient feature became its self-reliance and complete indifference to the cavil or judgment of his neighbors was primarily dependent for its direction in not a small degree upon this He possessed excellent faculties of observation and a very retentive memory, supplying in a great measure the routine work of the school-room, and there can be no doubt that at the time he was not at all averse to escape from the uncongenial labor of the latter. It is in the injudicious indulgence of this preference upon his part that is to be found the explanation of the neglect with which upon one occasion he reproached his father, the consciousness of his loss having led him, in 1813, to write the following letter, which a consideration of the foregoing remarks will show was decidedly unjust: "I have the proud satisfaction to know that my conduct, my labor, and my economy have enabled me to do one hundred times more for my relatives than they all together have done for me since the day of my birth. While my brothers were taught at college, I was the only one whose education was neglected. But the love of labor, which has very circumstance of its original exceeding sensibility."

In what way does biographer Arey show himself to be politically correct in downplaying the monetary cost of education in view of Pierre Girard's other guidance?

In the mere amount of money expended this statement was probably true. But it is the start in life which is most difficult to get, and for this Stephen was indebted to his father, notwithstanding the rather ungracious manner in which he had recognized his relative's subsequent claims upon him. But the stress under which this letter was written was sufficient to excuse it in a great measure, the more so as it is the only time he gave vent to his feelings in this manner, and the tone of conscious strength in it is certainly to be pardoned one who had indeed almost literally "made his way alone with means gained from his nurse, the Sea."

How does Arey show Girard's developing personality that needed correcting?

From his earliest childhood Stephen had been remarkable for precocious dignity and grave self-assertion, and with these masterful traits was coupled a passionate and rather domineering temper, which, when opposed, was displayed with considerable violence. His mother was still earnestly seeking to modify this character, so directly opposed to the usual careless high spirits of young French children, and to teach him the necessary self-control, when her death, which occurred while Stephen was yet quite a young lad, found him with the lesson still unlearned. The considerable influence which, as eldest son, he doubtless wielded in the immediate family after his mother's death, probably fostered the independence of character already natural to him, and his impatience of discipline, speedily reasserting its mastery, grew in time to be not only the most fruitful source of the unhappiness of his after life, but also the proximate cause of his leaving his father's home.

How did the arrival of a step-mother change the lives of the Girard family?

Not that he was at all unhappy at this period, however, for during the few years following his mother's decease no untoward event marred the peace of the family circle, and probably none would have arisen had not Pierre Girard selected a second wife in the person of Madame Giraud (née Lachapelle), an American or West Indian, who was, unfortunately, already the mother of several children. There is no evidence to show that Madame Giraud- Girard was unkind to or in any particular neglected her step-children; but it was not long before the discomforts of which a second marriage is so liable to prove the fertile source began to make themselves disagreeably manifest. Stephen had early found a grievance in the fact that the newcomer not only supplanted his influence in the family, but was also disposed to exercise control of his theretofore comparatively unrestricted liberty; while his step-mother failing to understand the peculiarities of the lad's disposition was unable to allay the distrust with which he had immediately regarded her. Stephen had always been amenable to kindly argument, being one of those natures which must be led and cannot be driven, and no especial effort having been made to win his regard, his dislike and jealousy increased from day to day, until, since he was not at the least pains to conceal his sentiments despite his father's frequent reproofs, it required but little foresight to predict that a speedy climax was inevitable. The crisis arrived one day while the family was gathered about the dinner table. Some action of Stephen's had called for a reproof from his stepmother, and her attempt to correct him proved to be the final increment which the lad's overburdened temper could not withstand. Restraining his feelings no longer, he burst into a torrent of passionate reproach, expressing so plainly the bitterness of his spirit that it was impossible for his father, who happened to be present, to pass the matter by without making of it a signal example. Astounded by Stephen's violence, apparently so disproportioned to the provocation, and indignant at his temerity, Pierre Girard, as he was able to stem the current of his son's indignation, rebuked him in the sternest manner, commanding him to make immediate present amends and submit cheerfully to family discipline in the future, or else to find a home for himself as soon as he was able elsewhere. But the young lad, having once lost his self-control, had gone too far to turn back. He was unwilling to confess himself an offender where he firmly believed himself to be the one aggrieved, and his father's command had hardly been finished before Stephen passionately replied: "I will leave your house. Give me a venture on any ship that sails from Bordeaux, and I will go at once where you shall never see me again!"

How does Girard make his break from his home and family?

Persisting in his refusal to make amends, it was evident that heroic measures were necessary, both for the lad's own sake and for that of the family, whose peace was constantly imperiled by his unmanageable presence. And while there can be no doubt that Pierre Girard felt deep compassion for his motherless lad when the heat of his indignation had subsided, yet it was still apparent something must be done to prevent such scenes of domestic insubordination. In this dilemma, serious thought was given the idea Stephen had broached himself, and the latter remaining firm in his obstinate attitude, his father found himself reluctantly forced to surrender his hope that his son might adopt a professional career, and consequently sought a business acquaintance, Captain Jean Courteau, master of the ship *Pelerin*, who was about to sail for Santo Domingo, one of the French colonies in the West Indies. Finding Captain Courteau willing to take charge of Stephen, a "venture" amounting to sixteen thousand livres was furnished the latter by his father, who bade his son farewell, as one may well imagine, with many regrets that the young lad's waywardness had made such a course a necessity.

What two events convinced Girard that he should swear allegiance to the Commonwealth of Pennsylvania?

First he was certain that the Continental Armies could make good the independence of the United States. Second, he was now sure that his bid to become a French Consul would not be realized.

Did Stephen Girard become a citizen of Pennsylvania?

Girard became a citizen of Pennsylvania. Herrick points out that Girard took the oath of allegiance and fidelity to the General Assembly of Pennsylvania on the 27th of October 1778. All who did so renounced allegiance to George Third, King of Great Britain, swore to bear true and faithful allegiance to the Commonwealth of Pennsylvania, never do anything prejudicial to the freedom and independence thereof, and discover and make known to some justice of the peace all treasons or traitorous conspiracies whereof they were cognizant.[5]

The oath was repeated the following year when the French Revolution had divided the country into two parties the Federalists and the Republicans. Girard remained a loyal and devoted citizen of Pennsylvania and repeatedly objected to being termed, in his ship's papers and other documents," a "naturalized citizen." He claimed that he was a "citizen" of Pennsylvania. He was as old a citizen of the United States as any man. If the test of citizenship were sacrifice for and devotion to the government under which one lived, surely Girard qualified as being a worthy citizen of Philadelphia, Pennsylvania and the United States.[6]

Was Pennsylvania citizenship a requirement for having a rental contract in Pennsylvania?

Yes, it was a requirement. This was the reason he moved to have his citizenship application processed quickly. There was also a stick that went with that carrot. Anyone travelling out of the city or county where he resided without a certificate showing that he had taken the oath was to be suspected of being a spy and of holding principles inimical to the United States, was to be seized, taken before the nearest justice of the peace, tendered the oath, and on refusing to take it, sent to jail, there to stay till he became loyal.

Who was Colonel Walter Stewart?

He was a twenty-one- year-old officer in Washington's Army which was camped in Mount Holly.

How did Colonel Stewart's billeting in Mount Holly impact the life of Stephen and Mary?

Colonel Stewart, being in a merry mood found that his spirits were rising somewhat above the level of rigid propriety could not resist the temptation—perhaps an idle frolic of the moment. [7] George Wilson writes: "While the beautiful and playful Mary Girard tended the store she would talk to the handsome colonel and share a laugh or two with him. Then he kissed her just as Girard entered the store. Stephen was angry with jealousy."

How did this matter end?

Girard had several options. He could report the colonel to his superior officer; he could demand an apology or he could insist on getting satisfaction in a duel. The pragmatic Girard accepted the colonel's apology.

When did France enter the war on the side of the colonies and under what conditions?

It was June 1778 that King Louis XVI agreed to enter the War of American Independence to help the budding nation against the British. This action gave encouragement to the Americans and helped greatly in the war effort.

What happened to Girard's first vessel named the *Water Witch*.

It is not certain whether Girard bought or had built the *Water Witch*. When the British left the city in 1778, the *Water Witch* was carried off with them and never again seen by its owner.[8]

George Washington (1732–1799). From the Portrait Gallery, Perry-Castañeda Library, University of Texas at Austin. Courtesy of the University of Texas Libraries, The University of Texas at Austin.

How did Washington's crossing the Delaware influence the lives of Stephen and Mary?

Stephen did not expect George Washington to cross over the Delaware into New Jersey. This action also surprised the British. To counter this tactic, British troops were sent directly to Mount Holly. Girard, who was planning to return to Philadelphia, thought it would be wiser to remain in New Jersey until the war ended.

How did Stephen tell his father about his marriage?

He wrote to his father: "I have taken a wife who is without fortune, it is true but whom I love and with whom I am living very happily."[9]

In 1780, Girard turned thirty years old. What was occurring in his adopted country?

On May 12, 1780, Charleston, South Carolina fell to the British after an effective siege. In Philadelphia, Ben Franklin, prompted by poor vision both near and far, and tired of taking his glasses on and off, invented bi-focals in the early part of the decade. It is unknown exactly when this occurred, with Franklin admitting to friends that he had been wearing double spectacles in 1784.

When did Stephen and Mary get back to Philadelphia?

They returned to Philadelphia after the British had been evacuated from the city. His was one of the first businesses to reopen.

How did Girard's professional life change after he got married?

Stephen became pleasantly accustomed to conducting maritime trade while keeping his feet on dry land.[10]

Was there a matter of unpaid debts that Girard allowed to go unpaid for several years?

Yes. He owed money to merchants in Bordeaux from back in 1774. Although Stephen's father reminded him of this debt on occasion, Stephen was in no hurry to meet this responsibility. Perhaps as a citizen of the State of Pennsylvania, he may have believed he was under no obligation to repay this debt.

Did Stephen ever solicit help from his father for his business?

In a letter to his father, Stephen wrote: "I therefore appeal to your fatherly love and friendship to procure from your friends as much commission and other business as you can."[11]

Girard was described as a King Midas in his business dealings. Was it true that everything he touched turned to gold?

He had plenty of good luck but Girard would have called it sound business practices but he was not always fortunate. For example, a schooner he had shared ownership in was wrecked on the Virginia coast a year after he had invested in it. In 1780, another schooner he owned in part was captured by pirates in the West Indies only two months after investing his money in it. In 1783, he became the sole owner of a schooner that he named *Mary* after his wife. It was wrecked three months later.[12]

Another of his contemporaries, Job R. Tyson spoke about Girard's business success: "We may cease to wonder at the magical transformations of his Midas touch. His secret lay in the patient application of a remarkably clear and sagacious intellect to the single work of accumulation, aided by inexpensive personal habits and the observance of general frugality. He sought through a long life the philosopher's stone with a sedulous and untiring assiduity."

Did the Pennsylvania Assembly ever doubt the validity of Girard's citizenship?

The assembly complicated matters for Girard in December 1778 by passing a new law that would cause Girard the need to pledge to another oath of allegiance.[13]

Did he cease all business with St. Domingo after 1776?

No because he went into partnership with his brother John (Jean) who took up residence there.

Was this John's idea in order to work with his brother?

John wrote:

> "I am at Le Cap, writing to my brother with whom I ardently wish to form a partnership. I believe that if he came here we could between us, do a great

deal of business, as one of us could look after the store, while the other was away on a voyage." John Girard, shortly before this time, had established himself as a commission merchant and trader at Le Cap. "Get," said Girard to him, " if you can, a solid insurance in France, buy a bark or schooner at Le Cap, load her with salt or syrup, select a good sailor and honest fellow for captain and come with the vessel to Philadelphia, where you will make a big profit on your cargo after deducting the insurance premium. Syrup is now worth four gourdes a gallon and salt twenty-four a bushel. When you arrive here, we might form a partnership to carry on the business in which I am engaged."[14]

John and Stephen kept regular contact: John would advise or forecast the market and Stephen would acquire and send the cargo with explicit instructions for the return lading. Thus, Girard did not have to rely upon the customary international "network" of merchants who traded on potentially inaccurate market prices.

While Stephen was awaiting the evacuation of the British from Philadelphia, was he still exploring other means of employment?

In a letter to his father he wrote:

"There is some prospect of the English evacuating New York, in which case the position of French Consul would become vacant. It is an honorable and very lucrative post and I humbly beg you to use your influence with your friends to get it for me. If, however, you should experience difficulty because of my being so far from you, send me if possible a letter of introduction to M. De Gérard, ambassador to this country from the Court of France, for the purpose of informing him who I am. I should be very glad to establish myself in New York where all my old acquaintances live."[15]

What advice did Stephen give his brother John concerning the purchase of farmland?

Stephen wrote: "The wisest course would be to invest 5,000 pounds in St. Domingo, in coffee, sugar or syrup and ship the goods to Philadelphia."

Was there a specific reason that Girard chose to make part ownerships in ships and cargoes?

He reasoned, perhaps, that to have several ships in which he had invested might have a better chance of avoiding disaster than a single ship into which he had placed a great fortune in wares.

What was the victory that gave the American Army the advantage and brought about the defeat of the British?

On September 5th, the French naval forces reached the Chesapeake Bay and sealed off the only escape route the British had.

Marquis de Lafayette (1757–1834). From the Portrait Gallery, Perry-Castañeda Library, University of Texas at Austin. Courtesy of the University of Texas Libraries, The University of Texas at Austin.

How did Yorktown play a significant role in the war?

Biographer George Wilson writes: "By September 11th, American troops were already at Yorktown under the command of General Marquis de Lafayette. Cornwallis made a tragic mistake by not attacking a relatively weak force in early September."

Was this a mistake?

By September 28th, some sixteen thousand American and French troops had gathered in a semicircle around Yorktown. They had now outnumbered Cornwallis by about ten thousand troops.

How did George Washington manage to hold together his army in such difficult times?

Washington gained his men's confidence, respect, and even love. His men followed him barefoot through the snow at Trenton. They wintered with him at Valley Forge, without proper food or clothes, or firewood. Surely they fought not only for independence, but also for Washington.

How did Girard manage to coordinate business operations with his brother John in The West Indies?

The only means of coordination was through the mail. This was difficult because the mail was slow—sometimes taking two months for a letter to arrive and the mail was not secure because of pirates and sea disasters.

Was this the reason that John Girard planned to visit Stephen in Philadelphia?

At the end of the war, John accompanied a cargo from St. Domingo to Philadelphia and visited his brother for both personal and business reasons.

What was Stephen's advice to his brother concerning John's travel to Philadelphia?

Girard wrote: "Take nothing but your clothes so as to appear to be a passenger on the ship's register on a visit. The British privateers are active. Above all bring no Negroes."[16]

Who accompanied John besides the crew?

John arrived with his black slave Hannah who was then in her twenties and Hannah's daughter Rosette—a light skinned girl who was clearly sired by John.

Who was Eleanor McMullin?

Eleanor McMullin was an attractive nineteen-year-old Irish girl that John had taken a fancy to. She had come to the colonies as an indentured servant and was bound by contract. John bought out her contract and planned to take her back to St. Domingo on his return voyage.[17]

Was it his plan to return with his two slaves as well?

No. He asked his brother Stephen to take both Hannah and Rosette.

Was the fact that Girard had accepted two female slaves from his brother a problem for Mary?

At first not so much, but as people began to notice and remark that Rosette had the facial features of the Girards, she complained to her husband.

Did Stephen plan to use Hannah as his brother had for bedroom duty?

There is no evidence that he had or that he had not wanted her for this reason but we do know that Hannah stayed with Girard until his death and that she was the first person he mentioned in his will.[18]

What provisions did the will have for Polly?

Polly who had been a member of Girard's household longer than any other woman, except for Hannah was given $300 a year for life. Emeline, Polly's niece who succeeded Polly as housekeeper, received the same amount as Polly.

Did Rosette remain in the household of Stephen and Mary?

After repeatedly asking John who had returned to San Domingo to send for the twelve-year-old Rosette, Girard packed her up and sent her back to live with John and Eleanor.[19]

Why did Stephen make this decision?

On one hand, Mary was always reminded that John had fathered the child and she was constantly angered by Rosette's presence. Mary had also felt that John had been unfaithful to her and was not as attentive to her as he had been in his letters.

Were Stephen and Mary happily married?

Stephen's biographers seem to agree that the early years, before Mary's mental illness, were very happy ones for the couple. James Parton writes: "Stephen was establishing himself as a merchant in Philadelphia and Mount Holly. Because of the war, he was unable to travel abroad which allowed him to cement their union. With the passage of time, their differences were no longer those that would enhance their marriage." Parton describes the early years together in this way: "Instead of bringing happiness into their home, his young wife merely embittered their lives. It was a union of mere fancy on his side and self-interest on hers. He was intelligent and industrious; she was ignorant and lazy. For about nine years, the couple managed to co-exist. In 1785 Mary began to show signs of mental instability. She was subsequently declared incurable."

6

Mary Girard's Illness

Partnership Problems, 1778

What was the Mount Holly house like that so pleased Mary?

The house had a story and a half and had a few acres of land.[1]

Did Stephen mention his marriage to his brother John?

No. In 1778, John wrote to Stephen. "And now my dear brother, tell me the news with you. They say that you are married. I hope so and that you are sharing the pleasure two married people are in condition to enjoy when they are really well matched." [2]

When did Mary's mental condition become worse?

She had erratic behavior during 1784 but in early 1785 she grew worse. The mental strain caused by the affliction of Mrs. Girard was telling on him. For a time he thought of placing her in the Pennsylvania Hospital, and early in the year obtained from the two sitting managers the necessary certificate as to her condition: but in June she was sent to the house at Mount Holly, and Girard determined to make a sea voyage. Again and again, therefore, he urged his brother to come to Philadelphia that he might "make a voyage, for I assure you I am very tired of the daily entertainments with which my better half provides me." "I must urge you to wind up your affairs so that you can get here by the next voyage of the brig. I can then get away in August and undertake a voyage which, if it turns out a success, will bring us a good deal of business and will thus be very lucrative."

Did Girard agree with the recommendation that Mary be hospitalized?

He resisted this recommendation for some time. He had hoped she could live quietly with her family in Mount Holly, by taking her out for drives in a carriage and giving her a life with as little stress as possible. He even considered a life for her in the West Indies but gave up that idea when her tantrums grew worse.

Pennsylvania Hospital, Philadelphia, PA. HABS PA, 51-PHILA, 39—34 (CT).
Library of Congress Prints and Photographs Division, Washington, DC.

How old was Mary when the doctors convinced Stephen that his wife would not ever be cured?

Mary was twenty-six. She and Stephen had been married only eight years. This was a difficult time for Stephen. Mary was ranting day and night. It was only when Dr. John Jones prepared an opium alkaloid did Mary calm down, allowing Stephen to get some rest.[3]

When did Stephen decide to take a mistress?

After two years of dealing with his wife's insanity and being told that she would only get worse, Stephen took a mistress.

How did Stephen meet Sarah Bickham?

Sarah or "Sally" had been a seamstress and had done some mending for him.

Did Girard simply hire her?

Yes. She was hired as a housekeeper and mistress. We must remember that there was no negative connotation to the position of mistress during Stephen's time. Her responsibilities included the supervision of the cleaning personnel and the services of a bedmate.

What was Girard's opinion of Sarah's looks?

He found her very attractive but not beautiful as was Mary. It took him some time to warm up to Sally but she managed to have Stephen fall in love with her.

Did Mary Girard ever recover from her illness?

Stephen Girard provided a good deal of comfort for Mary. While she was interred, she became pregnant and gave birth to a girl whom she named Mary. There has never been conclusive proof that Stephen Girard fathered this child nor any proof to the contrary.

What accommodations did Stephen provide for his wife at the hospital?

She had a spacious comfortable apartment on the first floor. She was allowed freedom of the hospital grounds and was permitted to have visitors with few restrictions.[4]

When did the hospital notify Girard that Mary was pregnant?

An official of the Pennsylvania Hospital notified Girard five months after she had been admitted that she was pregnant. Girard was asked to take Mary home so that she could have her baby there. Girard refused. He told the hospital official that he had no sexual relations with Mary for a very long time because of her illness and felt no responsibility for the pregnancy. He did however pay all the costs related to the birth.[5]

Do we know who the father was?

There is no record of that. There seems to be some question as to who the father was. The mother named the child Mary Girard but the infant died a few months after she had been baptized. The mother never recovered her sanity. For twenty-five years she lived in the hospital at 8th and Pine Streets in Philadelphia and died there in 1815. She was buried in the hospital grounds. Girard had been and continued to be a benefactor of the hospital which had sheltered his wife.

Did Girard ever petition The Pennsylvania Legislature for a divorce?

Girard petitioned for divorce twice but was turned down both times. It seems probable that Girard was considering as early as 1807 the plan for the institution which he was to found. Unless a divorce was granted, this plan would be placed in danger if his wife outlived him. Under the law of Pennsylvania his wife even though insane was entitled to all her rights of dower. Girard's petition for divorce or to have the dower rights of his wife set aside though repeatedly presented was never granted.[6]

Did Mary ever have moments of clarity of mind?

No. She sometimes would remain more tranquil but then she would slip lower. When she died, Girard made another donation to the hospital and continued to be its benefactor. She was buried on the hospital grounds. In *America's First Hospital*, author William H. Williams wrote: "Girard was by far the largest individual benefactor of the Pennsylvania Hospital."

What was Stephen's reaction to his wife's burial?

William Wagner, a clerk in Girard's employ wrote: "I shall never forget the last and closing scene. Mr. Girard stepped forward and kissed his wife and his tears moistened her cheek."

How was Mary's burial conducted?

The burial was conducted in accordance with the customs of the "Friends" who managed the Hospital where Mary had been a patient for so many years.[7]

Where was Mary buried?

A beautiful site was selected for Mary's grave at the north end of the hospital. Henry Ingram described this way: "A lovelier spot could hardly be found within the city, the smooth lawns, broken with occasional flower beds, shaded by tall sycamores and kept with Quaker-like simplicity and neatness."

Can the grave be seen today?

No. The actual site is now covered by the Clinic Building, erected in 1868.[8]

How did Stephen's brother John interpret Mary's madness?

He thought Mary had gone mad because she had failed to provide Stephen with children.

Did Stephen ever remarry?

Stephen never remarried; however, he did have mistresses for the remainder of his life. Polly Kenton expected after nineteen years of love and to become the next Mrs. Girard but Stephen decided not to be married again. It wasn't until 1843 that Polly Kenton entered a lawsuit against Girard's executors for wages due her. She was awarded $1500 for wages over six years.

John always wanted to live near and work with his brother. What was the beginning of their partnership?

In a letter to John, Stephen wrote that he always thought about the purchase of a brig to trade between Philadelphia and the Cap and proposed that John take half interest in the operation.[9]

How did the partnership develop in terms of a contracted length of time?

The firm was named S&J Girard Frères. All expenses and profits were to be shared equally for a period of five years.

What was in the first cargo that the firm sent to Le Cap?

The first voyage to Le Cap would carry wooden boards, hewn lumber, shingles, apples, onions and eight hundred barrels of fine sugar.[10]

Was it Stephen's responsibility to take care of the customs office in Pennsylvania?

Stephen who was very shrewd in these matters was able to escape the scrutiny of the customs office and paid no fees or taxes. Girard understood that the Federal Constitution did not then exist. The Articles of Confederation were still in force and under them Congress had no power to lay taxes, duties, imposts or excises.

In moments of controversy between the brothers, how did Stephen complain of their father's attitude of him?

Stephen often blamed his father of neglect. Girard wrote: "While my brothers were in school, I was the only one whose education was neglected...I paid for my support and for my few months of schooling out of my own pocket." [11]

What were some of the differences in personality between the two brothers that caused some friction in the partnership?

Stephen was daring; John was more conservative. Stephen would often cut corners in his dealings; John was true as an arrow. Stephen always wanted to push ahead; John wanted to buy a farm and live more simply.

What was John's interest in selling his business in San Domingo and moving to Philadelphia?

Aside from his devotion, even idolatry of his brother, he became infatuated with his pretty sister-in-law, Mary whom he had never seen. In letter after letter, he sent her increasingly warm assurances of his love and showered her with small gifts.[12]

How did this long-distance flirtation influence Mary's health?

Mary's physician Dr. Say noted an improvement but quickly took credit for it. He said it was because of the massages he had been giving her. Perhaps it was John's attention that brought an improvement in Mary's condition.

What was Girard's philosophy on not sharing his intimate thoughts and feelings with others?

Girard wrote: "I have noticed that no advantage results from telling one's business to others; it creates jealousy of competitors when we are fortunate or gratifies our enemies when otherwise."[13]

Girard remembered that his difficulties with John dated back to 1772 when he and John ran a brisk business with the Cap. What specific problem arose when Le Cap changed some of its tariff regulations?

Just as soon as their brig was nearing completion and after much of the cargo had been bought John sent his brother some bad news. Le Cap was closed to Americans. The old tariff which excluded all profitable exports for Americans was again in force. No vessels should come from American ports except those flying under a French flag. [14]

Did Stephen take his brother's advice and not go to San Domingo with a cargo under the American flag?

No. Stephen was sure there would not be a problem but there was. Their brig *Les Deux Frères* carried merchandise that was forbidden in American vessels. Flour which could no longer be unloaded in the Cap was a major part of the cargo. The flour had become overheated from the lumber on board and had turned bad. John became angry that his brother was never there to solve the problems that Stephen had created. John had to send the brig to the other side of the island telling the inspectors that the brig was destined for Jamaica and not Le Cap, thus avoiding trouble.

Did John manage to sell the cargo without trouble or paying duty?

Yes. At Stephen's urging, John unloaded the cargo, sold the flour by telling the bakers it was premium flour and lowered the price of the lumber which he knew Stephen would be angry about.

With all the difficulties of this cargo, were the brothers satisfied with their profits?

John was satisfied but Stephen was not and complained to his brother. John replied in writing: "You will always be the same, never content. This last voyage has given us a profit of 55,000 pounds."

Was the return trip of *Les Deux Frères* uneventful?

On the contrary, the captain and crew had to wait for John to put together another cargo for the return trip. He was counting on a cargo of sugar but the rains had made the sugar hard to get.[15]

Did Stephen and John ever work on the same ship together?

Yes, they worked together on the ship *Superbe* under Captain Jean Petiteau. The captain promoted Stephen to second mate for the voyage to the West Indies. This was a special honor for Stephen being only twenty-two years old.[16]

Who replaced Stephen in his apprentice (pilotin) position on that voyage?

With Girard in the now vacated post of pilotin was his younger brother John, newly graduated from Sorèze.

Was this voyage on the *Superbe* a successful one for the brothers?

Unfortunately it was not a successful trip. The *Superbe* ran into trouble, probably because Captain Petiteau was caught smuggling illegal goods into a carefully restricted port—Cap-Francais.[17]

How was this disaster to affect the two brothers?

The boys separated. John remained in America as colonial correspondent for his father. Stephen returned to France.

What happened to John in the months that followed?

John, the more sensitive of the two brothers, felt sad at not being with Stephen. John was in Louisiana when he fell sick with yellow fever. His illness made him even more in need of Stephen.

What brought about John's recovery from this illness?

He was nursed back to health by an attractive young slave girl named Hannah who was to become his mistress and the mother of their mulatto baby girl named Rosette.[18]

7

Privateering and Piracy

1778-1785

What was privateering in Colonial America?

The 13 Colonies, having declared their Independence, had only 31 ships comprising the Continental Navy. To add to this, they issued *Letters of Marque* to privately owned, armed merchant ships and commissions for privateers, which were outfitted as warships to prey on enemy merchant ships. Merchant seamen who manned these ships contributed to the very birth and founding of the young Republic. Girard had come to America just before the start of the War for Independence, and during that war engaged in two privateering ventures which ended disastrously.[1]

In this new venture Girard was not alone. With him were associated "M. De Neuville and Captain Marc who is to be in command," and " M. Baldesqui, captain in the corps of General Pulaski," a gentleman with some ready money with whom Girard had just formed a partnership. His reasons for taking this venture, he wrote Baldesqui, were that "Sales are very slow, money has gone up twenty per cent, and I am afraid that many will fail altogether. I have, therefore, taken one-third interest on account of our partnership in a schooner now lying off Egg Harbor and belonging to M. Le Chevalier de la Nau." Their one-third interest cost fifteen hundred livres. He was quite aware of the risk of the sea. If, therefore, Baldesqui had any fears for the safety of the vessel, or did not wish to embark in such a speculation, his interest could be sold and the funds invested in merchandise. The schooner was not destined to make the voyage to Le Cap. Captain Marc went to Virginia fell sick, and wrote Girard to sell his interest and get another captain. Girard accordingly bought the share of Marc for "fifteen hundred livres, Continental money," and late in October, 1779, the *Minerva*, commanded by Arthur Helme and carrying twelve cannon and a crew of seventy men, sailed from Philadelphia as a privateer.

To what extent did Girard involve himself with his friend Baldesqui?

In reviewing the reasons for taking Baldesqui as a partner and his value as such,

Girard said that in January 1780, Baldesqui promised, if the partnership were formed, he would sail at once for Cap Francais, would send merchandise valued at 60,000 livres, the sum of which should be added to the capital of the firm, and that he could procure for Stephen Girard & Co. "the most of the consignments that might be made from there to Philadelphia."[2]

With financial difficulties and disagreements, did the partnership succeed?

No. "Mr. Baldesqui might clearly see that Stephen Girard took him in his company in the hope that Mr. Baldesqui would keep the promise he had made to Stephen Girard," which he never did.

How does biographer McMaster relate an episode of privateering involving Stephen Girard?

"If your privateer is fortunate, as I wish it should may be, the cost of a trial will not amount to much." The trial was held in June and Captain Chadwick reported results. "He was at Onancock in Virginia on the eastern shore of the bay with a little fleet of four boats, the barge *Recovery* manned by twenty men, a second manned by twelve, a third by eight, and a fourth by six. His prizes were a sloop carrying four hundred bushels of corn and oats."

How was Captain Chadwick to be pursued legally for this event?

A record was established of all his doings which was put into motion the proceedings by the Admiralty Court at Baltimore for the condemnation of the prizes. What there happened is told by his correspondent. [3]

How did Girard react to this chain of events?

That same August day Girard wrote to Captain Chadwick and to his correspondent in Baltimore, George P. Keeports, instructing them to sell the *Recovery*. Mr. Keeports replied: "Agreeable to your desire I have enclosed for you an inventory of the materials of the barge *Recovery*. I have offered her by private sale, but cannot find any person inclined to purchase. I shall try her by public sale on Monday next; but am fearful she will not sell for near her value."[4]

How did Girard learn that Negro slaves were taken which made the court case difficult to win?

"I am sorry to inform you," Mr. Chase, Chadwick's attorney told Girard, "that it is my apprehension [that] Captain Chadwick will hold the weakest side for those Negroes he captured on the land, as he has no person to appear as an evidence but himself, and I am fearful of success."

How was this court case resolved in the case of the slaves?

On September 10th, the Court handed down its decision in the case of the Negroes taken from Lowrey and Seldon and ordered them returned to their owners. The attorney for Chadwick, Mr.Chase thereupon took an appeal to the Court of Appeals in Cases of Capture sitting in Philadelphia, and asked that the Negroes be sold and the money left with the marshal till the entire case was decided. This proposal was opposed by the attorney for the claimants.

What other than British and French ships did Girard have to be concerned with in 1794?

Privateering and warships were bad enough, but Girard had just had five of his ships taken—three by the French and two by the British. Now a new danger appeared—concern with the Barbary Coast pirates.[5]

Which countries sponsored these pirates?

They came from the coast of Africa and menaced the Mediterranean and the Atlantic Ocean. The Barbary States were Morocco, Algiers, Tunis and Tripoli.

What level of monetary loss did the United States sustain from these pirates?

Over a period of ten years—from the beginning of the Washington presidency through the presidency of John Adams, the United States paid almost two million dollars in ransom to free American sailors and their ships.[6]

What were Girard's initial motives for becoming a privateer?

Although Girard became a very patriotic citizen, at this stage in his life he regarded privateering as a form of legalized piracy. There was money to be made by capturing well-laden British ships.[7]

How did his first privateering venture fare?

It started with his 1/3 ownership of a two-masted schooner, the *Minerva*, on its first cruise after being repaired in Egg Harbor. The vessel, with Arthur Helme as master, ran into a storm and began to leak at every nail hole.

How successful was Helme on his first encounter with a foreign vessel?

In the distance he saw a schooner floundering in the storm with clearly nobody managing its direction. He boarded the vessel and found only dead bodies on board. It was the *Barbary* and it was filled with tobacco. This was Helme's only prize of the war.[8]

What further experience did Girard's crew have with privateering?

On several occasions, Stephen used his personal merchant ships against foreign enemies. However, he had little success. During one occasion, a heavy canon made his vessel go off balance. On another occasion, Girard suggested to Captain Chadwick that he cruise the Chesapeake to capture any ship belonging to the Tories.[9]

Was Girard a privateer in the negative sense of the word?

Girard had been a victim of privateering and had lost vessels at sea. He returned this action with action for the sake of his own protection. In many cases it was to help in the war effort against great odds and to bring down enemy ships that threatened the new republic. Among the important services Mr. Wildes, author of *Lonely Midas*, has performed is that of laying to rest, forever it is hoped, many of the bits of gossip concerning Girard and his college that have been repeated for generations. Among the most pernicious of these fabrications are that Girard established his fortune by privateering; and that he made an immense sum by assisting refugees fleeing from the slave insurrections. Mr. Wildes documents that these charges are without foundation.

8

Global Trade

1785–1793

How did Girard's business fare at the start of the 19th century?

Between 1799 and 1805, Girard had his heyday—more ships were sent out with bigger cargoes and with much bigger profits.[1]

What might have been a normal routine for sending out his vessels?

As an example, ships were quickly loaded. The captains were ordered to go to Bordeaux, sell their cargoes and reload with fruit and wine for Saint Petersburg. There they were to sell their cargoes and buy hemp and iron, and sail for Amsterdam. At Amsterdam they were to buy dry goods and sail for Calcutta.[2]

What in particular interested them in Calcutta?

Girard's biographer Hubbard suggested that they were to sell out their cargo and with the proceeds buy silks, teas and coffees and sail for America. These trips took a year to make, but proved immensely profitable.

As Girard opened his trade worldwide, did he personally manage to travel to places where his ships were destined—China, India, Russia and South America?

No. He was a stay-at-home trader. He was good at delegating responsibilities and trusted his captains and his supercargoes.[3]

What was his secret for enjoying so much success without seeing first hand these locations?

He had an intimate knowledge of the ports, the economies and the governments of these countries. He read books, studied dispatches and maps of the harbors. He also questioned his foreign agents in minute detail.

It has been said that Girard had a Scrooge-like character. Did he?

Biographer Harry Wildes writes that Girard, although denied the pleasures of a normal family life, usually had a large number of people around him in his home. Instead of being a lonely Scrooge-like character, he was remarkably generous, both to his numerous grasping and predatory relatives and to individuals and organizations in his adopted country. Girard was one of the most influential men of his day and contributed greatly to the early development of modern American business and finance. His advice and assistance were sought by presidents and statesmen.

What was Girard's first newspaper advertisement announcing the arrival of cargo from France?

On Monday, August 1, 1785, Girard advertised in the *Pennsylvania Packet and Daily Advertiser*: "Imported in the Brig *Two Brothers* from Marseilles French wine, Malaga wine, cognac, Castille soap, preserved fruit, Lucca oil, etc."

Why did Girard pursue a plan for global maritime trade?

As early as 1787, he became interested in a venture into China trade. The rumors were that such trade was extraordinarily profitable.

Did Girard ever go to sea again?

Since settling in Philadelphia, more than a decade earlier, he set sail once again in December, 1787 for Marseilles, France. The brig he was sailing was *Deux Amis*. He made a prolonged stop in Charleston, South Carolina. On leaving Charleston he spent thirty-two days crossing the ocean and then entered the Strait of Gibraltar. He continued on to the French coastal city of Toulon, then on to Marseilles.[4]

What was the reason for Girard's trip to Marseilles?

Girard had been percolating an idea for some time about going into a partnership with his agent in Marseilles on 50% ownership each for a vessel. The reason was that he wanted to have French ownership papers as well as French insurance so that he could access certain ports that were antagonistic to American trade. Girard had written to Samatan Frères at Marseilles telling of his proposed voyage to that city and offering to sell them a half interest in the brig *Kitty*, to ply regularly between their city and Philadelphia. "We should" was the reply, "be as much pleased as yourself to have a half interest in a French vessel to ply regularly between your city and ours. We should gladly be the owners; but the vessel must sail under the French flag, not the American, because two thirds at least, of the crew must be French. Let us have your views in regard to this. If it is possible to meet them we will do so."[5]

Is there a reason that Girard did not go to Bordeaux?

He still owed money to merchants in Bordeaux—almost two thousand dollars. Perhaps he was afraid his vessel would be impounded in Bordeaux and sold to pay his debts. His unwillingness to pay off his debts was a source of some embarrassment to his father. Girard could never honestly explain to himself why he delayed so long. The constant reminders from his father and brother were annoying to him. Hearing nothing from the father he now wrote to his brother John, just returned from Bordeaux, and asked what had been done. "I see on reading your letter to myself" was the reply, "that you ask for news of the funds you sent our father. There were several 6,000 livres to pay, but I believe that many would come to terms. You do not say a word about Pailher who has presented me a note against you for 1200 livres. I will wait until you speak of this to me before writing him. Take your own time."[6]

9

Family and Friends

When did Pierre Girard die?

He died on April 27, 1788. Stephen had not learned of his father's death until he had returned to Philadelphia from his voyage to France. Girard did not leave America again for the rest of his life. But at long last he repaid all his debts in Bordeaux. As Pierre's eldest son, Stephen became the owner of the house where he was born by virtue of the will. It was perhaps this money that he used to settle his debts in France.[1]

In later life Pierre had lost quite a bit of money. Why did he not accept Stephen's offer of a partnership?

On one hand it was a question of pride. Pierre had given virtually nothing to his oldest son. On the other hand, since his marriage to the wealthy Marie Jeanne, Pierre turned away from the sea and spent his time cultivating the land at Tresse.[2]

How did Girard deal with the new means of sea travel—the steamboat?

Not at all. All his ships continued under sail. It wasn't until 1838 that the first steam ship would cross the Atlantic Ocean.

Who was Sophie Fénelon?

Sophie was Girard's sister. She was married to Jean Fénelon. Some biographers have written that Sophie was mentally insufficient. At one point her father Pierre rescued her from a mental hospital. Sophie was smart in mind and as commercially apt as Stephen or John.[3]

Did Sophie own a business?

She helped her husband manage the Bordeaux Commission House and it was believed that her ability surpassed that of her husband. There were several points of conflict between husband and wife.[4]

Did Sophie and Jean have children?

While still married to Jean, they had a son who died in his youth and a daughter, Constance. (The reader will benefit from this information as it will explain the demands Sophie made against Stephen Girard's will).

We know that Stephen was not close to his brothers and sisters while they were growing up. Was his brother John any different?

Yes. John liked to imitate his brother in giving money to the needy; in this case to his siblings. Being a sensitive man, he might often ask his family how much they loved him. He wanted the reassurance of their love.[5]

Who was Monk?

Monk was the nickname for Stephen's younger brother—Louis Alexandre. He was called Monk as he was the only son to please his father by taking holy orders.[6]

When did the French Revolution begin?

The French Revolution began on July 14, 1789 with the storming of the Bastille in Paris.

What was the great benefit of selling wheat to France during the French Revolution?

So great was the demand for wheat in France that the entire cargo was marketed before it arrived for forty livres a charge, the government bounty of three livres, fifteen sous to go to the purchaser. The profit margin for the seller—was exceptional.[7]

Was there a corresponding risk?

The destruction of the French Monarchy had thrown its government into complete disorder which affected and discredited the whole commerce of France. The principal cities abroad, such as London, Amsterdam and Cadiz, were loath to negotiate paper in France.[8]

What kind of commercial war began at Le Cap over wheat and flour?

Girard was told that Le Cap was closed to American ships carrying wheat and flour to sell. To counter this action, Girard flew the flag of France and unloaded his cargo.

What other ruses did Girard's captains use to get around local Haitian regulations?

The captains were told to carry two different bills of lading showing that the cargo was not made up of prohibited items. Sometimes the captain stated that the cargo contained flour and wheat but the vessel was bound for a different destination. [9]

Was bribing custom officers ever considered?

With increasing frequency, Girard's captains smuggled goods aboard the *Polly*. Girard instructed his agents to offer custom house officers a few coins to silence them. Girard, however, was not prone to offer bribes because the cost would invariably escalate.

How did the activation of the US Constitution affect maritime trade for merchants like Stephen Girard?

Girard was pleased. At last he had only one set of requirements to abide by—no conflicting and confusing state laws to deal with. This made it easier to conduct trade with foreign countries.

Who was Timon Samatan?

He was Girard's agent in Marseilles. During the Reign of Terror, Samatan was executed on the guillotine simply because he was rich. All his property was confiscated.

Did Girard offer the family his support?

Stephen was quick to let Madame Samatan know he was willing to educate in America any son she wished to send.

Is this how he assisted the Samatan family?

As it turned out, Girard's help was not necessary. After Robespierre was put to death, the regime changed and all the money and property was returned to the family.

When did representatives of the thirteen states meet formally for the first time?

Beginning in May 1787 representatives from twelve states, all but Rhode Island met in Philadelphia for a Constitutional Convention. George Washington was chosen to head the Virginia delegation.

Were the sentiments about slavery the same for George Washington as they were for Benjamin Franklin?

No. Franklin abhorred the notion of slavery but had a few slaves who either ran off or died in their work. In later life he refused to own slaves. When George Washington was elected President of the United States and moved to Philadelphia, he had the opportunity to free his wife Martha's household slaves. Pennsylvania law required that slave holders moving to Pennsylvania could not keep their slaves beyond the six-month period after arriving. They had to be freed. Instead of freeing the slaves, Washington shipped them back to Virginia just before the time ran out.

Was George Washington a wealthy man?

When he became President of the United States he was one of the richest men in America. Upon marrying Martha Custis, he became very wealthy. He was the owner of 54,000 acres of land—8,000 acres in Mount Vernon. He owned 100 slaves.

What were the physical attributes of our nation's first president?

James Thatcher wrote: "His personal appearance was truly noble and majestic, being tall and well proportioned. His look and bearing was that of a man accustomed to respect and being obeyed. George Washington embraced a life like that of the English gentry. He could easily take his place among monarchs of Europe."

What other attributes did Washington have that would appeal to the American people?

Thomas Jefferson wrote that Washington was the best horseman of his age. He could hunt and ride for up to seven hours without resting and had exceptional stamina.

When Lord Howe arrived in America shortly after the signing of the Declaration of Independence, what significant exchange did Washington have with the famous General?

Howe had sent a letter to George Washington addressing it to "Mr. Washington. Esq." The letter was not delivered because there was no Mr. Washington in the army. There was, however, a General Washington in the army, a fact that Lord Howe chose to ignore. Washington later explained his position. If Lord Howe had come from London with the authority only to grant pardons, he had come to the wrong place. This attitude of the British was typical of everyone from King George down to the sergeants in the field towards Americans. It was patronizing and disdainful.

On September 15, 1776, Washington heard the roar of cannon from Kip's Bay. What had occurred and how did the General react?

Washington went to Kip's Bay and saw that his troops were in disarray. British warships took positions on Kip's Bay to provide protection for a flotilla of flat-bottomed boats that ferried 4,000 British soldiers to Manhattan. American forces under Colonel William Douglas put up meager resistance before breaking and running, Washington observed the scene from a hilltop. In anger and frustration he shouted, "Are these the men with which I am to defend America?"

Who was Nathanael Greene?

He was a good-natured Quaker from Rhode Island in whom Washington saw great potential. Although he knew little about the military, at age thirty-three he became the youngest brigadier general in the Continental Army. At Yorktown, Virginia, Greene proved himself to be one of Washington's most brilliant field commanders.

In 1790, when Girard was forty years old, what was happening in the United States?

The United States Census of 1790 was the first census conducted in the country. It recorded the population of the United States as of Census Day, August 2, 1790, as mandated by Article I, Section 2 of the United States Constitution and applicable laws. In the First Census, the population of the United States was enumerated to be 3,929,214. Congress assigned responsibility for the 1790 census to the marshals of United States judicial districts under an act which, with minor modifications and extensions, governed census taking through 1840. The law required that every household be visited, that the completed census schedules be posted in two of the most public places within each jurisdiction, there to remain for the inspection of all concerned. The aggregate amount of each description of persons for every district was to be transmitted to the president.

When did the colonies formally become The United States of America?

That took place in 1790 as well. Philadelphia became the capital of the new nation.

What was the catalyst for the slave uprising in San Domingo in 1791?

The catalyst was simply the outrageous conditions of the slaves kept by the French landowners. Learning that the French mainland had been taken by the revolt of thousands of people in Paris, the slaves of the West Indies took heart and began to seize and kill as many white settlers as possible. San Domingo was controlled by the French and had the largest enslaved population in the Caribbean. It had a booming sugar industry that had created the world's richest colony, with half a million enslaved Africans.

Were the conditions unusually harsh?

Slavery here was as harsh as anywhere. The slaves were treated as inhumanely as can be imagined. Many men were forced to sleep in cramped quarters without any ventilation whatsoever. They were beaten for the slightest real or perceived infraction. In many cases, the food they were given was spoiled garbage which they had to eat or starve. Some owners put tin masks on the slaves, to keep them from chewing sugar cane in the fields. Their overseers were not known to spare the bull whip on their workers.

The arrival of the *Polly* at Le Cap soon after the three dreadful days of plundering, burning and murder, and her return to Philadelphia with eight and thirty refugees gave rise to a story concerning Girard, which one of his biographers, Mr. Henry Atlee Ingram, thought necessary to tell and refute. "The year 1791 witnessed the horrible uprising of the slaves in the island of Santo Domingo, and many foreign merchants narrowly escaped sharing in the general massacre by taking refuge on one of Girard's vessels, commanded by Captain Cochran, then in port at Cap Français. Some of these refugees barely escaped with the clothing upon their persons, but others, more successful, saved large quantities of wearing apparel, household furniture, and silver, with which the vessel set sail for Philadelphia, where she arrived safely, loaded with the valuables. It has been said that Girard's fortune was largely increased by the subsequent failure of owners to claim many of these articles, but no reliable evidence has ever been adduced, while both Captain Cochran and Mr. Roberjot, one of the refugee merchants, who succeeded in saving nothing but a valise of valuable papers, vouched personally that all for whom articles could be found had been returned."

Did the African slaves attack the plantation owners?

Yes. They indiscriminately slaughtered men, women and children—all white people. Those whites who managed to escape said they had never seen such hate in the eyes of the Africans. This insane, blinding anger did not spare any white person in their paths. Their machetes cut through thousands of landowners as they tried to get aboard ships in the port. Girard had been warned in a letter from his brother John months before that an uprising was inevitable.[11]

How did the Stephen Girard's agent, Aubert, describe the horrible scenes?

"Hundreds of whites fled to the waterfront to escape the invasion only to be met by the mulattoes, who cut off their retreat. The blacks stormed the city, plundering and setting fire to property and killing many whites. The governor fled for his life alongside hundreds of now penniless refugees."[12]

How did Girard's agent attempt to save the jewelry and other valuables belonging to the fleeing slave owners?

Aubert, escaping with his family, had hidden all of the passengers' valuable possessions in barrels of coffee, or under the planks of the deck to protect them if the ship should be boarded once at sea. The captain of the privateer *Sally* (taken earlier by the British) observed the brig from a distance and decided to take it over. Having escaped the angry slaves on shore, the passengers now faced the destructive crew of privateers at sea. They almost demolished the ship in their search for valuables." They found the hidden cargo. "The value of the passengers' property," wrote Aubert, "amounted to about 100,000 gourdes, (£4550) and this loss deprives me of every resource." The formerly confident agent was despondent over his loss. "After 45 years at the Cape, where I accumulated a fortune over 3,000,000 (£140,000), I have been reduced to this! Nothing."[2]

What was Girard's reaction to the uprising?

Stephen Girard responded to the first news of the massacre with uncharacteristic concern for his agents. "After such a disaster," he offered, "I will ask you, as a true friend, to wind up your own affairs and mine and take advantage of my Polly if she still be in the harbor."[13]

Were the house servants involved in the uprising?

One Frenchman wrote: "When the trouble began we found that our own servants, who are very numerous, would join forces with the brigands and set fire to our houses; but, by the most watchful vigilance both by day and by night, we have escaped their plots. Nevertheless a number of servants were arrested and put to death. Others that we considered suspicious were put in a safe place. As a result of this wise precaution we are now a little less anxious, and may God keep us so for many a day."

Was Girard's ship the *Polly* in San Domingo at the time?

Captain Edger of the *Polly* had been waiting in port and had been ready to sail for three weeks but when he would sail was impossible to tell, for those who were cleared first were allowed to depart first.

What cargo did he have aboard?

His load included 42 hogsheads of sugar.

When was the *Polly* finally released for departure?

On October 7th, the *Polly* was allowed to sail after paying heavy duties assessed by the Colonial Assembly and undergoing a rigorous inspection. The rigorous inspection of American vessels practiced by officials on land, as well as by men-of-war, obliges them to truly declare their cargoes.

How long did the rebellion last?

It lasted less than seven weeks and during this time more than two thousand whites had perished in the uprising.

Did Girard profit by the instability and insurrection when the slave-holders of San Domingo fled from the crowds of angry people?

Stephen Girard just happened to have two vessels in that port. The planters rushed aboard with all their wealth and treasures. Many went back to bring more to the ships but several were killed along with their families before they could return. The possessions not claimed in Philadelphia became the property of Girard. In Philadelphia, he did whatever he could to help the refugees from San Domingo.

Did Girard buy more real estate with his windfall from San Domingo?

No. Instead he had several magnificent ships built and decided to enter the China and India trade. This trade contributed greatly to his fortune.

How did John Girard find conditions in the West Indies two years after the uprising?

At the beginning of 1793, John Girard, with whom relations had been mended with his brother, Stephen, wrote pessimistically: "The country is in a deplorable condition. The law has no force. Conditions are as bad as they were under white control."[14]

Where did the French families go that succeeded in escaping?

Many came to the United States. Stephen Girard gave financial assistance to the refugees that came to Philadelphia.[15]

Did these circumstances allow Girard to devote sufficient time to his business?

In 1780, circumstances made trade with New Orleans and San Domingo very profitable. He promptly engaged in it and in two years had doubled his worth. His personal tragedies during the years 1790–1793 were followed by general tragedy for the city of Philadelphia—an outbreak of a yellow fever epidemic.[16]

10

Outbreak of Yellow Fever

1793

What caused the yellow fever epidemic that devastated Philadelphia in 1793?

Since many refugees had been infected, it was assumed that the fever came with them from the West Indies. Girard noted that a stevedore fell sick while unloading the *Polly*. He was immediately purged and bled but his condition grew worse and died. According to biographer Wildes, Frenchmen such as Girard were accused of giving housing to people coming from San Domingo who may have been infected.

How was yellow fever described?

It was sometimes called the "black sickness" because of the color of the vomit, due to the amount of blood that was thrown up. It would kill about five thousand people in 1793.[1]

How did Hubbard describe Girard's courage during the epidemic?

"When pestilence settled on the city like a shadow, and death had marked the doorposts of more than half the homes in the city with the sign of silence, Girard did not absolve himself by drawing a check and sending it to a committee by mail. Not he! He asked himself: 'What would Franklin have done under these conditions?' And he answered the question by going to the pesthouse, doing for the stricken, the dying and the dead what the pitying Christ would have done had He been on earth."

Why did Girard take on such a difficult and dangerous task during the yellow fever epidemic?

Stephen Simpson wrote, "The yellow fever epidemic of 1793 excited all the energies of his mind, and brought into full play the latent benevolence of his heart. Stephen Girard and his companions stood forward in the shape of ministering angels to provide asylum for the sick. When Girard made a proffer of his services, it was not merely to aid by his counsel or cooperate by his money, in alleviating the calamity of his fellow citizens, but was to undertake in person the most laborious and loathsome duties."[2]

"Girard's Herosim" (during the yellow fever epidemic) illustration by G. F. and E. B. Bensell from James D. McCabe, Jr.'s, *Great Fortunes and How They Were Made,* 1871.

Why was the name "yellow fever" given to this illness?

The liver, kidneys and heart were affected which turned the skin yellow.

What were the conditions of the hospital where the infected patients stayed?

Prior to Girard's arrival, the conditions of the hospital on Bush Hill were deplorable. It was dirty, badly regulated, crowded and poorly supplied.

How many experienced nurses were available to care for the sick?

None. Nurses couldn't be hired at any price. They fled thinking merely being near the hospital would bring them certain death.

What did the hospital committee do for the sick?

The committee held a meeting of people whose loved ones had been contaminated asking for volunteers to work for the patients. The committee was astonished and pleased when two wealthy men in the crowd raised their hands. The first to volunteer was Stephen Girard and the second was Peter Helm. The record shows a statement by a committee member, Matthew Carey, about Girard: "...

sympathizing with the wretched situation of the sufferers at Bush Hill, voluntarily and unexpectedly offered himself as a manager to superintend that hospital."[3]

How did Girard divide the work for Helm and himself?

Girard took for himself the inside of the hospital—the more dangerous of the tasks and had Helm take on the outside.[4]

How did Arey describe the risks that Girard and Helm took in caring for the afflicted?

These men performed "the most loathsome duties... and the only reward possible was a nameless grave upon the heights of Bush Hill."

How long did this difficult task last?

For sixty days, Girard and Helm took care of all the people in their charge. Girard gave generously of his time and financial support to the afflicted.[5]

Did Girard become infected with yellow fever?

At the height of the epidemic, he felt a fever coming on but he managed to control and eradicate it with what he called "lavage" or constant washings. He had put himself at serious risk during this epidemic. While many in the city with the means to escape fled the city limits for a safer environment, Girard stayed to care for the sick and dying. "I shall accordingly be very busy for a few days and if I have the misfortune to be overcome by the fatigue of my labors I shall have the satisfaction of having performed a duty which we owe to one another." He managed to have a mansion converted into a hospital. When the outbreak subsided, The City Hall of Philadelphia hailed him as a hero.[6]

How did Philadelphia's Mayor Clarkson attempt to purify the air during the 1793 yellow fever epidemic?

At the suggestion of the College of Physicians, the mayor had the militia fire off blasts from a small canon. He also suggested that people carry camphor in their clothing.

Where did the disease seem to be concentrated?

The epidemic seemed to center around Water Street. People believed that a pile of rotting coffee that had been dislodged from a cart was causing people on Water Street to get sick.

Who made the suggestion to Mayor Clarkson to have the streets cleaned of dead animals and garbage?

Stephen Girard whose house was on Water Street made several requests that City Hall have the streets cleaned. The flies swarmed around rotting dogs, cats and rats in the street.

What were some of Peter Helm's functions at the improvised hospital on Bush Hill?

Helm who was a barrel maker by trade was handy with tools and helped with the construction of coffins for the dead that had to be removed for burial. When the death rate became too high, not all the bodies were given a coffin but were picked up by a designated wagon after sundown. Helm was also responsible for procuring housing for the newly hired nurses, and other staff members nearby.

Was Peter Helm not afraid of becoming sick with yellow fever?

Unlike Girard who had a scientific hypothesis for believing he was not in danger of contagion, Helm was a deeply religious man who relied on the Lord to protect him.

When was yellow fever classified as an aborviral disease?

It was not until 1900, that an army team of officers led by Walter Reed were able to discern that the fever came from the bite of a female mosquito.

Were most attempts at healing the sick ineffectual?

Yes. Doctors knew very little about this disease. Without understanding the problem, they resorted to purging and bleeding and often amputation. Doctors were often the cause of early death.

How did Philadelphia's population and businesses deal with the outbreak?

Half the population fled the city. The others remained in their houses. Most of the churches, the Great Coffee House, the library were closed. Of the four newspapers, only one remained open. To ward off the sickness, people smoked tobacco; others chewed garlic, or carried bags of camphor in pockets or around their necks. No one offered to shake hands.[7]

In the aftermath of the 1793 epidemic, did those people who had contracted yellow fever have any recurring symptoms?

There is no evidence that there were any recurring symptoms of the illness beyond the cold months of winter.[8]

What was the death toll of this epidemic?

From August 1st 1793 through November 9th, 1793, in a population of twenty-five thousand, (many residents were not counted because they would not return to the city until much later) there were four thousand and thirty one burials from the fever.[9]

During the height of the yellow fever epidemic, the dead had to be disposed of quickly. How was this done?

Every night, a horse-drawn carriage circulated through the streets. The call was made to bring out the dead.[10]

What was Girard's overall opinion of doctors?

It had often been said that Girard fancied himself as a sensible country doctor. He was quoted as saying: "I consider myself as competent as any (doctor) in the United States." Salt was Girard's favorite prescription for sores and cuts.

Girard disliked doctors and regarded them as ignorant imbeciles who killed more people than they healed. In his opinion, doctors were only good at bone setting. Girard was one of the first to speak out against bloodletting or bleeding. He criticized Dr. Benjamin Rush for weakening his patients by bleeding them. Many of them did not survive.[11]

How did Girard look back on his experience at Bush Hill?

Girard is quoted as saying: "Would you believe it, my friend, that I have visited as many as fifteen sick people in a day? And what will surprise you much more; I have lost only one patient, an Irishman, who would drink a little. I do not flatter myself that I have cured one single person; but in my quality of Philadelphia physician, I have been very moderate, and that not one of my confreres has killed fewer than myself."[12]

Benjamin Rush (1746–1813). Portrait by unknown artist. U.S. National Archives and Records Administration, NARA Identifier 532855.

Who was the young man who came to stay briefly with Girard and was struck down with yellow fever?

Girard wrote most tenderly showing his affection for the young man, Peter Seguin, and his deep distress at the illness which had overtaken him. Girard's letters indicated that he had watched all night by the bedside of this young man and no more tender solicitude for a member of one's own family would have been possible than Girard showed to one in need although Seguin was a comparative stranger.[13]

What was the daily death toll from yellow fever at the height of the epidemic?

By October 11, 1793, the daily death toll was one hundred nineteen.

When did the fever begin to wane?

By the first of December, the plague had started to subside.

Had President Washington visited Philadelphia during the epidemic?

He went to Philadelphia on November 10th and rode through the near empty streets but he determined that it was too soon to take up residence again. In December, he returned to stay.

Had yellow fever returned to Philadelphia in subsequent years?

Yes. The epidemic returned in 1797, another in 1798, a third in 1802, and a fourth in 1820. In each of these new crises, Stephen Girard was a leader in preventive measures and in the care of those stricken.[14]

> Philadelphia during the summer of 1802 was again visited by Yellow Fever. Early in June a vessel called the San Domingo Packet reached the Lazaretto, was detained there twenty-one days and towards the close of the month came up to the Vine Street wharf. A week later a carpenter, working on a ship nearby, was taken down with yellow fever and died, and in less than ten days eight others met the same fate. This led the Aurora to declare that it was certain a fever as virulent as that of '93, '97, and '99 had broken out at Vine Street near the San Domingo Packet, and to demand that the sick be instantly removed from the well. Thereupon the Board of Health made a visit to Northern Liberties, reported that all the sick had been removed and forbade all communication with the infected district.
>
> During a few days no new cases were detected and the Board announced that the fever had subsided; but July had not ended when the *Aurora* asserted that nineteen cases had appeared in the Northern Liberties, accused the Board of keeping the new outbreak quiet, and again demanded the removal of the sick from the well. Once more the Board visited the infected region, bounded by Vine, Callow hill, Front and Water Streets, reported they found but four persons sick with fever of a malignant kind, and assured the citizens that the rumors were greatly exaggerated and that notes had been left at the houses in the infected district recommending families to remove to the country as the best way to stop the spread of the

fever. If they had "no retreat," the Board would endeavor to find one. The fever soon spread to the city, whereupon the *Aurora* cried out that since the sick were not removed from the well, the well must remove themselves. The Board admitted that the fever was "very malignant" and entreated all who could to leave at once. The Editor of the *Aurora* then published an address to his "Fellow Citizens," told them there was "no remedy but in flight or frost," and announced the removal of his newspaper to Frankford. Flight now became general; so many went.

During the various yellow fever epidemics, did Girard's business activities suffer?

From 1783 to 1800, Girard shipped 175 types of items, from 25 locations, on 93 different vessels. These were some ships he built or owned between 1791 and 1810: *China Packet, North America, Superb, Rousseau, Montesquieu, Voltaire,* and *Good Friends.*

Who was J. H. Roberjot?

In 1794, this young man approached Girard for employment as a bookkeeper. Girard told him to improve his English and come back to see him. He did and got the job. Thirty-four years later, he was still working for Girard but in more important functions as a trusted business agent.[15]

What was Girard's estimated worth over the years of his accumulated wealth?

Late in life, an inventory of his estate revealed that he still owned four ships; namely, *Helvetius, North America, Rousseau,* and another whose name was not mentioned. Owning and leasing so many ships permitted Girard to expand his business to trade throughout the world. Marvin W. McFarland, who studied the Girard ledgers, states that by 1781 Girard's fortune was between fifty and sixty thousand dollars. Although the annual volume of his business rose to about $1.5 million in 1794, he was wealthy but not yet a millionaire. He estimated that in 1795 he was worth about $250,000, a very considerable fortune for the times.[16]

What were some of the items he shipped during this period?

Girard shipped and imported grain, wine, liquors, oils, tobacco, cloth, cheese, nails, sugar, coffee, cocoa, meats, and other necessary staples, using many agents in different ports to obtain the best local prices. He paid these agents well to protect his interests, but his papers include many letters scolding the agents for not getting what he considered reasonable prices. Girard's profits from shipping soared between 1790 and 1815, but international conflicts frequently interfered with his ventures. The French and the English were intermittently at war with each other and Girard's ships and cargoes were often confiscated.[17]

What important election took place in 1800?

The election of 1800 between John Adams and Thomas Jefferson was an emotional and hard-fought campaign. Each side believed that victory by the other would ruin the nation.

Federalists attacked Jefferson as an un-Christian deist whose sympathy for the French Revolution would bring similar bloodshed and chaos to the United States. On the other side, the Democratic-Republicans denounced the strong centralization of federal power under Adams's presidency. Republicans specifically objected to the expansion of the U.S. Army and Navy, the attack on individual rights in the Alien and Sedition Acts, and new taxes and deficit spending used to support broadened federal action.

Why did the United States want to go to war with France?

In 1797, the United States nearly went to war with France, because it harassed American ships trading with England. In 1805, England became master of the seas by defeating the French and Spanish fleets at Trafalgar. They blockaded Europe and often confiscated American merchant ships.[18]

Quoting from a book *Philadelphia in the War of 1812*, "The second war with England, toward which the country had been gravitating for many years, was brought very closely home to Philadelphia by reason of their important shipping interest. Large sums of money were invested in, and a considerable portion of the population was directly or indirectly sustained by, overseas commerce. The various embargoes of England and France during the Napoleonic Wars, the general invasion of the rights of neutral powers, and the impressment of their seamen by the belligerents, led to a feeling of great resentment in the United States."[19]

How did Girard manage to make a profit with ships being taken by privateers and pirates?

The constant interference with shipping caused a scarcity of some items, and

Girard's profits were huge when his ships did succeed in getting through the blockades. When England continued to harass American ships, Girard anticipated a conflict. In 1807, he started liquidating his overseas merchandise and collecting his foreign debt. The harassment of ships led to the War of 1812 and to Girard's decision to enter the banking business. The Bank of the United States, which Girard told Mr. Curwen had been refused a charter by the Legislature of Pennsylvania in 1812, was created by Act of Congress in 1791, at a time when there were but three banks in all the United States. The life of the charter was twenty years. At the close of this period, 1811, a memorandum from the President and Directors of the Bank, of whom Girard was one, praying for renewal of the charter, was presented to Congress; but it was not granted, and on March 3rd, 1811, the Bank closed its doors.[20]

Why did Girard decide to bring his European assets home to the US in 1811?

His assets in Great Britain and on the European continent were in jeopardy with Napoleon's armies running wild and England becoming more aggressive.

When did Girard reach the two million dollar mark in net worth?

According to Mercantile Papers, 31 December 1821, Girard became a multi-millionaire in 1811.

As his wealth grew, what single concern occupied Girard's mind, turning him into an activist with a cause?

Biographer George Wilson points out that Girard was concerned with the rights of Americans trading on the high seas. Girard was not successful with getting the first two Federalist Presidents, Washington and Adams to take a strong position against Great Britain, the most threatening nation. Girard continued his protests during the administrations of Jefferson and Madison.

Did Professor Wagner mention Girard's role in supporting the US government during the War of 1812?

Yes. In Lecture 5, he stated: "During the whole of the War of 1812, Girard's bank was the very right hand of the national credit. While other banks were contracting, it was Girard who stayed the panic."[21]

Some historians credit David Parish, who made a fortune speculating in silver and land in upstate New York, with the 1813 Government bailout. Although he owned lots of land, he was nearly bankrupt at the time.

How did Girard sum up the results of the War of 1812?

In a letter to his correspondent, Morton, in 1815, Girard wrote: "The peace which has taken place between this country and England will consolidate forever our independence and insure our tranquility.[22]

11

Banking

Domestic Arrangements
Foreign Policies
1793–1831

What was Girard's creed as a financier?

He believed to buy and sell for others on a commission basis and on a large scale was the safest and most profitable business.

Did Girard specialize in this endeavor?

His interest and expertise in foreign trade led him to exchange operations. He also firmly believed that a nation prospered best when the country enjoyed uniform and healthy financial conditions.

What did Girard do when he learned that the United States Bank was in trouble and that Congress was concerned about renewing its charter?

Girard supported a renewal of the charter and sent lobbyists to Washington to express his views. He then managed to secure a state franchise for the nation-wide operations of the bank. Through his London agent, he ordered Baring Brothers to convert all his European credits into cash in order to use the funds to purchase abroad all the United States stocks that could be obtained and to convert the remainder of his British pounds into approximately $300,000 and transfer them to the bank in Philadelphia.

Did this make Stephen Girard America's first hedge investor?

It is true that until Congress decided whether or not to re-charter the US Bank, Girard hedged his bets knowing that in either case, he would make a handsome profit on the outcome.

Did Girard work hard to help the US Bank survive this ordeal?

He worked the entire year of 1811 to help the bank survive. In November of that year, he realized that his efforts had been in vain. The US Bank was to close its doors. Faced with the problem of liquidating its assets, the bank turned to Girard for help. Girard agreed to buy the bank's buildings for $115,000. The value of the property was about three times this sum.

What made Girard think he would be permitted to buy the bank?

Girard was a firm believer that fortune smiles on the audacious. He had the capital, he had the property and he had the valuable services of George Simpson. After consultation with George Simpson in the spring of 1812 and having ascertained through him that there should be no problem in Girard's purchasing the bank as well as the cashier's house at a much reduced price, Girard pressed on. The deal was struck on May 12, 1812. It was also agreed that George Simpson would continue his services under the same conditions as previously.[1]

How did the public react to the change in bank management?

Most people never saw or knew of any change. The changeover was rather seamless. Some professionals were against an unchartered bank but few knew the details of the succession. The impression spread unchecked that Girard was closely affiliated with the US Treasury. This misconception gave Girard prestige and helped his business.

How did Girard capitalize the bank?

Girard deposited funds from checks he had drawn from other bank accounts. This amounted to $71,000. To that sum, he added $556,115 in securities he owned.

Did Girard earn a reasonable profit from his first year as bank manager?

By his own estimate, his first year earned him only about 3%. He was confident he would do better in subsequent years.

How did the professional banking community receive the new Stephen Girard Bank?

Two weeks after the opening of the new bank, only the Farmers' Bank of Lancaster and the Bank of Wilmington recognized Girard's bank. The Mechanics Bank of

Baltimore began relations with him a bit later. By September of 1812, two New York bank institutions recognized Girard as their Philadelphia agent.

Were other Philadelphia banks as welcoming as those from other states?

No, they were not welcoming at all. The four state-chartered institutions conspired to put Girard out of business. They resorted to unfair criticism saying to Girard's clients that they were risking their money in an unchartered bank. Some said that upon Girard's death the money in the bank would become part of his estate.

How did Girard handle that particular criticism?

He declared that upon his death, five trustees would immediately assume control of the bank's management and continue its operations.

At a time when Girard's fortune seemed limitless, he received many requests for donations or loans. Aside from buying bonds to support the War of 1812, did he lend money to any important government figures?

Correspondence shows that no less a person than James Monroe, President of the United States appealed to Girard for financial aid under the date of October 25, 1822. Monroe wrote at length from Washington saying: "his long employment in the public service under circumstances which had prevented him from giving proper attention to his private affairs and in positions which did not afford compensation adequate to his support had involved him in debts for which he wished to provide in such a manner as would be satisfactory to those to whom he was obligated and as would be also the least hardship on himself." To accomplish these ends, Monroe asked that Girard loan him from $25,000 to $40,000. President Monroe went on to say that he offered prime real estate as collateral for the loan. There is no evidence that this correspondence was answered.[2]

How did James Monroe perform for President Washington during his tenure as minister to France in 1794?

The *Liberty* had sailed for Bordeaux on the 25th of September carrying as a passenger the gentleman who was to succeed Monroe as Minister from the United States to the French Republic. The conduct of Monroe while Minister to France had been far from pleasing to President Washington. Monroe had reached Paris early in August 1794 to find the people rejoicing over the downfall of the infamous government of Robespierre, and the execution of the tyrant and his associates St.

Just, Couthon and Henriot. Though dead, their arbitrary decrees remained in force and the most arbitrary related to foreign commerce. A captain who entered a port of France with a cargo of flour, grain and tobacco was forced to sell it for assignats. The government was the sole purchaser, for all private trade had been suppressed. And when the assignats were paid not a livre could the captain expend for a return cargo till permission to do so was given him. Meanwhile he was fortunate if his ship was not boarded and the crew taken off and thrown into prison.

James Monroe (1758–1831). Pendleton's Lithograph [1828?] from a painting by Gilbert Stuart. LC-USZ62-117118. Library of Congress Prints and Photographs Division, Washington, DC.

What, according to Stephen Girard, was the second war for American independence?

The War of 1812 has well been called the second war for independence. Immediately following the Treaty of Ghent, Girard wrote to his correspondent in Bordeaux, "the peace which has taken place between this country and England will consolidate forever our independence and insure our domestic tranquility."[3]

The Signing of the Treaty of Ghent, Christmas Eve, 1814. Painting by Amédée Forestier, Smithsonian American Art Museum, Washington, DC. [Public Domain–United States].

How again did Girard show his true allegiance to the United States over France in 1812?

Correspondence at this time indicated the high regard in which Girard held America. A letter from Joseph Bonaparte held out to Girard a temptation to return to France and with his large wealth create a great estate. Girard refused point-blank saying that he did not wish to figure as a great proprietor in a country to which he would never go and under a government inimical to republicans.[4]

It seems that Girard treated Joseph Bonaparte very well. Did Girard ever disappoint Joseph by not granting a request?

He did disappoint Joseph in two matters. Bonaparte asked Girard to sell him the downtown property on Chestnut and Market Streets. Girard said "no"; unless Joseph were willing to cover the land with silver dollars standing on end. He also turned Bonaparte down by not moving his wealth back to France.

What happened when the bank charter was refused for renewal?

When the charter was refused, Girard was determined to use the funds he had drawn from London to establish a private bank of his own, bought the banking house and residence of the cashier of the old Bank of the United States on 3rd Street providing him with the information, employed its one time cashier, Mr. George Simpson, to act in the same capacity for him, and on May 23rd, he wrote Governor Simon Snyder of Pennsylvania providing him with information.[5]

Joseph Bonaparte (1768–1844) c.1811. Portrait by François Joseph Kinson. Wikimedia Commons [Public Domain].

Was there a law governing the purchase of a bank?

The law did not forbid any individual engaging in the business of banking, because, as yet, no one had ever established a private bank in Pennsylvania. The first man to do so was Stephen Girard.

Is it true that Stephen Simpson was critical of Girard's treatment of his bank employees?

Yes. Simpson wrote that Girard was generous to a fault with large donations for the beautification of the city but never paid his employees a penny more than agreed to in their employment contracts. Girard was a firm believer in the maxim "take care of the pence, and the pounds will take care of themselves."[6]

Did Stephen Simpson consider Girard to be unjust?

No. He said: "Stephen Girard had a sense of justice that was always paramount in his actions and never laid down a rule for others which he was not willing to observe himself."[7]

What provides us with the most information about Girard's character?

The Stephen Girard Collection contains numerous correspondences relating to his business ventures that sheds a strong light upon the development of his character, under a succession of sad and in some cases disastrous events, mingled with incidents and ventures of surprising success. "The subjects of public interest include his close business relations with France during the Reign of Terror, in which his personal friend and trusted correspondent, Mr. Samatan, of Marseilles, fell a victim to the guillotine; the Negro Slave Insurrection in St. Domingo, in which some of his closest friends were brutally murdered and others escaped only to die in abject poverty and suffering; the suppression of American trade in the Mediterranean by the Algerians and other pirates, and the depredation on American commerce by British and French cruisers in each of which he had a strong personal interest."[8]

With the return of peace between Great Britain and America in 1815, how was Girard's business faring?

Girard wrote that despite his large losses during the war and in addition to the capital which was employed in his banking operations and the money which he had invested in real estate and lands in the country, he had commercial capital sufficient to buy his goods for cash and to sell on credit without the necessity of discounting his paper.[9]

We've seen Stephen Girard as a sailor and as a merchant; what other professional interests did he have?

Above all he had an uncanny ability to make money. He would hardly think about making a purchase without thinking ahead about selling it for a profit. This is why he became interested in banking.

Where did Girard conduct his business?

Girard was operating his trading business from his home and counting room at 21 and 23 North Water Street, Philadelphia, a building that was demolished in 1845 to make way for warehouses, one of which later became the Girard Meat Packing Company.

What made Girard consider withdrawing his funds from the Second United States Bank?

In Girard's own words he said: "indeed when I take into view the increase of enemies to that bank I am alarmed and desirous to sell and realize what I have on hand this anxiety arose from my belief is owing to the improper management."

Did Girard change his mind?

Girard continued to transact a general banking business parallel with the Second United States Bank. His enterprise was so essentially personal and the amount of capital which he handled so great that he feared a possible disarrangement of the public finances.[10]

What single event gave Girard his first big step in banking?

When the charter for the First Bank of the United States expired in 1811, Girard purchased most of the stock as well as the building with its furnishings. His staff was small. He began his operation with eight employees—a cashier, two tellers, two bookkeepers, a clerk, a messenger and a janitor. George Simpson was given the responsibility of day-to-day operations.

Was the fact that Girard owned a bank that was unincorporated legal?

It had never been done before and Girard wanted to be sure so he hired two Philadelphia lawyers—Jared Ingersoll and Alexander Dallas to research the matter. But being the risk taker that he was, Girard opened his bank before his lawyers had their answer. As he anticipated, the lawyers told him it was legal.

What was the location of the First Girard Bank in Philadelphia?

This bank was located on South Third Street. In 1816, Girard influenced the Government to establish the Second United States Bank. Girard was appointed a board member of the bank and bought nearly a million and a half dollars of its stock. His involvement influenced others to purchase stock. He believed his involvement was necessary for the bank to succeed, but he disliked this appointment because he thought some of the other members were corrupt or incompetent. He accepted the appointment for only two years.

Stephen Girard had been called the "Napoleon of Merchants." Did Girard resemble Napoleon physically?

He did to a degree. Girard was described as being low in stature and squarely built. He was often clumsily dressed. His feet and hands were large, while his legs were short. His face was not attractive–wrinkled, colorless and stony. One eye was dull and the other blind–a wall-eye.[11]

What work habits made him similar to Napoleon?

Like Napoleon, Girard never undertook any great enterprise without hearing the advice of those best qualified to give a sound opinion.[12]

How did Girard's eye condition and the mean nicknames he was called affect his personality?

From his early years, Girard lived a life of reserve, kept his own counsel and neither received nor gave the confidences which come from intimacies of friendships.[13]

How did his appearance hurt his effectiveness?

Although he seemed cold, close, ungainly and ungracious, his mind was brilliant and always focused. He would often avoid social settings because of his looks but he was a superb business man. As far as his clothing was concerned—his coats were plain: however, they were made of the best broad cloth. It was said that he kept a pair of boots for each day of the week. His linen, cravats and the dress of his hair were after the fashion of the 18th century. In later years, his person was scrupulously neat, and every morning his French barber, one Dorphin, came to his house to shave and dress and powder his hair and retie his *queue* (pigtail) and brush his clothes. Osgood E. Fuller compares Girard to a monument:

Like a monumental bronze, unchanged his look,
A soul which pity never touched or shook
Trained, from his lowly cradle to his bier,
The fierce extremes of good and ill to brook
Unchanging, fearing but the charge of fear
A stoic of the mart, a man without a tear.

How did Joseph Bonaparte affect the habits of Girard?

One of Bonaparte's American achievements was to civilize Girard. In Joseph's company, Girard was less morose and friendlier. He smiled more and was more prone to play pranks on his friend.[14]

How did the man who saw him daily comment on Girard's apparel?

Simpson said: "What he saved (on buying) clothes, he expended in the embellishment of the city; but personal vanity, he had none to gratify." [15]

How was Girard in social conversation?

Girard had little to say except on business matters. He was impatient with idle chatter but loved to describe in detail his methods of closing a deal.[16]

What did Wildes say about Girard's reticence in boasting about his business matters?

In Girard's own words, he said: "I like to keep silent for two reasons. If I boast, I may make a rival. In the opposite case, should I lose my credit, people would believe I had ruined myself."

It is apparent that Girard learned to read English very well; he would continue to write in French. How was his spoken English?

He was never comfortable speaking English. His pronunciation was not clear. Biographer Wildes speaks of Girard's accent as a definite advantage. He drew the trade of other Frenchmen and Polish soldiers serving with the Continental Army. His hand-printed signs, partly in French and partly in English made his customers confident that his prices were reasonable.[17]

Was Girard as parsimonious in his food selection as he was for his clothing?

No. He enjoyed food and good claret. When in vigorous health up to the year 1824, he ate well.[18]

What were Girard's favorite beverages?

At dinner he drank the best French claret, rarely touching the heavier wines. In the afternoon he liked to have a tablespoon of Holland gin from stone crocks. His favorite beverages were cider in season and coffee of the strength seldom tasted by others.[19]

What did Stephen miss the most about his native country?

Girard was disappointed that Americans, unlike the French, did not understand the use of vegetables in preparing meals. He especially missed his beloved cauliflower. He was disappointed that Americans could not make good bread. He also missed the wonderful vineyards of Bordeaux and the wine he had tasted there as a young man.

Did Girard keep any pets?

He loved his breed of canary birds which was among the most choice and extensive in the world. His fondness for these birds was remarkable. He even encouraged them to sing by the use of a bird organ.[20]

Hubbard writes: "On each of his ships, he (Girard) placed a big Newfoundland dog- to keep the sailors company."

What was Girard's most marked mental trait?

He was able to anticipate events and reactions of people. His thought process was deep and thorough.[21]

How did Stephen manage his business affairs with his wife being incapacitated?

When Girard learned that his wife was an incurable lunatic, Girard was devastated. For two years, he tried without success to have the medical community help her. But in 1787, Girard finally recognized that his marriage was ended. He took a mistress, Sally Bickham, into his home to replace the lost affections of his wife. At that time, there was no stigma associated with the practice of acquiring a mistress. Girard no longer had a wife with whom he could continue a peaceful and compatible relationship. Sally Bickham would fill the void.

If not emotional love, what did Sally give to Stephen?

She cared for him and gave him pleasure but she also provided sensuous delights—presiding over the selection of food and making certain the kegs of fine herring were available. She reminded him to order anchovies when the ships went to France.[22]

Did Sally also help Stephen improve his appearance?

She worked on him to buy good clothes of a better cut, persuading him that it was more economical in the long run. She chided him not to shove the four inch receipt book into his small pockets. She was not very successful in this endeavor.[23]

How did the thirty-seven-year-old Girard, now with a mistress, manage his business responsibilities?

Like a lion. His astute business instincts led him in the direction of the trade with China, a decision that had him take the lead as a global trade prospector.

Stephen Girard standing on a Philadelphia waterfront wharf (posthumous portrait detail). From an 1885 painting by Frederick James.

With his wife incurably insane, what legal steps did he take concerning her?

Girard made his will, which obliged him to pay out some small amount for a lawyer's fee. "The latter tells me that the law of Pennsylvania allows the wife, during her life time, one third of the income from the real estate left by her husband at his death, and in addition she receives absolutely one third of the personal property, or, in case there are no children, one half of the said personal property. As I wish to be just, I think, that having been so unfortunate as to marry this unfortunate woman, it is my duty to see that she is provided for to the best of my ability."

Who was Martin Bickham?

One of those who benefited most by Girard's generosity was the brother of his mistress, Sally Bickham. Girard had taken her younger brother into his care many years earlier. Martin Bickham gained much from Girard's love and teaching; he was treated as the son Stephen Girard never had. With Girard as his mentor and protector, Martin was introduced to the business world when only fourteen years of age. Under Girard's tutelage, Sally Bickham watched with pride as her brother became an eager student, absorbing the business savvy that his benefactor so willingly put before him, and prospered as a lifetime employee. With Sally and her brother under the same roof, Girard lived the family life he seemed to enjoy. Martin became Stephen's friend and always the most important of his protégés.[24]

What made Girard so willing to have Sally's brother live with them?

Girard's closest associates affirmed that Girard had a need for children around him. It was for this reason that he invited the eight-year-old Martin to live with him and Sally.[25]

Was Martin ever a disappointment to Stephen?

Like Stephen, Martin made mistakes on starting out on his own. One serious mistake was the purchase of a ship he intended to use for buying slaves. When Stephen learned about it, he severely chastised his protégé.[26]

After Martin's bad decision to buy and sell slaves, did Girard forgive him?

Girard was very forgiving and urged Martin to come home to Philadelphia to resume his place in Stephen's home and counting house.

In what way did Martin Bickham mimic Girard's own behavior?

Like Stephen, he stayed away from—rather than face debt repayment. [27]

Young Martin asked Stephen about his first voyage as a new captain.

Girard explained that it was surprisingly very successful. He managed to pick up a cargo and take it to New Orleans. Because of his fluent French, he could make useful contacts and nice profits.

What occurred during his visit to France in 1788?

During his journey, in April of 1788, Girard's father died, though Stephen would not learn of it for months. Stephen Girard's inheritance amounted to less than one hundred dollars, an irony considering his own gathering wealth. He also inherited the house where his father had lived. This was also the house where Stephen Girard was born.

When Mrs. Girard grew worse and could no longer be kept at home, what measures did Stephen take?

In August of 1790, Girard had his wife committed to Pennsylvania Hospital as an *incurable lunatic*. This was not done without total awareness of the enormity of his actions. Girard, sparing no expense, made certain that there be effort made to ease his wife's discomfort; she was afforded every luxury possible.

When Girard finally agreed that he had to commit his wife to the hospital at the insistence of her doctors, how did Stephen express his feelings?

In a letter written in 1804, long afterward, to his friend Duplessis, Girard said: "As to myself, I live like a galley slave, often passing the whole night without sleeping. I am worn out with care." [28]

Who was William Wagner?

He was the founder and president of Wagner Free Institute of Science in Philadelphia. He was also a confidential friend and apprentice of Stephen Girard. He was known for a series of lectures he gave on Girard.

How was William Wagner able to describe Mary so well during her hospitalization?

Wagner, as Girard's apprentice, was usually tasked with paying Mrs. Girard's hospital expenses. He was able to see her often.[29]

What was Wagner's description of Mary Girard in the hospital?

He described her as "a dark-haired woman always sitting in the sunlight, still bearing strong marks of the beauty for which she was celebrated in early life."

What might have been Girard's life had his wife not suffered from mental disease?

The couple might have had several children, as Stephen's father had and he might have been less driven and more cordial. His role in life might have been that as a teacher of men and children and less tyrannical and judgmental.[30]

Did Girard suffer any financial setbacks by 1790?

After the dissolution of his partnership with his brother John, Girard's estate was valued at only thirty thousand dollars. This loss was due to troubled times—The French Revolution, the massacre at San Domingo and disturbed relations with England and France.

Were these the years of his great mercantile expansion?

Yes. By 1795, he had built his fleet from two ships to twenty-two ships and was worth more than a million dollars.

How, in retrospect, did Girard analyze his disadvantages during the period after the War of Independence?

America had no naval force. During the war, France provided America with protection on the high seas. Britain's warships and privateers were gunning for merchant ships flying under the American flag. President Washington declared American neutrality in the ongoing war between France and Britain.[31]

What was France's reaction to this policy?

France may have considered America to be ungrateful after France had gone to war for American independence.

How did Girard personally suffer under this neutrality policy?

In 1794, Girard owned five ships. All five of them had been seized by Britain and France.

Could Britain and France do this legally?

Both British and French warships could seize cargo and American ships in a liberal interpretation that these ships and cargoes would benefit their enemy.

What was Girard's point of view regarding Washington's decision?

The US should have remained on the side of France—if not for a sense of gratitude, then rather because the US could benefit from France's continued protection on the high seas until such time as the US could build its own navy.

At whose urging did Washington declare neutrality for America?

As in several other decisions, the Secretary of the Treasury, Alexander Hamilton had the President's ear.

What consequence did this decision have?

The Secretary of State, Thomas Jefferson resigned his position saying that neutrality in this case was a mistake.

Did Girard express his dissatisfaction with this policy as well?

Yes. He wrote: "The war now being carried on by the European pirates is very disturbing to our commerce... Our ships are not only stopped and plundered daily but even run the risk of being taken to the ports of these despots." [32]

In a letter to Alexander Hamilton, Girard asked that the Federal Government take steps to have his ship released from a French port. "Justice and the interests of a citizen of the United States may require."[33]

What was the result achieved by Girard's rally in support for a change in US foreign policy?

Focus was placed on three areas of concern: (l) better protection for US merchant ships; (2) compensation for loses due to confiscations; and (3) higher tariffs on goods exported to the US from countries failing to respect US shipping.[34]

While waiting for the nation to tire of having its merchant ships taken or destroyed, what remedy did Girard seek?

When both presidents—Washington and Adams failed to take measures to protect American merchant ships, Girard took matters into his own hands. He had guns mounted on the decks of his cargo vessels. He also sent ships out in convoys so they could protect one another. On a voyage to Cuba, his two ships carried 48 guns.[35]

What further information did Girard give to a crowd of interested supporters on March 18th 1794?

He accused Great Britain of violently seizing American ships; attempting to impose limits of American commerce; imprisoning American citizens and forcing some into the British Navy; encouraging Barbary States, especially Algiers, to prey on American ships; refusing to abandon British outposts on America's western frontier and fomenting war with Indians.

Was this rally effective for Girard?

It was very effective. Thousands in attendance started to bring pressure on President Washington and on Congress.

Was there a principal reason that John Adams did not seek a second term?

He had barely had a victory for his first term and because his popularity had suffered when so many ships were seized, he opted not to run a second time.[36]

What was the Sedition Act?

The Sedition Act prohibited any libelous attack by writing, printing, publishing or speaking of any criticism of the President, or any member of Congress. Punishment was a fine of $5,000 and from six months to two years imprisonment. Congress passed this Act in 1798.

When did Girard urge the government to open another national bank?

One day in March, 1830, his assistant cashier brought him a bundle of deeds just deposited in his Bank by Mr. Pratt, a trustee of the old Bank of the United States. No sooner had he looked them over than he wrote Mr. Alter of Pottsville: "At about four o'clock this afternoon Mr. Carpenter, assistant cashier of my bank, handed me a bundle containing several deeds written on parchment which embraced the lands expressed in the mortgage given to the old Bank U. S. by Messrs. Morris and Nicholson, all of which appear to be duly recorded as per annexed statement, which please to examine and compare with the book or books of record, and if you find that everything is in conformity and is sufficiently secured by the quantity and quality of the land, please to communicate me immediately all the information and observations which you have made, adding your remarks respecting the number of acres of coal land and your opinion respecting the highest price at which I can venture to purchase. "The aforesaid deeds have been kept in the dark and at last have been delivered to Mr. Pratt one of the trustees of the old Bank U. S. who has sent them to my bank where they shall remain until the sale of that property is over, which I have reason to believe will be in about 25 days from this date. "The lands in question were duly offered for sale by the Trustees of the old Bank, and Mr. William J. Duane was sent to obtain information "respecting the validity of the title of the old Bank of the United States, principally also the lawful Hens which may be on said lands or a part thereof, the number of settlers and their names, and the quantity of acres which each of them possesses, the epoch when they settled thereon, the nature of their title adding the quantity and quality of coal lands and of wood land unsettled. In short be so obliging as to take correct notes of all your remarks so that I may not be at a loss to fix the price which I should give for that property. In regard to yourself I recommend you to take good care of your health, and when you go to visit the lands to take a suitable carriage with competent and honest judges who are well acquainted with that part of the country and can give every correct information which you require. I wish it to be understood that I think it is correct to pay for the services of all the persons which will go with you."

Who in Congress was especially receptive to Girard's concerns?

James Madison in the House of Representatives introduced a bill that called for precisely the kind of changes Girard wanted. The bill passed in the House but failed in the Senate.

Was it hard for the American people to understand why Congress would not retaliate against countries that would ban American goods?

Yes. Madison wanted the US to ban products from countries that showed America no respect or fairness in trade.[37]

How was the banker Stephen Girard described?

As Girard lived on into the nineteenth century, he continued the eighteenth century style of dress wearing a white neckcloth and an old-fashioned full-skirted coat of the revolutionary period. He also continued the eighteenth century custom of wearing long hair in a pigtail down his back. In temperament he was intense, walking with a swift firm step; he was decidedly aggressive in speech and action.[38]

His dress was old-fashioned and sometimes shabby; a wide-brimmed hat, and the large-skirted coat of the last century. He was blind of one eye; and though his bushy eyebrows gave some character to his countenance, it was curiously devoid of expression. He had also the absent look of a man who either had no thoughts or was absorbed in thought; and he shuffled along on his enormous feet, looking neither to the right nor to the left. There was always a certain look of the old mariner about him, though he had been fifty years an inhabitant of the town. When he rode it was in the plainest, least comfortable gig in Philadelphia, drawn by an ancient and ill-formed horse, driven always by the master's own hand at a good pace. He chose still to live where he had lived for fifty years, in Water Street, close to the wharves, in a small and inconvenient house, darkened by tall storehouses, amid the bustle, the noise, and the odors of commerce. His sole pleasure was to visit once a day a little farm which he possessed a few miles out of town, where he was wont to take off his coat, roll up his shirt-sleeves, and personally labor in the field and in the barn, hoeing corn, pruning trees, tossing hay, and not disdaining even to assist in butchering the animals which he raised for market. It was no mere ornamental or experimental farm. He made it pay.[39]

12

Farmer

What was the beginning of Girard's foray into farming?

In 1797–1798, Girard came into the possession of two parcels of land aggregating seventy-five acres in what was then Passyunk Township; in that time he wrote to his French correspondent that he had lately purchased these two properties in the country situated three miles from Philadelphia on the road to Fort Mifflin.[1]

Did this letter to his French correspondent have a purpose?

Girard requested his correspondent to send by the ship *Good Friends* some roots of Muscat vines and any other good white grapes grown in France. In the same year he also directed that his Bordeaux correspondent send him twelve large hens and two cockerels specifying that he wished those with large combs.

Was Girard considered a competent farmer?

In 1830, the Horticulture Society of Pennsylvania recognized Girard's farms as being among the best.

What were some of the trees and plants that Girard had in the garden area?

The garden included an acre and a half of fine vegetables, including America's first artichokes and a variety of imported grape vines. Fruits, lemons, mandarin oranges, and the only known citrons grown in this country, filled his greenhouse. Finally, the report shows that the farm was profuse with jasmine bushes, and 20 feet high Marseillaise fig trees, and included 13 horses, 18 oxen, and 28 pigs. Later, the farms became the site of a federal housing project, a Government Depot, League Island (now Roosevelt) Golf Course, Girard Point Terminal, the Food Distribution Center and the Girard Estate homes.

How much time did Girard spend on his farming?

Although Girard remained active in banking until his death, as he aged, he devoted increasingly more time to his farm. It was located in Passyunk Township, now South Philadelphia and he called it the Places. He bought this farm and farmhouse in 1797 from George Copper who obtained it through default from Henry Seckel. Seckel used this farm to introduce and grow Seckel pears. It consisted of two lots totaling 75 acres. The east wing of the farmhouse was built about 1750.

Did Girard expand the farm from the original 75 acres?

Girard added the middle section to the farmhouse in 1800 and the west wing in 1825. He hired a caretaker, increased the productivity of the orchard, added crops and cattle and marketed his products. As the years passed, he purchased nearby acres, and when he died he had accumulated 583 acres.

When was the house on Water Street built and what was its basic design?

The house was built during 1795 and occupied sometime in August 1796, when he explains his delay in answering Mr. Douglas by saying that he had removed his counting house and that his papers were a little deranged. It was a four story, brick structure with a sloping roof surmounted by a railing and flanked by two great chimneys, one on either side. On an adjoining lot was the public counting house where most of his commercial business was done. The house was unpretentious but substantial but he like refined furnishings. He ordered from Bordeaux a mahogany sofa, twelve armchairs covered with blue damask or satin, finished as plain as possible. He also ordered three oval looking glasses with golden frames.[2]

On the ground floor there were two counting rooms, one private and the other public. There were steps leading down to the wine cellar and more steps leading to the first floor. On the first floor there was the dining room behind which was a tiled kitchen. The drawing rooms occupied the entire second floor. Sleeping apartments were on the third floor. Girard's room was in the rear. On the night table, Girard kept an unloaded brace of splendid blunderbusses with brass barrels and steel bayonets. The fourth floor was used by the servants.[3]

Is it true that Girard was one of the first residents of Philadelphia to use coal as a means of heating his home?

Yes. In William Wagner's Lecture 5, he speaks about Girard buying his coal from England which lasted him more than a year for each cargo. The rest he stored on his wharf.

What was Girard's library like?

He had about 150 bound volumes and 25 unbound pamphlets chiefly in the French language. He had the complete writings of Voltaire which were published in 1785.[4]

What books other than the works of Voltaire did Girard keep in his library?

Aside from the works of Voltaire, Girard's most extensive collection of books consisted of various dictionaries of agriculture one of these was a ten volume work under the title *Cours Complet d'agriculture*, edited by Rozier and published in Paris from 1791 to 1800. This was an extensive work of approximately six hundred pages in each volume.[5]

What other subjects interested Girard as seen in his book collection?

He was interested in building rustic houses, the economy of farm life, the goodness of nature and animal husbandry.[6]

John Jay (1745–1829). Painting by Gilbert Stuart and John Trumbull. National Portrait Gallery, Smithsonian Institution, Washington, DC. Billy Hathom, Photographer. Creative Commons CCO 1.0 [Universal Public Domain Dedication].

What farm property fruit trees gave Girard the most pleasure?

On the farm, Stephen had a small green house 25 feet long that was well stocked with lemons, mandarins, oranges and many other kinds of fruit all large and beautiful. There was a variety of citrons and a curious play of nature in some fruit that had the appearance of a half-closed hand. The tree which bore this singularly shaped fruit was said to be unique. Nothing of the kind existed anywhere in the United States.[7]

Turning to the politics of the time, why did President Washington send John Jay to England?

Washington believed that a conciliatory tone should be set in negotiations with the British, instead of exerting pressure on them to put an end to their aggressions.[8]

Was the Jay Treaty signed by both countries?

It was signed by John Jay and the British on November 19, 1794.

Why wasn't there a public outcry before the treaty was signed?

It had been kept secret from the public.

What was the final outcome of this agreement?

The American public was furious. It thought that Jay had given away the store. When Jefferson became president in 1801, he did not repudiate the treaty. He kept the Federalist minister, Rufus King, in London to negotiate a successful resolution to outstanding issues regarding cash payments and boundaries. The treaty broke down when it expired in 1805. Jefferson rejected a renewal of the Jay Treaty in the Monroe-Pinkney Treaty of 1806 as negotiated by his diplomats and agreed to by London. Relations turned increasingly hostile as a prelude to the War of 1812. George Wilson writes that in 1815, the Treaty of Ghent superseded the Jay Treaty. The angst that Girard suffered when the Jay Treaty was approved by the Washington administration years earlier was relieved when Thomas Jefferson became president in 1801. Girard worked on Jefferson's behalf toward his election and was rewarded when Jefferson made drastic changes in foreign policy, changes that Girard had wanted and was denied by the Jay Treaty. Jefferson also took other measures to gain safety for ships at sea from which Girard took pleasure and comfort. Jefferson was Girard's kind of president.[9]

What tangible results did the Treaty of Ghent secure?

Great Britain did not agree to end impressment of American citizens into the British navy but the practice did end. The harassing of American merchant ships did stop.

Did Girard always stand with Jefferson in political matters?

Although Girard was an admirer of Thomas Jefferson and was identified with numerous activities of the Republican Party, he was a firm believer in the United States Bank standing on this question against Jefferson and in support of Hamilton and the Federalist Party.[10]

When did the first United States Bank open?

The first United States Bank was opened in Carpenter's Hall in 1791 where it continued until 1797 at which date it moved to its new building on South Third Street. In addition, it established branches in different cities throughout the country. The bank operated under a charter granted by Congress for twenty years on January 23, 1810.[11]

How did Girard react when John Adams won the presidency?

Adams would represent the same politics as Washington in dealing with England. Adams was a Federalist and Girard was a Republican. Girard, as a party manager, served as treasurer and donated generously to his party. Pennsylvania, at that time, allowed only tax payers to vote. Girard would then pay the delinquent poll taxes for numbers of good republicans who had either been too careless or too poor to qualify as voters.

Did Girard take an active role in politics?

Girard participated actively in the presidential contest of 1800. In that year he was a candidate on the Republican ticket for a seat on the Select Council of Philadelphia. He was elected in a great landslide to the Republican Party. When in 1801, the Republicans in Philadelphia formed a committee for a public celebration on March 4th, Girard presented the "powder necessary to make the celebration a noisy one." The Committee of Arrangements thanked Girard for his donation of gun powder for the celebration.[12]

How did Great Britain react to the rapid rise of Napoleon?

The coup d'état of the 19th Brumaire which established the consulate in France was followed at once by the drafting of a new Constitution and its promulgation on the fifteenth of December, 1799. Napoleon, who easily gained the mastery over his colleagues, set himself at once to make peace with the powers of the Coalition and on December twenty-fifth addressed notes to Great Britain and Austria proposing that an end be put to the war. Great Britain rejected the offer, Austria did not accept, and in May, 1800, Napoleon made his famous crossing of the Great St. Bernard and descended on Italy. Marengo and Hohenlinden followed and in February, 1801, at Luneville, Austria made peace. Naples did the same in March; the other powers signed treaties during the year, and Great Britain, who for eight years had been at war with France, signed preliminary articles at London in October, 1801. The terms were discussed and finally settled at Amiens in 1802.

In December, 1801, the United States Senate ratified the Convention of September, 1800, which put an end to our war with France. As amended by the Senate, the Convention had been returned to Napoleon for his approval of the restriction which limited its duration to a period of eight years, and of the dropping of the second article which provided for a further consideration, some time in the future, of the question of damages for spoliations on our commerce. Determined to pay no damages, Napoleon saw in this action of the Senate a chance to be rid of a troublesome issue, and in giving his approval added the words that he did " accept, ratify and affirm the above convention, with the addition imparting that this convention shall be in force for the space of eight years, and with the retrenchment of the second article; Provided that by this retrenchment the two States renounce the respective claims which are the object of the said article."

On May 16, 1803, Great Britain declared war on France, but really on Napoleon, and opened a struggle which ended on the field of Waterloo. Great Britain blockaded the mouths of the Elbe and the Weser, and Napoleon, on July 15, by a decree barred from every port of France any vessel which had cleared from Great Britain.

How did Girard plan to use Amelia Island as a refuge?

With the belligerence of Great Britain on the one hand and the unpredictable aggression of Napoleon on the other, Girard decided to shelter his ship *Good Friends* with its cargo of more than a hundred thousand dollars in the Spanish port of Amelia Island (in present-day Florida). He had no intention of risking a loss of ship and cargo on the open seas. Events, however, conspired against Girard. The Spanish were driven off the island by American forces. Since some of the cargo consisted of British made items which were forbidden by American custom laws, Girard was faced with a large bill.

Battle of the Virginia Capes [French naval victory over a British fleet, 1781]. Painting done by V. Zveg, 1962. U.S. Navy Naval History and Heritage Command, Photo #NH 73927-KN.

How did Stephen's brother John interpret the naming of the vessel *Good Friends*?

John thought that Stephen's naming of the ship was a token that their fraternal quarrels had ended.

Were John Girard's efforts in trans-Atlantic trade successful?

John had not fully understood the dangers of trade on the high seas. With money he could ill afford, he bought a brig and hired a captain to sail it. Unfortunately, it was captured by the British which ended John's business career.

When did Girard's brother John die?

John died of tropical fever in the West Indies on November 4th 1803. He was fifty-five years old. After the death of his brother, Stephen took John's three daughters to his own home and provided for their maintenance and education and except for the brief time when two of them attended a boarding school, they continued to reside with him until their several marriages. He appeared to have enjoyed the companionship of these young women and with their assistance he gave hospitable entertainment to numerous visitors.[13]

Did Stephen continue this kindness after two of John's daughters were married?

Yes. When the women had children of their own, he liked to have them around the house and felt it his right to have the little people close by.[14]

Was it during this period, after the Napoleonic Wars, that Girard grew more attentive to his family, friends and French refugees?

Yes. The most familiar of all the French refugees was Joseph Bonaparte, King of Naples and later King of Spain who first came to New York incognito. At the outset, Joseph Bonaparte was coldly received in America but Stephen Girard became his close friend and trusted adviser. In addition, Girard welcomed other refugees who had sought safety in America following the wars. Girard also provided for the support of his aunt Ann Lafargue and his sister Victoire in France and extended aid to his brother Etienne when he made it known he was in need. The service of Girard to the children of his brother Etienne and the further fact that he had a strong attachment for his grand-niece Caroline Lallemand show Girard's love for children, his interest in education and his affection for the members of his own family.[15]

Where did Joseph Bonaparte live while he was in the Philadelphia area?

Joseph established himself at Bordentown, New Jersey to be within easy reach of both New York and Philadelphia. When in Philadelphia, he occupied a house belonging to Stephen Girard at the southeast corner of Twelfth and Market Streets in what was called Girard Row.[16]

Concerning the house wanted by Joseph Bonaparte, Girard wrote: "I have not yet been able to find a house that would suit you. The advertisement on this subject is still in two of our papers. Mr. Meany intends to rent one of his houses; one is new and is situated on 9th Street between Spruce and Pine and the other on Walnut Street near 10th. If the accommodation and the houses suit you, I am sure that the proprietor, whom I know very well, would give you your choice." Girard, unfortunately, had overlooked the little formality of consulting Mrs. Meany, who now wrote: "Mr. Bonaparte called on Captain Meany this morning to rent the house in which he now lives to which he in part consented, but as it would be very disagreeable and particularly inconvenient for me to move at this inclement season (December), and what I cannot possibly consent to, therefore if you will represent the case so as to abbreviate the difficulty you will ever oblige." The house in question was that on Walnut Street for which a lease to the Count had already been signed by Mr. Meany. The rent was to be $1200 a year."

How did Bonaparte's visits to Girard's home affect Stephen?

Often solitary and morose, Girard developed in his later years a more frequent tendency to smile, especially after the arrival of his friend Joseph Bonaparte and other guests that lifted his spirit.

How did his acquaintances in France hope that Girard would spend his money in the country of his origin?

They hoped he would bring his wealth to Europe and the opportunity he would have to be the guide and patron of French merchants and to engage in the cultivation of beautiful vineyards and the development of extensive herds in the fertile fields of Languedoc. Finally Girard was pictured as dying after he had founded a magnificent, benevolent institution in Paris, his name descending as a blessing to the poor and homeless.

How had life in France changed?

In a letter to one of his correspondents, Girard requested a "candid opinion respecting political events as far as it related (to) commercial interests." The events were well worthy of consideration even from a commercial point of view. The French Republic had ceased to exist. In its place was the Emperor Napoleon.

What effect did these events have on commerce?

The effects on world commerce were duly reported to Girard by his correspondents in accordance with his request. A Liverpool house, complaining of the dullness of trade, said: "This unusual depression is not to be attributed to any considerable increase in our general importations. The unsettled state of the continent has shaken that confidence so necessary to trade."

How did the Battle of Trafalgar prove Great Britain's superiority and change the conditions of war at sea?

The Battle of Trafalgar was fought on October 21st 1805 off Cape Trafalgar on the Spanish coast, between the combined fleets of Spain and France and the Royal Navy. It was the last great sea action of the period and its significance to the outcome of the war in Europe is still debated by historians. The French and the English were intermittently at war with each other and Girard's ships and cargoes were often confiscated.

What was the concern of the French when Wellington moved into Bordeaux?

The concern was that their lives would be once again torn apart.

Were these fears realized as the troops arrived in France?

After the occupation of Bordeaux, Madame Capeyron (Sophie Marie Girard) wrote: "It has fallen into the power of Louis XVIII. All I can tell you of my own knowledge is that the expectation of a real calamity which we believed would overtake us on the arrival of the English and Portuguese which was to be nothing less than death and pillage, has not happened and that everything passed off without any disturbance whatever."[17]

Did Girard hear again from Madame Capeyron on this subject?

As soon as the news arrived, Madame Capeyron made haste to tell it. "I reopen my letter to tell you that Paris has been taken in the name of Louis XVIII. Bonaparte has abdicated his Crown and they have allowed him an annual income of six million. The members of the Senate have all been made peers of France and their salaries are to be continued."

Did Girard ever marry his longtime mistress, Sally Bickham?

No, Sally left Girard to get married. In 1796, the family atmosphere was markedly changed. Sally Bickham had been Girard's surrogate wife for nine years. The parting was amicable and Girard was sorry to see her leave, but he did not spend much time alone.

How did Sally Bickham's leaving affect Girard?

Girard had never considered that Sally was essential to him. He had not known how deeply his feelings ran for her. Only after she had gone away with Charles Harrison did Stephen realize his deep fondness for the laughing girl.[18]

What realization did Sally come to regarding her feelings for Girard?

Her devotion to Girard was evoked more for his kindness to her brother than to Girard the man.

What happened to Sally Bickham after leaving Girard?

When Sally's husband died years later, she rented a smaller house that Girard owned. There is no evidence that she wanted to return to her former status but that position had already been filled by Polly Kenton. Somewhat desperate, Sally began to take up with various men and her reputation was the talk of the neighbors. When Girard heard about her lifestyle, he sent her a note, giving her three months to vacate his property.

How did Sally respond to the note from Girard?

Sally did not write to Girard but her sister Isabella did saying that Girard had acted improperly with Sally who had lived with Girard as his wife for eight or nine years. Girard ignored this letter.

What do we know about Girard's second mistress?

The parting of Sally Bickham was amicable and Girard was sorry to see her leave, but he did not tarry long in replacing Sally. Shortly after her departure, Girard took another mistress. Polly Kenton, a laundress, twenty-six years younger than Girard, and only twenty-six years of age, moved into the Girard house. Girard's fortune had grown considerably and at that time was in excess of $250,000, and he was well on his way to becoming a millionaire. Polly Kenton saw that as incentive to take on the role as mistress. She did not disappoint Girard, giving him all the comforts that such a relationship included. In return, Girard lavished upon her gifts of extreme extravagance, a contradiction to the austerity he normally exhibited, especially in business matters. But Polly was a woman cut from the same cloth as Girard; she worked hard and expected others to do the same. Aside from his love for her, Girard wanted to honor his mistress with gifts that would please her as a woman.

What might Girard have looked for in Polly?

Polly Kenton, happy, buxom, competent, was, although young, more mother than mistress. She symbolized, perhaps, the mother Girard had lost.[19]

How did Girard know Polly?

She had been coming to the house to take away the soiled laundry. Sally didn't like her because of her direct ways but Stephen did like her. It wasn't long before he suggested she take on the post as housekeeper. He didn't, however, move her into his home until he was sure he wanted it. He discovered that she was no nonsense and honest.[20]

According to many, who were the five most important persons in Philadelphia during that period?

It may be disputable but the names might be: William Penn, Benjamin Franklin, Thomas Paine, Stephen Girard and Walt Whitman.[21]

The names of Benjamin Franklin and Stephen Girard are often joined when speaking of philanthropy and development of their era. Is this an accurate statement?

Girard was inspired by Franklin. Girard observed the progress of the University of Pennsylvania which was founded by Franklin along with the Philadelphia Public Library, the Philadelphia Hospital and learned from the ideas and problems encountered by the planners. Girard was to create a school for poor fatherless boys many years later.[22]

Was Girard politically motivated?

He rubbed elbows with the greatest figures of the Colonial Period. He was a progressive but still managed to get along with the conservatives. Similar to Franklin, he wanted education to be within the reach of all people. Showing his willingness to support both sides of the aisle, Girard assisted in the raising of a liberty-pole in the Presidency of John Adams and gave his full backing to Thomas Jefferson. For as long as he lived, he held the name of Thomas Jefferson in high esteem.

Why did Girard feel especially close to Franklin, Jefferson and Paine?

All three spoke French and had great respect for the French people. Both Franklin and Jefferson had traveled to France on official business.

What did Girard have to say about Thomas Paine?

According to Elbert Hubbard, in the time of Girard, the names of Franklin, Jefferson and Paine were reviled, renounced and denounced by good society; and it was in defending these men that Girard brought down upon himself the contumely that endures—in attenuation, at least—even unto this day.

What did Paine teach Girard?

According to Hubbard, Paine taught Girard the iniquity and folly of a dogmatic religion: the religion that was so sure it was right, and so certain that all others were wrong, that it would, if it could, force humanity at point of the sword to accept its standards.

Why was it said that Stephen Girard was a master at lease agreements?

When business was slow, he would ask for a long term lease renewal which pleased the landlord. Girard's ability to sense an upward trend allowed him to make a fortune while still paying a modest rent. This he would do time and time again.

Many folks described Girard as tight-fisted and stingy. How does that explain his tremendous generosity and philanthropy?

It's true that there seems to be a paradox. Perhaps where Girard found illness or extreme poverty, he opened his heart and wallet. He was known to pay low wages to his employees but he considered the wages fair. When a ship captain in Girard's fleet wanted to transfer to another ship, he said: "You are discharged, sir. I do not make the voyage for my captains but for myself." To family members he was especially tight in his early years. They would ask for frivolous things and he would scorn them and tell them to work for what they wanted to buy.[23]

Could Girard be considered capricious and eccentric?

That is an accurate assessment. On one occasion, an esteemed Quaker asked Girard for a donation for the Pennsylvania Hospital. Girard replied: "Call on me tomorrow morning, Mr. Coates, and if you find me on a right footing, I will do something." The next day Mr. Coates had breakfast with Girard and received a check for five hundred dollars. When the Episcopalians asked Girard for a donation, he wrote out a check for five hundred dollars. Looking at the check, they asked Girard to add a zero to make it five thousand dollars. He took back the check to correct it but tore it up instead. He was capricious.[24]

How did Girard extend his influence into South America?

Girard recognized the importance of aiding the revolutionaries fighting for independence in South America. The leader of this fight to free the people from the power of the Europeans who controlled all the land and the wealth was Simon Bolivar.

Simón Bolivar (1783–1830). From the Portrait Gallery, Perry-Castañeda Library, University of Texas at Austin. Courtesy of the University of Texas Libraries, The University of Texas at Austin.

Who paid Girard a personal visit on behalf of Simon Bolivar?

It was Vincent Bolivar, Simon's brother. Vincent came to ask Girard's help to procure arms and money to support a revolution against Spanish rule in Venezuela. Girard was eager to help this worthy cause.[25]

How did Girard approach the US Government to cover his activities with Bolivar?

Stephen wrote a letter to Secretary of State Monroe, not to ask further assistance for the revolutionaries but to make sure he had not done anything illegal. He merely asked if it were possible for a private citizen to send arms to such a worthy cause. There is no evidence that Girard ever received an answer to this query.[26]

In his book, *Stephen Girard, America's First Tycoon*, George Wilson addresses the extreme plight of South America in the nineteenth century with its pervading poverty and overbearing upper classes. This was slavery at its most heinous form. In the chapter on Simón Bolívar, Wilson speaks of Stephen Girard's concern.

"Wars of independence were brewing in South America early in the nineteenth century. They were led by Simon Bolivar, who became known as the Great Liberator, and they were successful because there were brave men willing to fight to be free. Most importantly, victory was achieved because these men had arms and ammunition to fight with. Wars are not won by bravery alone.

Stephen Girard's role in supplying weapons and munitions to Bolivar and his freedom fighters is a noteworthy sidelight in the history of South America. Girard gave Bolivar the lift he needed when he needed it the most—when he was a nobody, when he was unknown, when he was unsung, when he was unheard of. Later, there were many who climbed on Bolivar's bandwagon, but it was Girard who led the parade.

When Bolivar, with few guns, little money and hardly any followers, first dared to dream of challenging and defeating the mighty European powers that were entrenched in South America, there were many who thought he was a fool. Nonetheless, Girard could see the potential for triumph against seemingly impossible odds. U.S. foreign aid had not been invented yet. Covert operations abroad were a nonexistent concept in Washington. A fledgling America was still shying from international entanglements. The laws of the United States frowned on unauthorized acts of war by private citizens against sovereign governments.

In spite of these deterrents, Girard financed the shipment of guns and ammunition to subjugated peoples in South America in the name of liberty and justice. He put weaponry in the hands of rebels desperately and urgently in want, rebels who were asking only for a chance to fight and perhaps to die for their objectives. Girard was not the kind to let legalisms stand in the way of a good cause.

There are many dimensions to this improbable story. It seems odd that a maritime merchant sitting in his counting-house in Philadelphia would become involved in the activities of an obscure would-be revolutionary thousands of miles away. Yet, that is what happened. It happened in part and indirectly because the slave revolt that had begun in St. Domingue in the early 1790s culminated in a fiery and bloody climax in the early 1800s when French plantation owners and their families were slaughtered in huge numbers Napoleon sent tens of thousands of French troops across the Atlantic in a futile effort to quell the uprising. Toussaint L'Ouverture, the leader of the rebellious slaves, was captured by the French and removed to France, where he died in prison in 1803. Nonetheless, former slaves continued to rebel and were successful in winning both individual and national freedom. The former French colony of St. Domingue became the independent country of Haiti, formerly founded in 1804."

Was President Madison indifferent to the plight of the South American revolutionaries?

From the start of Madison's first term, he was under the threat of war with Great Britain. He could not be responsible for starting a war with Spain even if he thought it was the right thing to do.[27]

What do we know about a plot in 1811 to have Stephen Girard kidnapped?

In retrospect, it seemed to be a comedy of errors. Incompetent men with no plan tried to kidnap Girard but he never felt he was in danger. The leader was declared insane and his helpers were acquitted. They thought that they would ask Girard to sign a few checks for them. Girard called them a gang of bunglers and laughed at them.

What were some of Girard's setbacks in the several years that followed?

Girard's persistence kept his ships on the high seas. Two of Girard's ships the *Voltaire* and the *Montesquieu* were wrecked, the former in 1822 and the latter in 1824. The conditions of foreign trade offered little inducement for him to continue. Markets abroad were unfavorable and commercial ventures often resulted in long delays.[28]

What happened when one of Girard's captains let his ship *The Montesquieu* fall into the hands of pirates?

Girard knew that it was carelessness on the part of the captain and he intended to fire him but at the same time he made a point of not humiliating him when he came into port with the ransomed ship.[29]

Were pirates also a problem on the open sea?

On one occasion, one of his captains reported a loss of ten thousand dollars having been robbed by pirates. Girard was not worried. He gave the man a present of one hundred dollars and told him he should be thankful his life was spared.

At what period did Girard's ability to read and hear begin to diminish?

According to Stephen Simpson who worked with Girard on a daily basis, Girard's left eye began to lose focus and his hearing was effective only in the higher registers in late December of 1822.[30]

Did this impair his ability to conduct business?

His ability to conduct business was not impaired. Although he was in his 73rd year, his humor remained the same; his new ideas continued flowing; his dynamic personality was unchanged.

When George Simpson, the bank's cashier for many years, died in December 1822, how did Girard react?

Girard called Stephen and said to him: "Your father, Mr. Simpson, was an old man, and old men must die. It is nothing uncommon. When one man dies, we must find others to do the business."[31]

Was Girard ever a patron of literature or the fine arts?

He was never a patron of the arts but we know from his admiration of Voltaire and the French writers of his age that he was not insensible to the charms and tastes of letters.[32]

13

Girard's Estate Planning

Family Needs
Lifestyle
1795–1799

In the planning of Stephen Girard's will, there was a requirement that no member of the clergy would enter the campus of Girard College. Does this mean that Girard was against organized religion?

Stephen Girard was not a religious man but he had no problem with others being religious. As far as the college was concerned, he didn't want young minds to be confused by conflicting dogmas. He thought that the young men who graduated from the college could make up their own minds. When asked to contribute to building a Methodist church, he said he would give a donation; not because it was a church but because it was a building that would contribute to the improvement of the city. To his father Girard wrote: "as to remembering the religion in which I was born as you bid me do I shall never forget it any more than I shall forget the pains you took to bring me up according to its precepts." When not placating his father, Girard might say: "Industry should be the deity of man. I observe the Sabbath by working."[1]

Did Girard anticipate the Church's reaction over his plan to bar clergy from his college? Did he ever formally break with the Catholic Church?

Girard only cared what the Church would think while his father was alive. He treated all denominations even-handedly. He made donations to them liberally and impartially, when he considered them worthy. Insofar as his feelings for the Catholic Church were concerned, he much preferred the purity and simplicity of the Society of Friends.[2]

What sad news had Stephen heard about his brother Etienne?

Mr. Morton, a French agent, notified Stephen in a letter that his brother-in-law had visited Perigueux; that he had seen Etienne Girard without making known the purpose of the visit; that he found him the father of two sons and four daughters, who were without education save such as the father could give, and that he was in grave circumstances. By the same ship came another letter from the brother showing in detail the extent of his resources, his income and the real need of at least three thousand francs a year.

Christ Church, Philadelphia.
The Church was founded in 1695; main body built 1727–1744. LC-DIG-ppmsca-18123.
Library of Congress Prints and Photographs Division, Washington, DC.

What was Stephen's reaction to this news?

Girard wrote to Morton: "I never did know that my brother was married till the epoch when Lord Wellington was advancing from Bayonne, towards Bordeaux. At that moment my sister Capeyron wrote me a very alarming letter and informed me that he was married, had several children and did not possess sufficient means to support them. Being still disposed to aid my relatives as far as prudence will permit, I beg that you will be so obliging as to pay on my account, to said brother E. Girard, five thousand francs to be applied to his & family use, and for the education of his daughters."[3]

Did Stephen address the education of Etienne's sons?

Girard wrote: "In regard to his two boys I will thank you to place them in a good college or suitable school, under competent masters, who will inculcate in the high activity, good morals, and force their education as far as their brain will admit."[4]

Simpson writes: "Girard's friendship toward his brother Etienne in France was exemplary. He succoured him from prison, relieved his wants, discharged his debts and settled him comfortably as a vintor in the neighborhood of Bordeaux."[5]

Who was Fabricius Girard?

Fabricius was Stephen's nephew and son of his brother Etienne. Although he and his brother were brought to the United States in order to help Etienne by taking on the expenses of their keep and their education, Fabricius later disappointed Girard and went on to be an active player in the attempt to break Stephen's will.[6]

In view of Stephen's generosity towards his brother Etienne, his wife Marie and their two sons Fabricius and Auguste, why did they join ranks with other family members in attempting to have Girard's will set aside?

It may have been simply a matter of greed. They all wanted more than they received.

How did Girard react when his brother wanted to keep his sons at home but wanted Girard to pay for their schooling in Bordeaux?

Girard saw through his brother's attempt at wanting an open-ended obligation or blank check. He wanted a good education for the boys in America; so, he told Etienne that it would be education in the US or nothing.

Did Girard realize he was opening the flood gates to other relatives near and far to get him to give them pensions as well?

Stephen was astute and knew very well what was being attempted. He was selective in giving money to only those family members in dire need.

Did Fabricius get his life in order after failing to break Stephen's will?

No. The college he tried to eliminate by his and his family's greed would be the institution he applied to for a teaching position in French. He was given the job perhaps because the Trustees thought he was as bright as the Founder of Girard College. He taught there for only a couple of years.[7]

Daniel Webster (1782–1852). From the Portrait Gallery, Perry-Castañeda Library, University of Texas at Austin. Courtesy of the University of Texas Libraries, The University of Texas at Austin.

How did Daniel Webster's arguments add to the misconceptions that people got about Stephen Girard?

138

In his attempt to break Girard's will, Webster used derogatory comments, many of which he took from Simpson's writings to attack the will. In failing to have the will set aside in favor of Girard's family, Webster left the court with the opposite impression than he originally intended—Girard was not a miser, not a racist or an atheist.[8]

How did Girard's success in making money work against him in public opinion?

Philadelphians forgot his great service as a courageous humanitarian. Seeing him as a millionaire and noticing his simplicity made them more suspicious.

Were there any other instances that showed Girard's lack of interest in religion?

Girard had a dislike for organized religions. He was angered by the quarrels between sects and controversies over creeds. Although raised as a Catholic, he did not attend mass. He much preferred the simplicity of the Society of Friends.[9]

There has been evidence throughout his life that he thought each person should make religious decisions on his/her own without undue influence by the various churches. Children, especially, should be protected from such influence. Although ship owners would often name their vessels after the saints, kings or beautiful women, Girard named his new ships after the philosophers he respected i.e. Voltaire, Rousseau, etc. Surrounded by Christian churches he had helped to build, Girard remained uncommitted. If he were asked about laboring on Sunday, he would reply that the sin lay in idleness. For him honest labor was holy.

How was the success that Girard achieved viewed by his business competitors?

They thought Girard was just lucky. Poring over the enormous volumes of business correspondence, we see clearly that he planned his operations meticulously. Luck had little to do with his success. Girard always struck a hard bargain. He held firmly to his side of the agreement but insisted that he be given his full due. Girard was one of the most influential men of his day and contributed greatly to the early development of modern American business and finance; his advice and assistance were sought by presidents and statesmen. At times the stubborn courage of his convictions enabled him to attain heroic stature. On the whole, however, one who knows the sources must commend the author for handling a Herculean task in his usual expert way. The documentary records left by Girard constitute a mass of material that would take years to read and digest. By his selection of materials Mr. Wildes has presented Girard as a human and not a mythological figure.[10]

What were Cheesman Herrick's remarks on Girard's luck?

Great volumes of his letters and papers preserved in a room of Girard College show that his success in business was not due in any degree whatever to good fortune. "Let a money-making generation take note that Girard principles inevitably produce Girard results. The grand and fundamental secret of his success as of all success was that he understood his business. He had a personal and familiar knowledge of the ports with which he traded, the commodities in which he dealt, the vehicles in which they were carried and the dangers to which they were liable."[11]

Were these prosperous times for merchants?

To those engaged in trade and commerce with foreign countries or between the States, to those engaged in business of any sort at home or abroad, the fourth of March, 1789, marked the beginning of a new era of commercial and industrial prosperity. The old confederation had been swept away. The Constitution, framed at Philadelphia in 1787, had gone into effect as to the eleven ratifying States; the first Congress under that instrument of government had assembled at New York; and in that city on the twenty-ninth of April the first President of the United States took the oath of office. Henceforth no State, without consent of Congress, could lay duties on imports or exports nor ever again issue a bill of credit, nor make anything but gold and silver coin a legal tender for the payment of debt.

What was the taking of Girard's ship, *Montesquieu* all about?

In 1813, a British frigate captured the *Montesquieu* as it entered the mouth of the Delaware River. Girard's ship was returning to Philadelphia fully loaded with valuable merchandise from Canton invoiced at about two hundred thousand dollars. Rather than risk taking the ship to a British port, the captain flew a truce flag and accompanied the *Montesquieu* to the Delaware River. Britain demanded a ransom of 93,000 dollars for the return of the ship. Girard quickly paid the ransom and the *Montesquieu* was returned. As it turned out, even with the money paid in ransom, Girard made a profit of about a half million dollars from the sale of his merchandise. Not only did Girard make an enormous profit but he had the enemy conduct his ship safely to his home port.[12]

Did Girard ever write about his love of work?

In one of his letters of 1820, to a friend in New Orleans, he wrote: "If I thought I was going to die tomorrow, I should plant a tree nevertheless to-day." [13] It was a favorite theme for him, when he grew rich, to relate that he began life with six pence and that man's capital was his industry.

How did Girard describe his activities as he grew older?

Of himself Girard said that he lived like a galley slave, constantly occupied and that he'd often passed the night without sleeping. He added that he was wrapped up "in a labyrinth of affairs and worn out with care."[14]

Did Girard like to sleep late in the morning?

Absolutely not. On one occasion when building a large ship, Girard had arrived at the shipyard before any of the workmen and carpenters. He would often lose his temper at any tardiness.

Did Girard's eating habits change in his later years?

In the later years of his life, Girard was a vegetarian. In these years he reported himself as eating nothing but vegetables and what he called "ship bread"-a form of hard crackers-no meat, no animal fat, no butter or any milk or milk products. These frugal tastes coupled with extreme care in his habits of drinking and his active out-of-door life preserved Girard so that he passed the fourscore mark in tolerable health and strength.[15] He was so happy with his growing good health that he thought vegetarianism might even restore his sightless right eye.

What did Girard do to explore possibilities for curing his right eye?

He wrote to the only doctor he trusted in Paris-Dr. Jean Deveze. The doctor told him it was, in his opinion, impossible to restore the sight but he gave Girard some ideas on keeping his right eye clean and the skin soft on his eyelid.[16]

How did Girard describe his hard work?

Of his life of unremitting toil, Girard also wrote: "When I rise in the morning, my only effort is to labor so hard during the day that when night comes I may be enabled to sleep soundly."[17]

How was Girard's work schedule described?

The early morning and the forenoon he spent in his counting house; the middle of the day, he worked at the bank; the late afternoon and evening were given over to his farm. He continued this schedule into his advanced years.

How did Girard explain his strict ethic in not paying his employees a penny more than was fair?

He thought that one of the duties which a rich man owes to society is to be careful not to disturb the law of supply and demand by giving more money for anything than a fair price.

Did he practice this philosophy in dealing with members of his own family?

That is largely true. He rescued his poor relations in France from want, and educated nieces and nephews in his own house. His gifts, however, to them were not proportioned to his own wealth but to their circumstances. He considered that his treatment of his family members showed largess on his part. They did not think so.

It has been said that despite his impatience with mediocrity, his patriotism was never in question. Is that so?

That is true but it is also true that his patriotism did not hurt his succeeding in business and helped him to build his enormous wealth. Still no one could doubt his sincere attachment to his adopted country.

How does Mayo describe Stephen Girard's lifestyle?

Mayo seems to think that "by our standards, he was a loner—no guests came to his house, he had no hobbies. His only recreation was his garden and his farm in what is now South Philadelphia at the Passyunk area. His life was his work. He would often say that his work made him happy and the money was only a byproduct. Despite the uncertainties of shipping worldwide, Girard's business enterprises continued to prosper; his wealth increased accordingly, but he remained a simple man, luxuriating only in a penchant for good food, fine wine and his mistress.

As he approached the middle years of his life, he seemed to more enjoy his work and the increased demands made on him physically and emotionally. He shared his increased wealth willingly with those around him, giving considerable sums to charity, and afforded care and consideration for those whom he employed."[18]

Was the farm a business venture?

Girard was interested in scientific agriculture but with his practical turn of mind he sought to make his farm pay. He introduced rare vegetables and cultivated them with the same business success that attended his other activities. He made his farm profitable.[19]

"It is a singular feat and is fully illustrated in the history of Girard that men who commence (business) life at the earliest period, generally, if not always, succeed the best."[20]

Aside from the excellent fruit and vegetables that he served at his dining room table, where did Girard sell his farm produce?

Girard maintained two stalls in the South Second Street Market where the produce from his farm was sold.

How does Girard speak about his efforts with his vines?

"I have taken much pain with grape vines. Our severe winters are a great obstacle to their progress. For these few years past, I lay them down and cover them with earth in the fall and take them up in April. They appear to do a little better. The last season, I had some good fruit. I have about 250 of the best sort imported from France and Spain except one vine which is pretty large and raised from the seed of a grape imported in a jar from Malaga. Out of that vine, I had last season several fine large grapes in full maturity."

How was Stephen Girard described in Osgood E. Fuller's *Napoleon of Merchants*?

Imagine the figure of an old man, low in stature, squarely built, clumsily dressed, and standing on large feet. To this uncouth form, add a repulsive face, wrinkled, cold, colorless, and stony, with one eye dull and the other blind–a "wall-eye." His expression is that of a man wrapped in the mystery of his own hidden thoughts. He looks–

"Like monumental bronze, unchanged his look
A soul which pity never touched or shook
Trained, from his lowly cradle to his bier,
The fierce extremes of good and ill to brook
Unchanging, fearing but the charge of fear
A stoic of the mart, a man without a tear."[21]

Was Girard ever happy?

He was quoted as having said that work not possessions made him happy. His work ethic was admirable. He was demanding in the tasks of his subordinates but was more demanding of his own work. In writing a letter of congratulation to his brother who had recovered from an illness, Girard wrote: "as for myself, I have not the same good fortune for without any illness of the body I have that of the mind I fear that I have lost forever the peace which a certain success should procure for life in this world."[22]

14

The War of 1812

Real Estate Interests
1812

What were the causes of the War of 1812?

The causes of the war were many. The second war with England, toward which America had been gravitating for many years, was brought very closely home to Philadelphia by reason of Great Britain's important shipping interest. Large sums of money were invested in, and a considerable portion of the population was directly or indirectly sustained by overseas commerce. The various embargoes of England and France during the Napoleonic Wars, the general invasion of the rights of neutral powers, and the impressment of American seamen by the belligerents, led to a feeling of great resentment in the United States. The main problem was that England still treated the United States as part of its Empire. England seemed to forget that the War of Independence ever took place.

Since many differences could not be settled peacefully what happened?

President Madison signed an Official Declaration of War against Great Britain. The United States needed to show the world that it could stand on its own, and that it would not be bullied by any nation.

Why did many citizens think that this was folly?

The young country did not need war; it was too busy building and expanding a nation. Besides the US Treasury was in the red and a war would be a costly expense.

Who was the Secretary of the Treasury in 1812?

Albert Gallatin was Secretary of the Treasury.

How did the President of the US and Mr. Gallatin expect to pay for a war?

A bond issue was floated in the amount of sixteen million dollars, of which only six million had been sold. It was then that Stephen Girard of Philadelphia and John Jacob Astor of New York and other smaller financiers were approached for the remaining funds. Stephen Girard invested a bit over eight million dollars and John Astor about two million.

Was this not a very risky investment?

Had the war not been won with the money of these men, the new nation might have collapsed and history might have been written in another way.

What concessions did Stephen Girard request of the government in exchange for his support?

He asked for none. Girard was happy to help his adopted nation in its hour of need. By purchasing risky government bonds, he proved to be a true patriot.

What more did Girard offer to give after providing the US Treasury with critical funding?

He offered to provide the US Government free use of his fleet of ships and volunteered to serve personally in the war effort without pay.

When did the War of 1812 end?

The war ended in 1814 by the signing of the Treaty of Ghent. Girard had given his nation a lesson in patriotism and courage and more importantly a love of country.

What ironic situation did Girard face with the Treasury Department?

Girard provided a substantial loan to the US Treasury Department to support the war with Great Britain, risking his entire fortune and then some. At the same time Gallatin was suing Girard for perceived infractions that Girard's ship *Good Friends* had been accused of.[1]

How did the abdication of Napoleon Bonaparte affect the attitude of Great Britain toward her former colonies?

After the defeat of Napoleon at Leipzig in 1813, the surrender of Paris to the

Allies in March, 1814, and the abdication of Napoleon in April the situation of Great Britain changed completely. She was now free to give serious attention to her war with America, and in August a British squadron entered Chesapeake Bay. Troops were landed; the city of Washington was captured, and the Capitol, the President's house, the Treasury building, the Departments of State, of War, two private dwellings, a tavern, a newspaper office and two rope walks were set on fire. This done, the British returned quickly to their ships.

As fear gripped the country, what measures did Girard take to protect his investments?

To this fear that the city was in hourly danger of falling prey to the enemy, Girard had concerns of his own. He gathered up his goods and sent them by wagon to Reading. Having chosen that town as a place of deposit, Mr. Edward George, at the end of August, was sent there to arrange for the safe keeping of Girard's possessions.

How did Joseph Bonaparte hope to involve Stephen Girard after Napoleon's final defeat and exile on the island of St. Helena?

According to David Stacton who wrote extensively about the Bonapartes, a ship owned by Girard was being prepared for a long voyage to a faraway island in 1821. These preparations were halted when word was received that the fifty-one-year-old Napoleon had died.

Is there a specific example of Girard's boldness in his commerce?

There are many examples. Girard's business judgment was probably as nearly infallible as was that of any other merchant in all history. He combined boldness and daring in operation with prudence and conservatism—the same foresight which led him to invest in cotton during the period of the embargo when the market was flooded.[2]

Did Lafayette return to America after his courageous and generous participation in the American War of Independence?

Lafayette returned at the urging of President Monroe in 1824. Girard had the pleasure of serving on the committee for Lafayette's visit. George Wilson, a Girard biographer, mentions the surprise that Lafayette expressed that Philadelphia had not erected a monument to George Washington.

At what point in his career did Stephen Girard become interested in real estate?

From 1825 to 1830 most of the money Girard made came from the banking business, and as it accumulated, he invested in real estate. His most valuable purchase was seventy-two tracts totaling 29,494 acres in Schuylkill and Columbia Counties in Pennsylvania.

What specifics did the deed of the land show?

The deed issued to Girard by the trustees of the late First Bank on April 30, 1830, lists the 67 tracts of land by name and also the five tracts of land situated in Mahoning Township called: Clear Springs; Six Springs; Mill Seat; Three Springs; and Pleasant Valley. These five tracts later proved not to be a part of the Estate.

The deed to Girard was recorded in both Schuylkill County and Columbia County on May 10, 1830. The recording in Columbia County was necessary as the five separate tracts by that time were a part of that county.[3]

What further real estate did Girard invest in?

The money made by Girard during these years, 1825 to 1828, came from his bank, and seems to have been largely invested in real estate. Since 1812, there were forty-one purchases: farms in Passyunk and Moyamensing, houses and lots on Chestnut, Spruce, Water and Front Streets, Third, Fifth and Eleventh Streets at a cost of $366,652. Out of the city he had acquired a great tract in Louisiana.

What real estate did Girard consider buying for the school he planned to create for poor white fatherless boys?

An item of interest in Girard's correspondence of 1807 is the purchase from John Dunlap of the block of land between Market and Chestnut Streets, and Twelfth Street. It was on this tract that Girard originally intended to locate Girard College.

At what cost did the seller set this property?

The cost was one hundred thousand dollars. This block, exclusive of improvements, rose in worth to more than six million dollars, and earned in the year 1909, in addition to interest on the cost of the improvements, nearly two hundred thousand dollars net, which was more than enough to support the college as originally planned by Girard.

When did Girard begin to give serious thought to writing a will?

After the peace of 1815, Girard began to consider what he should do with his millions after his death. He was then sixty-five and still expected to live many more years. It was not until he was seventy-eight that he entered into serious consideration of a plan for the final disposal of his immense estate.

Did Girard continue buying property after 1815?

Between 1815 and his death in 1831, he purchased nearly 200,000 acres and many buildings. During the last nine months of his life, he purchased two houses on Walnut Street, sixty acres in the Neck (South Philadelphia), land on Spruce Street, a house on 6th Street, houses on Coates and John Streets, houses on 3rd Street, a house in the Neck fronting on the Schuylkill River, stores on the wharves and docks, and land in Schuylkill County.

What were some of the properties owned by Stephen Girard at the time of his death?

When he died, he owned the choicest land and buildings throughout old Philadelphia (now Society Hill). Some properties were near 2nd and Spruce Streets, along Chestnut Street, Walnut Street, the block surrounded by 11th and 12th-Market and Chestnut Streets, Front and Delaware, 5th Street, Water Street, 2nd and Delancy Streets, 3rd and Philip Streets, and the area of today's Penn's Landing. His properties in the Neck included 583 acres of farmland and several tenements.

What were the investment interests in Girard's later years?

Girard's physical abilities were diminishing in the advance of his years, but his mental acuity remained at a high level; he saw opportunity where others did not. Coal and the railroad became a new, exciting and profitable challenge for him as he approached the twilight of his life. He purchased land in upstate Pennsylvania. The value that Girard perceived in making his bold venture was to be accrued as coal mining would bring him new riches. He was then seventy-nine years old. When he turned eighty-one, he invested in railroading, the vehicle that would carry the coal to the markets he envisioned would be there. Girard had previously been appointed to act as receiver for the First Bank to make final distribution of its assets.

His investigation as to the reason for the long delay in revealing the existence of these lands as belonging to the First Bank probably showed that coal had been discovered in the Pottsville region, mines had been opened, and that coal had been transported on the Schuylkill Canal since 1825. It would also seem possible that land speculators knowing of the coal discoveries had possibly influenced the trustees–or at least the trustee knowing of the existence of these deeds–to withhold any action on these tracts until the last possible moment.

Undoubtedly, this information convinced Girard that these lands had great value and he decided that his business interests would be better served if he acquired them. The trustees had held the tracts for 19 years, and shortly after the deeds were turned over to the receiver, Girard, an advertisement appeared in a Philadelphia newspaper that these tracts of land deeded to them by the First Bank would be sold at public auction at the Merchant's Coffee House on April 17, 1830. The auction was held as scheduled and Stephen Girard, being the highest bidder, purchased the 67 tracts for $30,000.

Did these coal lands prove to be a good investment for Girard?

The lands were exceedingly valuable. After litigation and compromise, they had been reduced to about nineteen thousand acres of which only about five thousand were coal-bearing. Up to the beginning of 1942, they produced about 119,869,794 tons of anthracite.[4]

What was the purpose of the Danville and Pottsville Railroad, 1826–1840?

The purpose of the proposed Danville and Pottsville Railroad was to open both the Shenandoah and Mahanoy Valleys, connect them by a tunnel, and mine the coal from the lands encompassed. On April 8, 1826, the Pennsylvania legislature passed an act which incorporated the Danville and Pottsville Railroad Company and granted it the right to hold not more than 1,000 acres of coal lands.[5]

What was the professional opinion about the effectiveness of this railroad?

Chief engineer, Moncure Robinson estimated that the railroad was twenty years ahead of its time just as Girard's anthracite was ahead of its time by a generation.[6]

What can we learn about the vessels that Girard sailed, leased or owned during his lifetime?

It's a long complicated answer. Let's start at the beginning when Girard was a young man.

On what vessels did Girard serve as a pilotin?

Girard's first service, as a pilotin, was with the *Pélerin*; the date was 1764. He performed apprenticeship duties on six vessels between 1764 and 1772. The vessels were: *Gloire*; *Dorille*; *Esperance*; *Superbe*; *Les Deux Frères* and the *Pélerin*.

What were the years that Girard served as mate or lieutenant?

He served in these capacities between 1772 and 1776. The word "lieutenant" was imported from the French language into English. *Lieu* means place; *tenant* means holding. The officer holding the place of or seconding the captain is the lieutenant.

How many vessels did Girard own or partially own over the years?

He was the owner or part owner of 24 vessels.

What were the types of these vessels?

They were mostly brigs and schooners at first. As Girard's fortune increased and the voyages became longer to include South America, China and India, he added ships to his inventory. Confusion among the ship names may be due to the fact that Girard's captains were told to carry dual papers for their vessels, especially in dealing with trade to the Cap where capricious tariff restrictions caused American ships to become inventively deceptive.

How did the idea materialize to establish a home for orphans?

Girard had thought about this possibility for many years. Without revealing the reason for his inquiries, William Duane, his lawyer-friend, would gather information during his travels and discuss them with Girard.

Did Thomas Jefferson influence Girard's plans for a school for orphans?

Girard founded his college with the idea of helping the helpless. Thomas Jefferson's ideas on education impressed Girard greatly. Girard once made a trip to Monticello; and he spent two days at the University of Virginia. This was really remarkable, because time for Girard was a very precious commodity.

How did the wording "poor white male orphans" come into the will?

In Girard's day, girls were rarely educated. All they needed to know, they learned at their mothers' side. The thought of educating an African slave was also beyond his scope of understanding.

At Girard's death what was the assessed value of his real estate holdings?

He owned prime property and buildings that generated enough revenue to allow his estate to continue growing long after his death. George Morgan's book, *The City of Firsts, A Complete History of Philadelphia*, reported that in 1926, Girard's property in the city, excluding Girard College, was assessed at $20 million.

When did Girard purchase the property on which Girard College would be built?

On June 6, 1831, Girard paid William Parker $35,000 for the forty-five acre farm located on Ridge Road in Penn Township, then in suburban Philadelphia. By codicil to his will he changed the location for his school to the Peel Hall farm. William Duane, his lawyer, indicated the change was made because Girard preferred that the college be built outside the congested city.

15

Accident and Death

1830–1831

How was Girard's health described by Mr. Simpson?

Stephen Simpson remarked that Girard's eyesight and hearing were beginning to suffer which may have led to his accident.

What do we know about Girard's accident?

He was seriously injured while crossing the street near Second and Market, on December 22, 1830. The December 22, 1830 issue of *The United States Gazette* reported that he was knocked down by a wagon whose wheel hit his head and lacerated his ear. He returned to his banking business after remaining secluded for two months.[1]

Another newspaper added however that Girard was quite able to help himself, that he retained his self-possession perfectly and seemed more pained by the fact that the accident had attracted attention than by the wound which he had received though it was said that the wound was far from trifling. Girard later wrote that the wheel of the wagon went over his head.[2]

How did Girard react when he was faced with needing a surgical procedure as a result of his accident?

He was quoted as saying: "Go ahead doctor. I am an old sailor and can stand pain."[3]

Was Girard seriously hurt?

He was hurt more seriously than he thought. He was confined to bed for two months as inflammation set in, which he also blamed on the doctors. He was in excruciating pain and chased his clerk from his room, wanting to hear about no business.[4]

How might one describe the year between Girard's accident and his death?

Although weakened by his accident, Girard was bent on carrying out a full schedule of activities. His mind was still clear, although his sight and hearing were diminishing. Had it not been for influenza that seized the city of Philadelphia during the cold month of December and did not spare Girard, but weakened him further with pneumonia, he might have lived many more years.

What were the last words spoken by Stephen Girard before he died?

After lying in a stupor, he arose from his bed. Placing his weak, thin hand on his forehead, he exclaimed: "How violent is this disorder! How very extraordinary it is!" He then died without speaking again.[5]

When did Stephen Girard die?

Stephen Girard died on December 26, 1831 during an influenza epidemic in Philadelphia which had taken a high toll of the city's population. He contracted the disease that quickly developed into pneumonia and proved to be fatal. His death came about six months after his purchase of the forty-five acre farm. At the time of his death, Girard had well passed his eighty-first year. For more than fifty-five years, he had been a resident of Philadelphia; yet such was the secluded life he led, so careful had he been to keep his affairs, both private and business, to himself, that nothing concerning his life was known. The sketches of his career, therefore, which appeared in the newspapers of the city after his death, were wanting in detail and of no value.[6]

What occurred at the time of Girard's death?

When Girard died, the authorized trustees of his will took possession of the assets of the bank, proceeded to close its affairs as speedily as possible transferring the assets to his executors as a part of his estate.

How did Girard behave, knowing he would not survive his attack of influenza and pneumonia?

As he never exhibited any concern for his life, he now displayed no fear of death which was meeting him, as he always hoped, in the midst of active labor.[7]

Was Girard alone at the moment of his death?

His faithful slave, Hannah, was at his bedside when he died. She had served Girard for more than fifty years and was generously rewarded in Girard's will.

What comments did Stephen Simpson make when Girard died?

Stephen Simpson wrote of Girard: "As a citizen Mr. Girard discharged his duties with exemplary zeal fidelity and rigor. He was repeatedly elected a member of councils; and gave his time, which to him was always money, to the improvement of the city. As a director of the bank and insurance company, he always did his duty never falling short of his portion of labor and often exceeding it."

What prejudices did Girard face during his lifetime?

Girard lived in a time when there were intense political, national, racial and religious controversies. That he was a Frenchman brought against him from some quarters a prejudice which was strong against that nation. Girard's religious independence made him the object of intolerance during his life and particularly so after his death. His identification with the pronounced republican views of the time brought much political antagonism upon him, certain it is he had a cordial dislike for the English and after the Jay Treaty, he wrote terming it "infamous" and calling the English a "worthless and contemptible nation." After citing some of the indignities which England had heaped upon America at that time and America's seeming supineness he concluded: "I must say our government deserves it." As a Frenchman, Girard was naturally identified with the republicans in the demonstration against Jay's Treaty with England.[8]

How was Girard's funeral reported?

The account of the Girard funeral which appeared in the United States Gazette relates that after the members of the family came, the mayor, the recorder of the city, the city councils and the members of a society of which Girard was a member arrived.[9]

How soon after Girard's death was the will opened?

On the day after his death, the will was opened in order that any directions, or wishes, regarding his funeral might be duly respected. None were found, but it then became known that large bequests had been made to the City and many charitable and benevolent institutions, and it was decided to formally invite them to be represented at the funeral.[10]

At Stephen Girard's funeral what were the comments made by Nicholas Biddle?

Mr. Biddle said: "He has now taken his rank among the great benefactors of mankind. From this hour that name is destined to survive to the latest posterity and while letters and the arts exist he will be cited as the man who with a generous spirit and a sagacious foresight bequeathed for the improvement of his fellow men the accumulated earnings of his life."[11]

It was Nicholas Biddle, Girard's friend, Director of the Second Bank of the United States, and Chairman of the Building Committee who recommended that the architect include Grecian columns on the main building of the college. Biddle's home, Andalusia, built about 1794, has similar columns.

How did the people of Philadelphia react to Girard's funeral?

For more than forty years, Philadelphia had not seen so many people in attendance at a funeral. There were about three thousand people crowding the streets. Not since the death of Benjamin Franklin had there been such a large turnout.

Where was Stephen Girard buried?

He was buried in the vault he built for Baron Henri Lallemand, his nephew, in the Holy Trinity Catholic Cemetery at Sixth and Spruce Streets. Bishop Kendrick refused to permit a Catholic burial mass because the Masons would not remove their ceremonial aprons. Twenty years later, his remains were reinterred in the Founder's Hall vestibule at Girard College behind a statue by N. Gevelot, a French sculptor living in Philadelphia.

How does Professor Wagner speak of this statue?

Dr. Wagner said that the face was copied from a death mask taken at the direction of Dr. John Y. Clark. He continued that the artist Gevelot had never seen Girard but was obliged to formulate details from descriptions by untrained observers.[12]

Statue of Stephen Girard, Girard College, Founder's Hall front vestibule in front of his sarcophagus by sculptor, Nicholas Gevelot. HABS PA, 51-PHILA, 459-20. Library of Congress Prints and Photographs Division, Washington, DC.

Statue of Stephen Girard (side view), Girard College, Founder's Hall. HABS PA, 51-PHILA, 459-19. Library of Congress Prints and Photographs Division, Washington, DC.

At what point during his eighty-one years did Girard at last begin to enjoy the luxury his vast wealth could easily afford?

Having wealth was not about having luxury. He was more attuned to the Quaker philosophy which held to a simple life with no ostentatious display.

16

The Execution of the Will

College Construction Planned
1831

The will was considered an important document in the history of endowments. Why was that?

Girard's will is a classic in American law. It served as a model in the creation of endowments by such important philanthropists as Joseph Williamson, Charles E. Ellis and Milton Hershey. The will was controversial. It offended his family, the religious community, and later females and non-white minorities. Shortly after Girard's death, *The Pennsylvania Gazette* published the will's content.

Did the public show surprise at the contents of the will?

People were shocked at the estate's value and how Girard left nearly all of his seven million dollars to charitable causes. Girard designated the City of Philadelphia to administer the estate, and this act became a significant point that led to the will's dismantling.

How was the will dismantled?

For a long time, the will remained intact. However in time with controversy growing, the court ruled that no public institution, in this case the city, could enforce restrictions that were contrary to the Constitution's 14th Amendment that guarantees equal rights to all citizens.

Was there more than one will written?

Girard's first will was written in 1787. Horace Binney, a famous attorney, prepared the second one in 1826. That will was significantly revised in 1830 by William J. Duane. The final will is dated February 16, 1830, but after Girard bought additional property and changed the location for his school, two codicils were published. Girard was a benefactor to many. Consider these facts to appreciate the significance of his generosity. In 1826, a typical monthly wage for a mill supervisor was $48. A skilled worker earned between $14 and $18 a month, and a laborer made about $8 a month. The combined earnings of a father, mother, and one child working in a mill was about $350 per year and they paid about two dollars ($2.00) a month to rent a mill house.

What were some of the larger bequests made by Girard?

> 280,000 acres and about thirty slaves in Louisiana, to the City of New Orleans, providing they were administered by his friend, Judge Henry Bree.
> $500,000 to Philadelphia "to layout, regulate, curb, light, and pave a passage or street, fronting on the Delaware River, to be called Delaware Avenue and extending from South or Cedar Street all along the east part of Water Street."
> $300,000 to the State of Pennsylvania to improve canal navigation and enact laws that would permit Philadelphia to improve its port.
> $30,000 to the Pennsylvania Hospital, and from its interest, his black maid Hannah was to be paid $200 each year for the remainder of her life.
> $10,000 to the Orphan Asylum of Philadelphia.
> $20,000 to the Pennsylvania Institute for the Deaf and Dumb.

Was Mrs. Girard mentioned in the will?

The name of Mrs. Girard does not appear in the will. She died in the Pennsylvania Hospital, September 13, 1815.

When was Stephen Girard's will contested for the first time?

E. Alfred Smith, a Girard College graduate and an attorney, in an undated paper titled *Stephen Girard and His Will*, reveals that the will was contested and defended several times in the past. The first contest occurred in 1833. Girard's heirs centered their attack on $66,418 worth of real estate bought by Girard after the execution of his will. The plaintiffs maintained that Girard could not bequeath land before he owned it. The heirs won this argument, but did not succeed in getting the entire will set aside. Girard's siblings and their children were awarded four thousand acres of Pennsylvania land that Girard purchased after writing the will.

Did the family attempt to contest the will again?

The family attempted to break the will again in 1836. They claimed that Philadelphia lacked authority to administer the will, that the number of beneficiaries was vague, and that the will conflicted with the laws of Pennsylvania regarding "rights of conscience." Daniel Webster who was a celebrity having recently won several important decisions was eager to shine again when he was retained in the effort to get Girard's will nullified. Among other issues, Webster contested Girard's right to include a restriction banning clergy from the college. Webster claimed that the restriction was contrary to public policy and Christian morality. The word "godless" was used in an attempt to describe Girard as a hater of all clergy. He also wanted to insist that Girard had no right to restrict the institution to only "poor white boys." Webster said that the college was not a charitable institution and should not be treated as such. The Supreme Court rejected Webster's arguments and upheld Girard's will unanimously in 1844.

How did the will specify the endowment for the school for orphans?

The residual of his estate, approximately five million dollars, both real and personal, he left to the City of Philadelphia to construct and maintain a school for "such a number of poor male white orphans, as can be trained in one institution, a better education, as well as a more comfortable maintenance, than they usually receive from the application of the public funds." He declared that no part of his Pennsylvania real estate should ever be sold and rent from the properties should be used to maintain the properties and maintain his school.

How much money did the will set aside for the construction of the college?

Girard set a limit of two million dollars to construct the school.

How did the will treat the maximum number of students to be enrolled at one time?

He directed that the school be large enough to accommodate three hundred "scholars" and the necessary staff. He described, in architectural detail, the dimensions and features of the school and required that it consist of a main building and four out buildings.

Did the will address the construction of a wall around the school?

Girard directed that the school "be enclosed with a solid wall, at least fourteen inches thick, and ten feet high, capped with marble and guarded with irons on the top, so as to prevent persons from getting over." The testator intended the tract should be surrounded by a stone wall, and had opened a quarry on the estate and begun to provide the stone. He designated that as the site of the college, and to render the entire site as secure from intrusion as possible, give the orphans ample space for exercise and provide room for agricultural and mechanical pursuits.[5]

How did the construction of the wall surrounding Girard College differ from the requirements of the will?

The will required that the wall be ten feet high and fourteen inches thick and that it be a mile and a quarter in length. These requirements were met. However, the will also specified that the wall be topped with a marble cap with iron spikes. This requirement was ignored by the builders.

What were the ages Girard thought best for entry into the school?

Girard stated: "As many poor male white orphans, between the ages of six and ten years, as the said income shall be adequate to maintain, shall be introduced into the college as soon as possible."

Were there preferences as to filling vacancies according to home locations of applicants?

He specified that should there be more applicants than vacancies, preference be given to the orphans from Philadelphia, then Pennsylvania, then New York City, his first port of entry in North America, and finally New Orleans.

Did Girard specify the subjects of instruction for the students?

He directed that they be instructed in "Reading, Writing, Grammar, Arithmetic, Geography, Navigation, Surveying, Practical Mathematics, Astronomy, Natural, Chemical, and Experimental Philosophy, the French and Spanish languages, and such other learning and science as the capacity of the several scholars may merit or warrant."

Were there specifics in the will as to when students should finish their studies?

The will is not very specific, it merely states: "The students were to remain at the college until they were between fourteen and eighteen years of age unless they were declared unfit." Then they were to be "bound out by the Mayor, Aldermen and Citizens of Philadelphia" to "suitable occupations," consulting, "as far as prudence shall justify it, the inclinations of the several scholars, as to the occupation, art, or trade to be learned." (James Parton spoke about the difficulty of placing young boys as apprentices at graduation in industries where grown, experienced men were working.)

What restrictions were identified in the will?

The will contained these restrictions. The excess income not necessary to maintain the college was to be invested in "good securities," thereafter to remain a part of the capital. "In no event, shall any part of the said capital be sold, disposed of, or pledged, to meet the current expenses of the said Institute, to which I devote the interest, income, and dividends thereof, exclusively." None of his money or estate could be used for anything except for that specified in the will. Separate accounts were to be established for each endowment.[6]

How did Henriette Girard Clark express her position for opposing Girard's will?

"The heirs of Girard never believed it was their relative's intention to deal less liberally with them after his death than he had unintermittingly done during his lifetime that his published will reflects an adverse ascendency gained after his intellect had been seriously weakened."[7]

What sort of accountability for use of funds was stipulated?

Girard required that a yearly report of the expenses, expenditures, and growth of his estate be submitted to the State Legislature and published in the local newspapers.

What restrictions were placed on the clergy?

He prohibited clergy from entering the college or holding a position on its staff. This restriction, he said, was to isolate the students from the confusion of the conflicting doctrines that existed among the various religions. However, he encouraged the lay teachers to teach the principles of Christianity and directed that they "instill into the minds of the scholars the purest principles of morality," so that later in life the student would be wise enough to select the religion of his choice.[8]

How was the design of the college's main building previously described?

"It was magnificent in design and proportion, with its spacious surrounding colonnade of thirty-four Corinthian columns." It has been called "the most perfect

Greek Temple in existence. It is similar to the Madeleine Church in Paris, France."

From what we've learned about Stephen Girard, he was a hard-working, generous but demanding tycoon with simple tastes. How can we reconcile the ostentatious plan for the main building of the college with the man?

The redesigned main building, standing today as Founder's Hall, is not what Girard intended. "Girard was a great admirer of the habits, customs and manners of the Society of Friends, their frugality, industry and temperance, the plainness of their public and private buildings, their strength, convenience and neatness, and complete adaptation to the uses for which they were intended, combined with a practical economy in their construction." Had Girard been alive, he would not have agreed to the design of Founder's Hall.

Parton comments:
> The city of Philadelphia entered upon the possession of the enormous and growing estate with which Girard entrusted it. If Girard were to visit the banks of the Schuylkill, would he recognize, in the splendid Grecian temple that stands in the center of the college grounds, the home for poor orphans, devoid of needless ornament which Girard particularly disliked?

Who was retained as the principal architect of the Main Building?

Thomas U. Walter was chosen to be the architect, but his original designs were not the ones used to construct the college. Those plans proposed porticoes approached by large flights of steps in the front and rear of the building. Nicholas Biddle influenced the redesign of the Main Building to include surrounding columns. The building committee claimed that they were necessary to support the weight of the roof.

What do we know of Walter's background?

Walter was the son of a bricklayer. When he designed Girard College he was only 29 years old and already a Professor at the Franklin Institute. He was the architect for many of the buildings in Bucknell University. He designed the reconstruction of Biddle's home, Andalusia that also looks like a Greek temple. In 1861, he replaced Robert Mills as the United States Government Architect and while in that position, he designed the dome and wings of the nation's Capital, completed in 1863. He and John McArthur were the architects for the Philadelphia City Hall.[1]

When did the construction begin on Girard College?

The final plans for the college were approved by Council on April 29, 1833, and ground breaking occurred on May 6, 1833. The corner stone of the Main Building was laid on July 4, 1833. Nicholas Biddle addressed the dignitaries present to witness the cornerstone placement. "From the time that stone reached the earth, the name Girard was beyond oblivion. He has now taken his rank among the great benefactors of mankind." Biddle concluded with the following: "In the name of Stephen Girard we dedicate the college to charity, education, morals, and Country." Encased in the cornerstone are the Will, coins, a $5 and $10 note with Stephen Girard's signature, a newspaper of the day, and a scroll containing the following inscription:

> THIS CORNERSTONE OF THE GIRARD COLLEGE FOR ORPHANS WAS LAID ON THE FOURTH DAY OF JULY 1833 IN THE PRESENCE OF THE MAYOR, RECORDER, ALDERMAN, SELECT AND COMMON COUNCILS OF THE CITY OF PHILADELPHIA, AND THE TRUSTEES OF THE GIRARD COLLEGE FOR ORPHANS, BY THE BUILDING COMMITTEE CONSISTING OF JOHN GILDER, CHAIRMAN, JOSHUE LIPPONCOTT, JOHN R. NEFF, DENIS MCCREDY, JOSEPH WORRELL, JOHN BYERLY, EPHRIM HAINES, AND SAMUEL V. MERRICK. THE ARCHITECT IS THOMAS U. WALTER, THE GENERAL SUPERINTENDENT IS JACOB SOUDER, THE SUPERINTENDENT OF MARBLE WORK IS FINDLEY HIGHLANDS, AND JOHN P. BINNS IS THE CLERK OF THE WORKS.

In the planning process did Girard make any allowances for the possible future inclusion of female students?

No. The thought was nowhere on the horizon. There were, however, several institutions for girls that Girard donated to regularly: Poor Sister Rose's, Widows' Asylum and Female Hospitable Society; and the Magdalen Society which cared for more than 200 outcast girls.[2]

What did the will specify for buildings on the campus?

Besides the Main Building, the will called for four side buildings and Walter submitted the plans in 1835. He called them numbers one, two, three, and four. This designation lasted until 1927. No.1, later designated Allen Hall, contained four dwellings for the staff. No.2, now Bordeaux Hall, contained 4 dormitories, 2 section rooms and toilets to serve 100 students. No.3, now Mariner Hall contained the dining rooms for all, and parlors for the staff. No.4, now Merchant Hall, contained small dormitories and an Infirmary.

What did Walter announce in his final report on the Main Building?

In his final report to the Board, Thomas U. Walter, in talking about the Main Building, says "The reverberation of sound in these rooms, in consequence of their magnitude and their arch-formed ceilings, render them wholly unfit for use: They are, however, constructed in exact accordance with the will, and these results were anticipated in the earliest stages of the work."[3]

Was there any mention in the construction plan for any facility that could be used in the training of future seamen so dear to Girard's heart?

When Girard became rich and powerful he did not forget the seamen and their interests in his will. He stated that he was a member of the society for the relief of poor and distressed masters of ships, their widows and children and to this society he bequeathed ten thousand dollars. His plans for Girard College didn't include a course on sailing as a trade.[4]

When was the construction of the college completed?

Construction of the college was completed on November 13, 1847, after many delays. Construction proceeded exceedingly slowly, often interrupted by litigation initiated by Girard's family and public critics. Some people claimed that many delays were intentional because so many bodies of governing people and officers involved with the construction were "eating up a large portion of the fund which Mr. Girard devoted to the education of the poor orphans." In 1842, the State House of Representatives conducted a hearing to determine "if the City of Philadelphia knowingly or willfully violated the conditions of Stephen Girard's will in the construction of the college." Duane, Girard's attorney, testified that Girard considered himself a builder and had he lived he would have supervised the building of the college. Duane stated that Girard had a mason evaluate the stone on the property and he concluded that it was inadequate for the buildings, but satisfactory for the wall. Duane testified that Girard considered columns to be in bad taste and hated them so much that he considered removing them from the front of his Bank. Duane concluded his testimony by stating that the proposed college was more like a temple and not what Girard had in mind and surely not appropriate as a college for poor orphans.

17

Girard College

1832

"Girard College for Orphans." Lithograph, ca. 1845 by James Fuller Queen. Street view of Founder's Hall and other buildings. LC-DIG-ppmsca-24858. Library of Congress Prints and Photographs Division, Washington, DC.

Who was the first President of Girard College?

The first President of Girard College was Alexander Dallas Bache, who was a Professor at the University of Pennsylvania. He was elected President in 1836, and although he traveled extensively in Europe preparing the Girard College curriculum, he left the position before the college opened, to become president of the Philadelphia Central High School.

How many students were admitted to the college during the first year of operation?

On January 1, 1848, Dr. Joel Jones, successor to Dr. Bache, welcomed 95 boys to the college. Of the 95 boys, all but 31 came from Philadelphia. Before the year was out, another 100 boys were admitted.

What were the operational costs for the first year?

The total cost of operating the college for the first year, including salaries of the staff, and all other expenses amounted to approximately $51,000 of which $22,000 was spent for clothing and subsistence for the children.[1]

What were some of the problems with the construction that were encountered during the first year?

On November 11, 1848, the college had its first disaster when a break occurred in the reservoir of the Spring Garden Water Works, located just north of the north wall near 24th Street. Its flood swept away 125 feet of the northern wall then crossed the campus and removed a similar amount of wall on the south side. Shortly after the college opened, lighting of the buildings was converted from oil to gas for economic reasons.[2]

Who was Dr. Allen?

Dr. William H. Allen after whom Allen Hall was named was the third president of the college. He entered into this position in 1850 and remained in office until 1882.

Was Stephen's original estimate of a student body of 300 students quickly met?

The enrollment of 300 was easily met. It was held at that number until 1863 when the decision was made to increase the enrollment not to exceed 520.

Were there health problems among the boys?

In 1851, the college was struck with an epidemic of dysentery that resulted in the death of four students. The doctors, after unsuccessfully attacking the problem, decided to send all the students home for three weeks. This succeeded in terminating the epidemic. It is interesting to note that in the early years a couple students died each year, but the causes where not mentioned in the reports.

With only a few buildings finished, where were the classes held?

In 1856, plans were being developed to divide some of the rooms in the Main Building (Founder's Hall) to increase the number of classrooms. The third floor of the Main Building was found to be useless during the summer months because the small fan-type windows were inadequate to ventilate the build-up of summer heat. Additionally, the existence of the huge skylights in each room contributed to the accumulation of heat.

Founder's Hall, Girard College HABS PA, 51–PHILA, 459–4. Library of Congress Prints and Photographs Division, Washington, DC.

To whom was the will entrusted for its administration?

At first, the City Council had the responsibility for administrating the will.

Why did that change?

Because of the constant changing of Council members and the desires of political parties and their agendas and the events and demands of the times, a change was also necessary in the Administration. After some seven years, a law was finally passed which established changing City Council membership. The administration of the affairs of the tracts was affected by the Board of City Trusts consisting of a more permanent membership, which would administer the affairs of all City Trust's including the Girard Trust. The Board of City Trusts officially took over on February 25, 1870 and its first action was to publicly state "that regardless of the conduct of operations of other city departments, the management of the Girard Estate by the previous members had been well managed."

Who were the executors of Girard's will?

He appointed these executors: Timothy Paxson, Thomas P. Cope, Joseph Roberts, William J. Duane, and John A. Barclay. John H. Irwin, Samuel Arthur and S. H. Carpenter witnessed the will.

Aspects of the will were discussed by William J. Duane, Girard's lawyer and confidant, before a Committee of the Pennsylvania Legislature on February 25, 1842, and documented in *Report of The Majority and Minority of the Select Committee, Relative to the Estate of Stephen Girard*, published in 1842. Duane said that he and Girard spent several months discussing the content of the will. Often, when dining at Mr. Girard's country home they discussed law, politics, religion, endowments and architecture.

To Girard, discipline was a natural law, and subordination a proper duty owed by junior employees to their masters. When, therefore, the Revolution broke its bounds and, under the leadership of radicals struck at the basis of society, Girard recoiled from it, but he remained a bourgeois with strong prejudices against the trash who came in to take over.

Duane described Girard as "a good judge of language, none better and the bones and muscle of the will were all Mr. Girard's, whereas I put in the flesh and the color." Duane revealed that Girard conceived the idea to build a school for orphan boys in 1826. Duane convinced him to build the school outside the City. He and Girard had many conversations about the school after the will was written. He believed that the main building would not have columns had Girard lived during construction. Girard never suggested columns and in fact despised them. He believed columns to be "appropriate for Temples and not suited for poor orphans." Duane believed that had Girard lived longer he probably would have revised his building specifications, favoring simplicity.

What were the set asides?

Over the years the Courts have set aside nearly all the restrictions contained in the will. Today the college educates other than white, other than male, and other than orphan children. Clergy have been permitted entrance to the grounds. Most of today's students would not qualify for admission under the original terms of the will. Also, contrary to Girard's direction, most of the real estate property has been sold and today the Estate is nearly totally dependent on investments other than real estate.

The philosophy that preserved the sanctity of wills was set aside. How did this happen?

The family attempted to break the will again in 1836. They claimed that Philadelphia lacked authority to administer the will, that the number of beneficiaries was vague, and that the will conflicted with the laws of Pennsylvania regarding "rights of conscience." The lower court ruled for the family. The case was appealed to the Supreme Court where Daniel Webster represented the family and the famous Horace Binney with John Sargent defended the Will for the City. Among other issues, Webster contested Girard's right to include a restriction banning clergy from the college. Webster claimed that the restriction was contrary to public policy and Christian morality. The court rejected Webster's arguments and sustained the will.[3]

When the Consolidation Act of 1854 extended the boundaries of Philadelphia by merging the Old City and twenty-eight other townships and boroughs, the family claimed that the consolidated municipality lacked the right to administer the will. The family's claim was denied.[4]

The Court ruled against the family in 1863 when they contested the right of Girard or any individual to restrict sale of his possessions.[5]

Again, the family was unsuccessful in 1880 when they tried to obtain the excess moneys that accumulated since Girard's death, claiming they were not needed by the school.[6]

In Philadelphia v. Fox, 64 Pa. 169 1870, the creation of the Board of Directors of City Trusts was upheld. In that case the family claimed that selection of the Trustees by the Judges made it impossible for the Judges to remain impartial in a conflict.

In Field v. Directors of Girard College, 54 Pa. 233 1867 the Court declared that the City Council could not contravene the will's direction.

In the Soohan v. Philadelphia case, 33 Pa. 9 1859 the court defined Girard's use of the word "orphan" as a fatherless child. This ruling was necessary because some people believed it was necessary to lack both parents to be an orphan.

Because the will was so often successfully defended, it was considered sound and defensible. It was not until the 1950s, that courts began to consider social changes and political expediency, when interpreting the constitutionality of a man's last wishes.

When were the remains of Stephen Girard moved to Founder's Hall?

On January 9, 1851, Girard's remains were taken from the grave at Trinity Cemetery and moved to Girard College, and placed in Founder's Hall. Months later after completion of a sarcophagus, the casket holding the remains of Girard was placed in the sarcophagus in the front foyer of Founder's Hall. A life-size marble statue of Girard stands before the sarcophagus giving the students and visitors who can view it from the roadway below an impression of dignity, authority, and a peaceful aura of simplicity, competence, and durability.[7]

18

The Aftermath

Building for the Future
1832

How would the wealth of Stephen Girard stack up with other rich men of the United States?

He amassed his enormous wealth as a merchant and a banker; if this wealth is viewed as a percentage of GDP, he was one of the five richest men in American history.

How can Girard's achievements be summarized?

In his life, Girard was "Junior officer of eleven ships, master of four, owner of twenty-four; director, in person, of world-wide trading operations for more than a half a century; first and foremost private banker in Pennsylvania; wartime financier to the United States Government; farmer in Philadelphia, landowner in eastern Pennsylvania and in Louisiana; richest citizen of the United States; philanthropist, founder of Girard College."[1]

How did his biographer Cheesman Herrick describe Girard?

He wrote: "Girard was a father to the fatherless and a friend to the widows. The boldness, the originality, the magnificence of Girard's philanthropy entitled him to a place among the true lovers of mankind, great in life and doubly great in death."[2]

How did James Parton reflect on the state of Girard College, its Board of Directors and the difficulties of their task in 1864?

Sixteen years have gone by since the college was opened. But it cannot be said that the policy of the Directors is now fixed. These Directors, appointed by the City Councils, are eighteen in number, of whom six go out of office every year, while the Councils themselves are annually elected. Hence the difficulty of settling upon a plan, and the greater difficulty of adhering to one...Four times the President has been changed, and there have been two periods of considerable length when there was no President...

How did Elbert Hubbard describe the college he saw in action?

"At Girard College there are now constantly more than two thousand boys, who have a home and school advantages. There are certain grave dangers about institutional homes for children, in that there is a strong tendency to kill individuality. But certain it is that Girard College has ever labored, and in a great degree succeeded, in minimizing this tendency. It is the proud boast that any boy who is graduated at Girard is able to take care of himself—he can do things that the world wants done and is willing to pay for." [3]

Who was the first graduate of Girard to serve on the Board of City Trust?

In 1911, Louis Otto Heiland, a graduate of the college, was elected Secretary of the Board of City Trust. He was the first graduate to hold a position with the Board.[4]

What were some of the basic changes Dr. Herrick introduced early in his presidency of the college?

He changed all the lavatories, adding hot water, individual sinks, showers to eliminate the community baths, and tile to improve sanitation. He asked that President's quarters be built so that No.1 building might be better used to relieve the overcrowded student dormitories. He hired a grounds-keeper to improve the campus appearance, to plant new trees and care for the aging ones.[5]

How can we explain why a man who had shown such generosity and courage during a lifetime of helping the sick and the poor, of showing more patriotism than many of our colonial leaders, why his name is not only little known but sorely ignored in our American history books?

James Parton writes:
> Never was there a person more destitute than Girard of the qualities which win the affection of others. His temper was violent, his presence forbidding, his usual manner ungracious, his will inflexible, his heart untender, his imagination dead. He was odious to many of his fellow-citizens, who considered him the hardest and meanest of men. He had lived among them for half a century, but he was no more a Philadelphian in 1830 than in 1776. He still spoke with French accent, and accompanied his words

with a French shrug and French gesticulation. Surrounded with Christian churches which he had helped to build, he remained a sturdy unbeliever, and possessed the complete works of only one man, Voltaire. He made it a point of duty to labor on Sunday, as a good example to others. He made no secret of the fact, that he considered the idleness of Sunday an injury to the people, moral and economical. He would have opened his bank on Sundays, if any one would have come to it. For his part, he required no rest, and would have none. He never travelled. He never attended public assemblies or amusements. He had no affections to gratify, no friends to visit, no curiosity to appease, no tastes to indulge. What he once said of himself appeared to be true, that he rose in the morning with but a single object, and that was to labor so hard all day as to be able to sleep all night. The world was absolutely nothing to him but a working-place. He scorned and scouted the opinion, that old men should cease to labor, and should spend the evening of their days in tranquility. "No," he would say, "labor is the price of life, its happiness, it's everything; to rest is to rust; every man should labor to the last hour of his ability."

When several of his associates were together, did Girard contribute to the conversation? What did biographer Elbert Hubbard say?

"He talked little, but he had a way of listening and making calculations while others were arguing. Suddenly, he would reach a conclusion and make his decision. When this was done, that was all there was about it. The folks with whom he traded grew to respect his judgment and knew better than to rob him of his time by haggling."

Did anyone from personal knowledge of Stephen Girard write disparagingly about him?

Yes. In spite of all his deeds, Girard was maligned by Stephen Simpson in his book, *Biography of Stephen Girard*, released within three months after Girard's death. He wrote derogatorily about Girard and many myths about Girard can be traced to this book written by an ungrateful employee. Simpson's father George had been the head cashier in Girard's bank and while there, he obtained employment for his son Stephen. When Stephen Simpson's father died, the son did not, as expected, receive the father's position. Many years passed before people like Professor William Wagner, a close friend and prodigy of Girard's, and the philanthropist who endowed the Wagner Institute at 17th and Montgomery Avenue in Philadelphia, convinced the public of the inaccuracies and distortions contained in Stephen Simpson's book. In one of Wagner's lectures, given before the Pennsylvania Historical Society in 1882, he said, "Anyone who reads Simpson's biography of Stephen Girard will perceive that the whole account is embittered and venomous and that wherever he could find an opportunity to falsify or pervert he improved it to the utmost. He tortured facts to suit his purpose."

Were all the facts in Simpson's book false?

Cheesman Herrick wrote: "In fairness it should be said that Simpson supplied very commendable and outstanding facts about Girard's life." In this he was referring to Girard's bravery during the yellow fever epidemic. Stephen Simpson, Girard's first biographer and one who showed no wish to flatter him wrote: "No man perhaps ever possessed so great and perfect a genius for trade and commerce as Stephen Girard—not that superficial trick or mere cunning that exults in a dash of speculation but that sound penetration and various knowledge of the products of countries and the state of markets; the seasons and climates of various nations which constitute what may be termed the mental chart of the intelligent talented and liberal merchant combined with a constant observation of the political and domestic situation of countries and their international relations as they tend to influence their pacific or belligerent attitude towards one another."[6]

What has been stored in The Stephen Girard Collection?

The Stephen Girard Collection, housed at the college, is a priceless collection of furniture, plate, china, and other effects mostly accumulated by Girard during the period 1780-1830. Also stored are his preserved original papers representing one of the largest collection of records involving commerce between 1776 and 1831.

Did the Girard papers include business correspondence over the years?

Among the Girard papers are 36,000 letters received by Girard, 14,000 sent by him, numerous ledgers containing nearly every transaction conducted by Girard, and one of the finest collections of nautical maps. The collection includes many of the original drawings submitted by the architects that competed to construct the college.[7]

Was the meticulous method of his record keeping reflected in the collection of his papers?

Girard was orderly and efficient and recorded almost everything. He seldom discarded anything. When he died, the papers were in specific order and it has been written that he could find any paper within a few minutes. During an inventory, unfortunately, shortly after his death, that order was forever disturbed. At least three unsuccessful attempts were made to restore the order.[8]

How did Dr. John Bach McMaster get involved in studying Girard's papers?

He was interested in writing about Stephen Girard. In March 1913, the Board of Trustees appropriated $5,000 and commissioned Dr. McMaster, a Professor of American History at the University of Pennsylvania, to write a biography of Stephen Girard. Many have asked how McMaster managed to gather so many facts about Girard's early years. The professor went to France and got his information by talking to people and studying records.[9]

Did the McMaster study reveal personal information about Girard's family?

The papers include a view of Girard's personal matters such as his quarrels with his brother John and their complete estrangement for a period of two years. Then they reveal Stephen's patience and his generous response when, broken in health and fortune, John applied for assistance.

Did the papers make mention of Girard's two nephews?

There are accounts of the marriage of his niece Marie Antoinette Girard to John Hemphill, and the arrival in Philadelphia of two nephews, sons of his brother Etienne, who would live with Girard and whom Girard would pay to have educated.

Have there been any relatively recent findings of papers belonging to Stephen Girard?

Founder's Hall windows were sandbagged in 1941 to prevent possible damage to Girard's relics should an air raid occur. In the process of moving the rare articles from the third to first floor of Founder's Hall, many books belonging to Stephen Girard's personal library were discovered, along with other papers and volumes. There are approximately 600 books still remaining from Girard's personal library. Many have been rebound. After years of research, Dr. William F. Zeil, in 1981 compiled and published A Catalogue of the Personal Library of Stephen Girard, 1750–1831.[10]

In 1950, historians began to realize the importance of the Girard papers, especially when studying the economics of colonial America. The papers were examined by state historians and a Harvard professor. Ten more large footlockers full of ships' records, that had never been opened, were discovered. The following year an air conditioned vault was constructed in the basement of Founder's Hall and in 1954 safes containing Girard's papers were moved into it. A court decree in 1953 placed the original Girard Will under the care of the college. It was delivered to the college on May 20, 1954 by the Philadelphia Register of Wills and placed in the basement vault.

Were any other genres used by those writing about Girard?

Lanie Robertson wrote a one-act play, *The Insanity of Mary Girard* in 1976. It explores the treatment of the mentally ill in 18th century America. Earlier, an historic play about Girard was written in 1922 by John Louis Haney and Frederic A. Child. It gave an accurate description of Girard as a merchant of wares.[11]

What can be said about a book written perhaps by Stephen Girard that was published after his death? It was a book about dreams.

The book is titled *The Mystic Dream Book of Stephen Girard*. It was possibly written by Girard, but maybe not. At some time in his life, he may have chosen not to publish it. The book was published in 1866 with a copyright date of 1885 by Rufus C. Hartranft.

  An example of the information offered is as follows: "Nothing which is natural is entirely useless. Dreams must be intended for some purpose. About one-third of our existence is passed in sleep; and during sleep we often dream. Why is this? Does the mind naturally and irresistibly act in a certain way, while we sleep, and this without any possible useful purpose? Certainly not. Common sense, philosophy, and history will contradict this supposition. Mankind, in all ages and countries, have agreed in believing that dreams have a spiritual origin, and to a certain extent, a useful purpose."

  Sample of the contents: "Therefore he who is desirous of receiving true oracles by dreams, let him abstain from supper, from drink, and be otherwise well disposed, to his brain will be free from turbulent vapors; let him also have his bedchamber fair and clean, exorcised and consecrated, then let him perfume the same with some convenient fumigation, and let him anoint his temples with some unguent efficacious hereunto, and put a ring of dreams upon his finger; then let him take one of the images we have spoken of, and place the same under his head..."

What was the subtitle to this work?

The subtitle was, *A Complete Guide to Wealth, Health, and Happiness. Consulted Daily By This Eminent Man. Taken From the Arabic of Publisher for the Trade. 1886.*

At his death, what was the value of this real estate?

The value of the estate was estimated at $6,699,233.09.

Has the overall cost of all his real estate been estimated?

The cost of his real estate everywhere was $1,741,834.46.

Why did Girard pursue wealth?

Stephen Simpson wrote: "Girard pursued the acquisition of wealth in order to base his renown on the benefits he would confer upon after generations—to have the songs of people unborn chanted in his praise."[12]

When did the Board of Trustees discover Girard's actual birth date?

In 1885, the Board sent a query to Girard's church in Bordeaux for information on Stephen's date of birth. They discovered that Girard was not born on the 21st of May as they had thought but on the 20th. This query was made for the establishment of Stephen Girard's Founder's Day Tribute.[13]

Has there ever been a statue of Stephen Girard erected in Philadelphia?

A statue of Girard was dedicated in 1897. It was placed on the West Plaza of Philadelphia's City Hall. It stands a bit over nine feet tall. It was later moved to the West Plaza of the Philadelphia Museum of Art. Massey Rhind was the sculptor.

Why was Major Richard S. Smith fired from the college presidency?

This occurred in 1867. It appears that Smith ran Girard College like a reformatory school. He was fired for excessive brutality and torture and apparently it was allowed to continue because certain Board members of his political party concealed it until some of the incidents were described in the newspapers. [14]

What was it in the existing conditions at the college that Major Smith found objectionable?

"One of Girard's biographers described it this way: The poor white male orphan, dwelling for eight or ten years in comfort almost amounting to luxury, waited on by servants and machinery in all domestic requirements..."

What had Major Smith proposed to ameliorate the "softness" of the boys?

To remedy all these evils, Major Smith proposed to add to the college a Manual Labor Department that would alleviate the tedium of the college routine and assist the physical development of the boys.

How did the start of the Civil War affect the college?

The year 1861 saw the beginning of the Civil War and, like every war thereafter, it caused problems in Girard College. Prices for supplies inflated so high that expenditures substantially exceeded appropriations. Economies in every facet of the school were implemented. As students were bound-out, their vacancy was not filled. Some of the employees were released. Eighteen percent inflation occurred mostly in clothing and food. Many original Girard students were of the age that they become involved in what was called a "causeless and unjust rebellion." To prepare the students for the war, four companies of 60 students each were formed and drilled almost daily. This began the high school Battalion Corp.

Did Girard alumni enlist for service in World War I?

In the 1917, Dr. Herrick, who was then President of the college acknowledged the dedication of the Girard boys in their defense of the country during WW I. One boy took what Herrick called "French leave" to enter the service, but Herrick mentions that, unlike the past when boys "hopped the wall," most of the boys waited until they graduated before joining the service.

Where were the high school classes held?

They were being held in Founder's Hall. This was an inadequate arrangement, so President Herrick's priority was to build a new high school. On March 19, 1914, the cornerstone for the High School was laid.

When did the first Junior High School come into being at Girard?

In 1915, the will of Stephen Girard was used as a text-book for study by the older boys. This year the concept of "Junior School", a step between Elementary and High School, was initiated.

How many students were enrolled at Girard in 1919?

The number of students in the college in 1919 was 1,583, and it was costing $1.2 million to operate the college. James E. Lennon, a Girard graduate, was elected President of the Select Council (today's City Council), and in that capacity became a member of the Board of City Trusts.

When were the three executive homes built?

In May 1930, the Board authorized construction of three executive houses. In 1932 the new residences of the President, Vice President, and Superintendent of Household were occupied. The cost to build the three executive residences was $102,000. That permitted Building No. 1, Allen Hall, to be converted to dormitories.

When was the new area for the youngest students built?

On January 1, 1930, 150 new students moved into the House Group, six new buildings at the west end. One of the most outstanding features of the new "cottages" for the youngest children was the tower that stood at the west end of the Main Road.

When was it decided that Girard College needed a new chapel?

In September 1930, the Board authorized an architectural competition to construct a new chapel. Ten architects competed and their drawings were displayed at the downtown Architects Club. An impressive judging panel including the Dean of the Fine Arts School at Yale University, and the Professor of Design at the University of Pennsylvania School of Fine Arts judged the plans and selected the architectural firm of Thomas, Martin & Kirkpatrick and Turner Construction Company to be the contractor.

When was the new chapel completed?

The new chapel was completed in 1933. In the college's earliest years the students were required to attend fifteen religious services each week—two each day Monday through Friday, one on Saturday and four on Sunday. The services were conducted by lay people.

Did the Great Depression affect the spending at the college?

The Depression finally was felt in the college in 1932, and austere financial practices were implemented that saved $250,000. Staff salaries were reduced, purchasing of clothing and supplies was curtailed, and some school trips were eliminated.

When did the college have to be quarantined?

In 1939, the college imposed a quarantine because of the large number of scarlet fever cases. The first case was detected on January 4th and by March there were 30 cases. A quarantine was placed on the boys leaving the college and mobility within the college was restricted. Easter vacation was canceled.[15]

What was the cost of basic food and maintenance in 1939?

The *Steel and Garnet* wrote the following: "Household problems at Girard assume small town proportions. All the bread used daily was made in the bakery by four men who turn out 1800 loaves daily. In the kitchen 1200 pounds of meat and 150 gallons of milk were consumed daily. Fifty tons of coal were used daily. In the laundry, 40 women were employed to insure a change of clothing twice a week for each of the 1385 students."

What cost restrictions had to be made after the bombing of Pearl Harbor in 1941?

The United States was at war in 1942 and it impacted the college. More of the staff were granted leave. There were significant shortages of supplies and most items were rationed. The students were required to do more care-taking. Shops made products for the armed service. Excursions were eliminated due to lack of transportation. Physical education was increased to prepare the boys for service life.[16]

When did President Truman visit Girard College?

The year 1948 was the year Girard College celebrated its centennial—one hundred years since the opening of the college. Naturally, the highlight of the year was Founder's Week. Continuous events were held—speeches on education trends, needs of the youths, curriculum, the college history, Stephen Girard, and a play "Stephen Girard" staged at the Academy of Music. The highlight of the week was a visit to the college by the President of the United States, Harry S. Truman on Founder's Day, May 20th, and what a good time he had. He joined with the students and ten thousand guests in honoring Stephen Girard and Girard College.

What did Martin Luther King Jr. say about the all-white policy of Girard College?

In August 1965, the Rev. Dr. Martin Luther King Jr. stood outside the high stone walls encircling Girard College in the city's Fairmount section. "It is a sad experience to stand at this wall in the 20th century in Philadelphia, the cradle of liberty," Dr. King told 3,000 demonstrators massed outside the school Stephen Girard established in the 19th century to educate orphaned white boys. "It is a kind of Berlin Wall to keep the colored children of God out." Three years later, the racial barriers fell, and four black students enrolled in the free boarding school for elementary and secondary students.[17]

When were the first nonwhite students admitted to Girard College?

On March 6, 1968, the U.S. Supreme Court ruled that Girard College had practiced discrimination and had violated the Fourteenth Amendment. On September 11, 1968, Girard College admitted four African American boys and two Asian American boys. It remained an all-male institution until September 3, 1982, when girls were admitted for the first time.

When was the college battalion eliminated and why?

In 1969, the new President of the college, Dr. Kingsley Lawrence eliminated the battalion, apparently disliking its image of military discipline. Before the end of his first year, he apparently concluded that his experiment in liberal discipline was a failure so he outlined his future plans in a letter dated Aug. 24 1970. Lawrence, unlike all Presidents before him, did not publicly publish an annual President's report, an act apparently not questioned by the Board.[18]

What were these plans?

He appointed a disciplinarian and insisted upon a strict code of behavior. He threatened to discharge any boy unable to conform to his "Standard of Student Appearance, Conduct, and Behavior."

What major event occurred in 1982 that would alter the makeup of the student body?

A major event occurred in 1982. Until then, the "male" provision of the will was unchallenged. However, in the 1970-1980s, women's rights movements were influencing people. The court was ruling "all men" clubs and organizations to be illegal. Rather than wait for the will to be challenged, then spend considerable funds in a useless defense, the Board decided to petition the court to permit acceptance of girls. On September 3, the court directed Girard College to accept girls. This action was another in a long line of court-mandated deviations to Girard's will.[19]

What was the main issue causing cutbacks on all services and programs over the years?

It was simply that inflation of costs became unmanageable. For example, the student population was 1733 in 1940 and the cost to operate the college was $1.7 million. In 1999, the population was 580 and the cost to operate the college was nearly $10 million.

What relatively recent crisis did Martha Woodall report on regarding Girard College?

The board that oversees Girard College asked Philadelphia Orphan's Court for permission to suspend the boarding and high school programs in the fall of 2014 to help restore its ailing finances. In its petition, the board asked the court to modify the will of Stephen Girard, the merchant banker whose 1831 bequest es-tablished the boarding school for poor children on a 43-acre campus in Fairmount. The filing comes nearly eight weeks after the Board of Directors of City Trusts announced that dramatic change was necessary to avert financial ruin.

What does the future hold for Stephen Girard's college?

In the same way that Girard was unable to predict how his dream for the college would develop since its conception, we can do no more than hope that the bright minds and innovative spirit of the future will carry the dream along.

(Note to the reader: The questions and answers offered in this book are a small fraction of those that might have been included; consider them to be only representative. The remarkable life and legacy of Stephen Girard have inspired many books and will continue to do so in the future. My fervent hope is that along with the heroes of the colonial period, school children will all be taught and will long remember the greatness of Stephen Girard.)

Review of Essential Facts

Early Life

Stephen Girard began life with a handicap which made him uncomfortable in groups. His right eye was grotesque, had no vision at all and served only to repulse those around him. The only person to show him unconditional love was his mother who died when he was still a boy. This is hardly an auspicious beginning.

Stephen did however have other attributes: he was intelligent, courageous and kind. As a child growing up in the outskirts of Bordeaux, France, he had his share of hurtful remarks thrown his way by mocking children. His brilliant mind however allowed him to rise above the pain he suffered by making his father understand he was more than ready to become a man. He was the eldest of nine children which did not give him much time at his mother's knee. So many births, so much fatigue weakened her and finally took her away.

Born on May 20, 1750, Girard could not have known as a boy that he would become the wealthiest person in The United States of America, that a day would come when he would put this entire fortune at risk to come to the aid of his adopted country at war. And yet, our school children never hear or read about him.

Pierre Girard, Stephen's father had gone to sea at thirteen. He was a solitary man who spoke very little to his eldest son but was pleased to see the boy interested in sailing. Pierre had been a hero in the War of the Austrian Succession. In 1744, a British fleet attacked the seaport of Brest with the intention of destroying French warships stationed there. Pierre's ship caught fire and, risking his life, he put the fire out. Louis XV awarded Pierre the Cross of Royal and Military Order. Stephen had his first experiences on board ship with his father who taught him navigation as well as cargo handling.

With his father he traveled to the West Indies and to the American colonies. Stephen very quickly made acquaintances and was hired by one ship owner after another in jobs of growing importance.

Stephen had a very inquisitive mind and would often volunteer for jobs just for the experience. When he finally qualified for the rank of captain, he was too young for the position but due to his seriousness of mission, he found that his captain had fudged on the application by a year and a half.

His unhappiness at home explains to a degree why among the hundreds of pages he was to write in his lifetime, there was hardly a mention of his early childhood.

When Stephen's mother Odette died, his father invited Odette's half-sister to come and house-keep for the family. This young, sixteen-year-old girl named Anne Marie took care of the children during the day and against her better judgment took care of the whims of Pierre Girard at night. Stephen was angered at this turn of events. Not only had he lost his mother but his main confidant Aunt Anne Marie now took the side of his father in many household disputes.

Wanting to get out of the house, tired of being an office boy, Stephen asked his father if he could go aboard one of Pierre's ships as a *pilotin* or apprentice under Captain Courteau. The ship was the *Pélérin* and was to sail on a trading voyage to Haiti. Stephen was finally going to sea as a real sailor. He was fourteen.

Going to Sea

There was ambiguity in Pierre's attitude toward his eldest son's education. On one hand he wanted to see this bright boy go to Sorèze for the formal training that would prepare him for a career in law or the priesthood. This avenue, however, would cost money that Pierre was reluctant to spend and would take Stephen away from any earning possibility that would clearly help support the family. On the other hand, Pierre could easily see Stephen learning *le métier* of maritime trade from the basics to being a ship captain one day. Besides, the boy was ready to face the hardships of living on board.

Girard had sailed before but never in the official status of a pilotin. He would learn all the secrets of loading, stacking cargo, inventory as well as the finer points of being a budding officer. He would leave his childhood behind with father and his aunt as well as all the kids. As a pilotin, he reported to everyone—the seasoned seamen, the supercargo (the person responsible for cargo security), the junior officer and the captain. Instead of just being his father's gofer, he would now answer to a shipload of strangers that resented him for being the owner's son. Stephen knew that the captain would be responsible for him and make sure he would return safely.

He was off to the Sugar Trade Islands in the West Indies and the delights of facing a new world of excitement. He would do his best to match his father's heroism for which he had been recognized by the King of France.

Girard was bright and eager. He was glad that the sea had offered him a release from his father's tyranny but he was grateful for the start his father had given him. Those in the crew that expected Stephen to show signs of sea-sickness were certainly surprised. Clearly Stephen had the genes of his ship faring forbearers. To vary that maxim, he hit the deck running. What little spare time he had from his many chores, he devoted to the study of navigation. When later asked how he felt about going to sea so young, he said: "The sea is in my blood and I have made my way alone..." Do we know if Stephen had time to read during his first voyage? According to his biographers, he worked twice as hard as the other mariners. His strong arms and nimble feet had him climbing and running all day. He could see better with one eye than others could with two. After ten months, Stephen returned home but was in for a big surprise. His aunt Anne was no longer there. She had been replaced by a woman Pierre decided to marry for sound financial reasons. His stepmother was Marie Jeanne Géraud, an older woman from San Domingo. She was a widow with fertile vineyard lands in Tresse. Pierre was definitely in love with her dowry. From that time on, Stephen kept in touch with his aunt and provided her with an income in later years, supporting her until she died.

As the years went by, Girard continued to go on voyages mostly to the West Indies and returning to his home near Bordeaux. It was clear that he wanted to go off on his own as soon as he could manage the finances. Returning from one voyage, he learned that his brother John was attending classes at Sorèze and would be interested in going to sea with Stephen when he completed his studies. Stephen decided a few months at serious studies at Sorèze might come in handy, especially in mathematics and navigation; so he began his brief period of formal studies. Stephen made it clear to all who would listen that he paid for his studies out of his own savings.

In 1772, Stephen was twenty-two years old and had made his way from pilotin to second mate. He was at that time working under Captain Jean Petiteau. There became a vacancy in the first mate billet and Petiteau was pleased to promote Stephen to it. Stephen then requested that his brother John fill in the second mate position. John had just completed his studies and was pleased to be given a job next to his brother. The ship *Superbe* was going to Cap Francais in San Domingo. Misfortune marked this voyage.

Trouble in San Domingo

For both Stephen and John it was important that this trip to Le Cap Francais be successful. A far as their individual responsibilities were concerned the voyage was successful. Stephen excelled in his management skills as first mate and John was delighted to be working with his brother in his first paying job after his graduation from college. John worshiped Stephen as younger brothers often do. And Stephen certainly liked to have some familial witness to his rising success.

But there was trouble in Le Cap after the cargo had been unloaded. Captain Petiteau was caught smuggling illegal goods into a carefully restricted port—Cap-Francais. So how was this disaster to affect the two brothers? The boys had to separate. John traveled to Louisiana to work as a colonial correspondent for his father. Stephen returned to France. This proved to be a great challenge for Stephen because he had to sail the Superbe back to Bordeaux without its certified captain. Again, he showed his extraordinary skill in this maiden voyage as captain.

John who was more sensitive and certainly more sentimental than his brother was very disappointed.

While John was in Louisiana, he fell ill with yellow fever. Away from home, in a strange city and seriously ill, John needed his family more than ever. He was nursed back to health by an attractive young slave girl named Hannah who was to become his mistress and the mother of their mulatto baby girl named Rosette.

Sailing and Trading on His Own

The West Indies Islands cover an area of a little more than ten thousand square miles. There were seven hundred thousand African slaves overseen by fewer that thirty-eight thousand French slave owners. Stephen saw it as a difficult situation to say the least, seething with unrest. The principal products for export by these West Indies islands were sugar and coffee. From Bordeaux to the islands, Girard noted in his journal, would typically take between 57 and 65 days each way, depending on good sailing weather.

At the age of twenty-four, Stephen could handle any unusual emergency at sea. He was young, strong and cocky. He was about to learn however, an important lesson—know your clients and know their needs.

The fact that he had been to Haiti before did not guarantee his success in trading. He had no money of his own so he bought merchandise on credit in Bordeaux , using his father's good reputation as security. He intended to sell the entire cargo for a decent profit and return to France, pay his debts and have money of his own. Unfortunately, this did not happen. Not only did he fail to make a profit, he failed to sell his merchandise.

The principal reason for Girard's failure in trading in Port au Prince in 1774 was his inexperience. He allowed some Bordeaux merchants to dump junk on him that they could not sell in France. The goods were badly selected for the market in Haiti. Girard had purchased these items on credit and was standing to take a serious loss.

This was the principal reason that Girard was never to return to his native city. His merchandise sold at a loss of 25 per cent. He was unable to pay the merchants from whom he bought the goods, and fearing imprisonment for debt, should he go back to Bordeaux, he sought a discharge from the roll of the ship.

Out to Sea for Thomas Randall

The important lesson that Girard learned from this disastrous trading experience was that Haiti did not need trinkets but food. He was resolved then to sell American beef and flour in exchange for sugar, coffee and cacao.

A series of voyages to New Orleans on vessels owned by Thomas Randall, who befriended the energetic Girard led to a highly profitable business association for both of them. Stephen Girard began to develop an appreciation for the potential of the American market, buying sugar and coffee in the West Indies to sell in the new nation, while in return shipping American goods to the West Indies, an arrangement that allowed him to quickly accumulate considerable capital.

As a consequence of his good work, Captain Randall saw to it that Girard was rewarded for his conscientiousness. And in a few years, he began by commanding small vessels. He was constantly observed by his supervisor and was taught the tricks of the selling trade. It was not done through smiles or making compliments or social maneuvers. Stephen worked harder that anyone on board and would volunteer for any job that was available.

July, 1774, Girard sailed for New York, taking with him sugar and coffee purchased with the proceeds of the sale of his Bordeaux goods. In New York he probably sought employment by some merchant who traded with San Domingo.

Captain Randall had full confidence in his protégé who was a quick learner and eager apprentice. Randall constantly tested Girard, urged him on to learn lessons that others might not be ready to take on; telling him to solve hypothetical problems on nautical knowledge of the day. A genius like Girard would learn quickly and well.

Girard could sense that American merchants were entering into a new era of prosperity. Previously, America's international trading pattern had been directed by English rules, taxed by restrictive levies, and subject to the risks of a hundred years of Anglo-French and Anglo-Spanish wars. Now, with the British evicted and a failed harvest in France, the demand for American food and staples rose in both Europe and the West Indies.

In 1789, Philadelphia merchant John Lewis observed with relief: "Philadelphia seems to enjoy a better trade at present than it has done for some time past."

In April 1789 Girard entered into a relationship that he would describe to his brother in more endearing terms than his own marriage. "Jean," he wrote, "I have decided to buy a charming little brigantine...the figure of a woman is the figure head." When he bought the *Polly*, Girard saw these opportunities. "As regards this venture," he wrote, "I am entering it in the firm conviction that the ports of the French Islands will be open to Americans for the introduction of flour."

The *Polly* was a brigantine, the trading ship of choice for West Indian and European trade, with two or more square sails on the foremast and a fore and aft sail on the main mast. This English design held the advantage of increased tonnage over both coasting sloops and schooners, averaging from "half again to more than double the tonnage" of these older ships. Although slower and less maneuverable than the smaller trading ships, the *Polly* offered affordability and large holding capacity. To command his new ship, Girard enlisted William Edger, a captain familiar with the West Indies. Rather than contract for a commission on each voyage, Girard offered a straight salary of 7 pounds, 10 shillings a month. Here he broke with colonial tradition.

Along with naming his ships after women—both real and mythical, Girard liked honoring the names of great men in history whom he admired. Claude Adrien Helvetius (1715–1771) was such a man. He was a French philosopher who devoted himself to the world of ideas. He was a student at college Louis-le-Grand and excelled in his studies and was awarded a much-sought- after post at court and later became chamberlain to the queen. What may have influenced Girard was Helvetius' willingness to leave the court and the lucrative lifestyle to pursue his studies. He traveled to England and Germany and was received at the court of Frederick II. He became one of the Encyclopedists. His writings include *Essays on the Mind* which was condemned by the University of Paris and publicly burned. Girard had this book in his personal library when he died.

Claude Adrien Helvétius (1715–1771). Engraving by Augustin de Saint-Aubin after a painting by Louis-Michel van Loo. Bibliothèque Nationale de France. [Public Domain-US].

Montesquieu, an important philosopher whose writings were dear to Girard, was to remind citizens of his greatness, each time they saw Girard's ship bearing the name of that philosopher sailing into the harbor of Philadelphia. Montesquieu's mother died when the lad was only seven years old. His mother came from noble ancestry which greatly enhanced the family of Jacques de Secondat the father. Like Girard's father the boy was sent off—not to sea but to the Catholic College of Juilly where he spent the next ten years. Again we have a boy who makes a great career for himself despite the little assistance he received from his family. His *Persian Letters* mocks the French society for its silly and absurd customs—not unlike the mockery of Moliere. Girard seemed to idolize the iconoclasts and quietly cheered them on in the privacy of his library. With the writing of *The Spirit of the Laws*, Montesquieu attacked both the government of laws as well as the Catholic Church. The Church banned the book.

By the middle of April, 1776, Girard was at Cap Francais and a month later sailed from San Domingo, as master and half owner of the bateau *La Jeune Bébé*. (Which he had the pleasure of naming for a woman he had known in New Orleans). High winds and seas beset the boat from the start, and on the second day out, according to the log, a great wave "threw off two hogsheads of fresh water stowed to leeward." On the seventh day, "the sea frightful," says the log, several great waves broke over the ship, the third of which unwedged the masts, cracked

191

the jury mast and swept overboard a third hogshead of fresh water stowed to starboard. The crew greatly feared that they would die of thirst.

Knowing that they would not survive with only one hogshead of water, Girard turned the ship into the port of Philadelphia. He explained his actions in this way: "I believed that on these coasts I should meet with some vessels of the King of England which would supply me with water or grant me protection on entering some port."

Philadelphia 1776

Storms had battered the sloop and Girard's crew was sick and almost ready for mutiny. On May 20, 1776, sixteen days after he left Le Cap Francais, he signaled a British frigate that was blockading the port city of Philadelphia to request water. Instead of sending water, the captain came aboard to search for weapons and gun powder. Although Girard did not have enough currency, he was able to convince the captain that the sloop's cargo could serve as collateral. Girard saw that the port and the harbor were sealed by British naval squadrons. His sloop needed repair but he made his way as far as possible before he realized the folly of trying to enter a busy commercial port without the help of a local pilot which then was ordered to lead Girard's sloop into the harbor of Philadelphia.

It was purely by accident that Girard landed there for the first time, instead of going on to New York where he knew people and places to get his vessel dry docked. He was not particularly concerned with the uprising in the British colonies. As a Frenchman trading with the West Indies he would not be involved in a rebellion of Americans against their king. Ships, commerce, and the accumulation of fortune alone occupied his thoughts.

McMaster provides a vivid description of the life of the city as Girard saw it. "On the streets he saw Colonial America. The post rider, the lumbering stage wagon, the chimney sweep with his number on his cap, the bellman, the porters with their loads on their backs, the drayman with his long-tailed dray, the slave, the slave merchant, the apprentice boy, the constable wandering about his ward during the day, the watchmen with their lanterns patrolling the streets at night, the poor debtors letting down their caps, by strings, from the windows of the prison in hopes that some charitable passer-by would drop into them a few pence, the women drawing water from the pumps along the streets, were figures familiar enough to Girard."

The city Girard saw on the bank of the Delaware River, menaced often by sea storms which he considered bad luck, was to fill him with interest and fascination. Some biographers say it was on May 20th, his birthday others say it was in June 1776 that he landed in Philadelphia. The fortunes of a sailor's life thus brought Girard to a city that was first in population, and first in trade and commerce, among the cities of the thirteen colonies. At that time, Philadelphia was America's largest city and the second largest English-speaking city in the world—London being the largest. The population of Philadelphia that year was about 35,000. In June, the colonies had not yet declared their independence from Britain but tensions ran high. Breaking away from the motherland meant making enemies of one of the strongest naval forces in the world which could cause the new republic considerable grief. Girard had a lot to learn as he took his position.

Meeting Mary

Stephen Girard, the merchant sailor, looked around and saw that there was little chance he could go out to sea with the British Navy sealing off the ports. Girard was thankful that his English was bad and his accent atrocious. At least he would not be taken for a rebel. He took some time to explore Philadelphia. He learned that the city was bordered on the north by Vine Street and on the south by Cedar which later was to be called South Street. On the east border was the place where William Penn first landed on what was to be called Philadelphia as he traveled the Delaware River and on the west, the city was bordered by the Schuylkill River.

He decided he would become a land merchant somewhere near the busy port on the river. With the sale of some of his cargo, he rented a house with a shop front on Water Street. There he was able to store some of his cargo and sell what he had at retail prices. This kind of business was not foreign to Girard for he had done it as a young man for his father in France.

Walking along Water Street one day, near the corner of Vine Street, he saw the most beautiful servant girl going to the pump for a pail of water. She was an enchanting brunette of sixteen, with luxuriant black locks curling and clustering about her neck. As she tripped along with bare feet and empty pail, in airy and unconscious grace, she captivated the susceptible Frenchman. Not a poet, Girard understood, in observing this beauty, that this was a reason that poetry existed. He made her acquaintance by offering to pump the water for her which she happily accepted. Soon he made himself at home in her kitchen, bringing claret and fresh vegetables that he would cook for her. He smiled, looking at the water pump just outside the store window–it was a wonderful bit of luck and a means to meet Mary, more affectionately called Polly.

How could a young attractive girl be drawn to a man ten years older than she who was not physically attractive, with an unfortunate eye deformity? But there was attraction. Perhaps she saw in him a man of experience and means. As a servant girl her options were few and this man Stephen she believed had determination and intelligence. Mary Lum could offer nothing more than her youth and her beauty. However it happened, neither one discouraged the encounter. In short order, he proposed marriage and she accepted. The marriage took place on June 6, 1777.

Stephen wanted to know if Mary's family was in maritime trade as well. Mary told him that her father, John Lum, was a shipbuilder. Biographer George Wilson speaks of the unfortunate death of John Lum three months before his daughter's wedding. Cheesman Herrick reports that John Lum had built a small vessel for Stephen for local trading trips and that Girard named the vessel *Water Witch.*

The only honeymoon they were to have was to stay on board his boat while it was still anchored in the harbor—for only a couple of days. Then the British army moved on land to occupy Philadelphia. Stephen and his new bride moved to Mount Holly, New Jersey, taking his bottling business with them.

Trouble in Mount Holly

A year before meeting Mary Lum, Girard met a beautiful woman in New Orleans by the name of Bébé Duplessis. She was French which pleased Girard but he found her to be too light and nimble a wit. In conversation, he was unable to match her repartee. Mary was more direct and honest.

Mary did not bring many other attributes to the marriage. She had no education; she couldn't cook; she was not good with figures and could not be counted on to tend the store. She pleased Stephen; however, by saying she wanted children. He was flattered that such a beauty wanted him.

This time, rather than pay rent, Girard decided to buy a house in Mount Holly. On July 22, 1777, Mr. Isaac Hazelhurst sold Stephen his first home of a story and a half which included a few acres of land. The price was 528 pounds and nineteen shillings in Pennsylvania currency.

Girard benefited greatly from the arrival of Lord Howe and the British troops that occupied Philadelphia. He made considerable money selling claret to the British officers who came to his house in Mount Holly. On returning to Philadelphia, these officers turned a profit by reselling the claret to the troops.

Stephen did not mention his marriage to his brother John; John, however, found out about it. In 1778, John wrote to Stephen. "And now my dear brother, tell me the news with you. They say that you are married. I hope so and that you are sharing the pleasure two married people are in condition to enjoy when they are really well matched." Stephen did not miss his brother's irony but he decided to write to his father about his marriage. He wrote to his father: "I have taken a wife who is without fortune, it is true but whom I love and with whom I am living very happily."

Trouble came in the form of a twenty-one-year-old officer in Washington's Army which was camped in Mount Holly. This fact had an impact on the life of Stephen Girard and his new wife. Colonel Stewart wandered into the shop one day while Stephen was out and being in a merry mood, perhaps helped along with a drink or two, found that his spirits were rising somewhat above the level of rigid propriety and he could not resist the temptation—perhaps an idle frolic of the moment. While the beautiful and playful Mary Girard tended to her work, she talked to the handsome colonel and shared a laugh or two with him. Then he kissed her just as Girard entered the store. He became jealous and very angry. Girard had several options. He could report the colonel to his superior officer; he could demand an apology or he could insist on getting satisfaction in a duel. The pragmatic Girard accepted the colonel's apology.

Soon after the incident with Colonel Stewart, the British evacuated Philadelphia and Girard and his wife returned to the city with a decent capital piled up from his Mount Holly trading. Seeing that the War of Independence had succeeded and believing that his other interest, that of being named French Consul would not materialize, Stephen decided to pledge his allegiance to the Commonwealth of Pennsylvania. This meant that he would become a naturalized American citizen. Moreover, Girard understood that citizenship was a requirement to have a rental contract in Pennsylvania.

A Friend in Need

It didn't take Stephen long to analyze the situation with the British occupation of Philadelphia. With his experience as a mariner and a merchant, he understood that the young republic could not succeed against the British without enlisting Great Britain's longtime enemy to the cause, a country that understood the quest for freedom and independence, a country with a strong army and a stronger navy–France. Stephen anticipated that the founding fathers of the

United States would approach the French government. Benjamin Franklin and others would plead their case.

Louis XVI (1754–1793). From the Portrait Gallery, Perry-Castañeda Library, University of Texas at Austin. Courtesy of the University of Texas Libraries, The University of Texas at Austin.

What he did not anticipate was that the federalist leanings of George Washington, who felt more kinship with England than with France, gladly accepted the support of France but never intended to return the favor when France needed it. General Lafayette, a French nobleman serving in the American Army, convinced the French King Louis XVI to send overwhelming forces against the British to assist the Americans. It was June 1778. This action gave heart to the Americans and helped greatly in the war effort. When George Washington made the bold decision to cross the Delaware, his decision affected the newly married couple Stephen and Mary. Seeing that the French had joined the American forces against the British, the couple believed that the war would soon end and began making plans to move back to Philadelphia. When George Washington surprised the British with his move over the freezing water of the Delaware to land in New Jersey, the British moved thousands of troops into the Mount Holly area. Stephen changed his plan and decided not to return to Philadelphia yet, not wanting to draw attention to himself or his business at that time. Together they watched about fifteen thousand British troops leave Philadelphia and head right to Mount Holly.

With France now fighting on the side of the American patriots, Great Britain had to revise its military strategy. Holding Philadelphia was now too risky. French troops immediately took control of New Jersey. And what was the victory that gave the American Army the advantage and brought about the defeat of the British? On September 5th, the French naval forces reached the Chesapeake Bay and sealed off the only escape route the British had. This brought Yorktown into play and led to its significant role in ending the war. Girard biographer George Wilson writes: "By September 11, American troops were already at Yorktown under the command of General Marquis de Lafayette. Cornwallis made a tragic mistake by not attacking a relatively weak force in early September." By September 28th, some sixteen thousand American and French troops had gathered in a semicircle around Yorktown. They had now outnumbered Cornwallis by about ten thousand troops.

What was relative apathy on the part of Girard in 1776 when he first arrived in Philadelphia, concerning the destiny of the new nation had turned into a deep fervor and support for his native country and his adoptive country as they chased the British out. The British would not admit they had been beaten. They knew the vulnerability of the United States, which had no navy of its own and not much of an army. The British would continue to conduct a war of harassment against America by seizing its merchant ships and warships almost at will. It would not be until the War of 1812 that Great Britain finally knew and accepted that their colonies were lost to them forever.

Some Happiness Then Madness

During the war, Girard had to bide his time before resuming his trading on the open seas. His mind, however, was in constant motion with plans and strategies. His maritime trade started to boom. He took a partner, in name only, because he had no intention of delegating anything more than grunt work. His hard work brought him satisfaction. Soon he was recognized for the expert he was. Life was looking up for Stephen Girard.

Since the end of the war, the British were continuing to menace American merchant ships. Not only did they take the cargoes but took possession of the ships as well. It was as if the British had refused to accept their loss of the colonies. After all, they may have concluded, had it not been for the French, the American colonies would still be British. Stephen taught himself to be a privateer and take booty of his own. The US Government approved of private citizens taking on British warships and merchant vessels. Girard had his ships mounted with canon to drive off any pirates, including the British. Despite his requests to President Washington to provide protection for his ships, no official help was forthcoming. It would be several presidential administrations before Girard's pleas were heeded. Girard's success continued with trade in the West Indies. With his brother John, he made great strides financially. John was satisfied but Stephen had a more rigorous analysis of his earnings and profit. He was called lucky but his success was not luck but careful analysis of the markets and anticipation for future needs of his clients.

He was reasonably happy at home but there was the beginning of tension with Mary. She seemed to lose her focus on the home she had built with Stephen. In early 1785, the happiness that Girard had realized at home started to unravel. Mary would suddenly shout out incoherently and in uncontrolled anger. These outbursts became more and more frequent. Girard feared the worst. Mental instability and violent rage were signs of impending insanity. Stephen's brother John who had come to visit his brother and sister-in-law in Philadelphia came to see that his harmless flirting with Mary by letter now seemed to anger her. She could not bear to see John's two slaves Hannah and her daughter in the house. Even in her confusion she knew that John had fathered the young mulatto girl Rosette. John had hoped to make his stay permanent in a farm near Philadelphia but Stephen discouraged this idea. Stephen reasoned it was bad enough that John planned to leave both slaves with Stephen. Now with Mary's condition growing worse, he was sorry he had agreed.

During the eight years of his marriage, Mary had not produced a child. Stephen was certain that the fault was Mary's. After all, the Girard brothers and sisters alike had never had a problem in having children. Now Girard was faced with an insane wife.

For two years he had her examined by doctors from the hospital. Girard reasoned that life in Philadelphia was perhaps too stressful so he had Mary go off to Mount Holly with her family to find some peace. Her condition grew better for a while and then it grew worse. The doctors recommended that Mary be hospitalized but Girard resisted this recommendation. He had hoped that carriage drives in the country might clear her mind. He even considered that a life in the West Indies might help her. In 1787, Girard had to accept that his wife was incurably insane and had to be hospitalized.

Having spent more than two years without the companionship of a wife, Girard decided to take a mistress.

Mary's Departure / Sally's Arrival

Mary had agreed to marry Stephen with hope and optimism. Her own family had little to offer her. Although her father called himself a shipbuilder, he was without property and had few financial resources. Now Mary, at the age of twenty-six was declared incurably insane. Several times, Girard had refused to have his wife committed despite her ranting and screaming day and night. Dr. John Jones managed to prepare an opium alkaloid for Mary which helped her get some needed rest. Girard finally agreed that the doctors were right. Mary needed full time professional attention that only a hospital could provide. After only eight years of marriage, Mary was interned in the Philadelphia Hospital.

It must be said that an unmarried woman taking on the household responsibilities as a mistress was not considered a pejorative role in the eighteenth century. Stephen needed a housekeeper and a companion. And surely Girard would not be considered unfaithful to his wife. Sarah or Sally Bickham was a Quaker and only eighteen years old. She had been working as a seamstress for a few years and had the occasion to do some mending for Girard. Having observed the young woman for a short period, he proposed that Sally become his housekeeper and his mistress. Her responsibilities included the supervision of the cleaning personnel and the companionship of a bed mate. Was Sally a strict Quaker in her fundamental beliefs? Sally had a liberal interpretation of the teachings. She had a fun-loving personality and elaborate tastes.

Girard considered his new homemaker to be attractive but not beautiful as he considered Mary to be. It took him some time to warm up to Sally who had a bright mind and a clever sense of humor that Girard did not always appreciate. Soon her organizational skills and her ability to manage the household won him over. At that point he invited Sally to share his home.

Mary's hospital accommodations were excellent by the standards of the day. Girard spared no expense. She had a spacious comfortable apartment on the first floor of the hospital for the first seven years, and for the next eighteen years, she was moved to a second building, called the New House. This facility was reserved for patients suffering from mental illness. When she was reasonably stable, she was allowed freedom of the hospital grounds and was permitted to have visitors with few restrictions. Unfortunately this freedom turned out to cause difficulties for the Pennsylvania Hospital as well as for Stephen and Mary.

An official of the hospital notified Girard five months after she had been admitted that she was pregnant. Girard was asked to take Mary home so that she could have her baby there. Girard refused. He made it clear to the hospital official that he had had no sexual relations with Mary for a very long time because of her illness and felt no responsibility for the pregnancy. When the hospital wondered if they should allow Mrs. Girard to stay there, Girard offered them an additional sum for her monthly upkeep and offered to pay all the costs related to the birth. Mary gave birth to a girl on March 3, 1791. Stephen allowed the child to have his name and she was baptized Mary Girard. Unfortunately little Mary was not strong enough to survive. She died in her mother's arms on August 27, 1791.

There was some speculation as to who the father was but Girard made it clear that the child was not his. The birth provided Girard with his reason to seek a divorce from his wife. The State of Pennsylvania denied his request saying only a wife caught in *flagrante delictu* would give grounds for a divorce.

Mrs. Girard never recovered her sanity. For twenty-five years she lived in the hospital at 8th and Pine Streets in Philadelphia and died there in 1815. She was buried on the hospital grounds. Girard had been and continued to be a benefactor of the hospital which had sheltered his wife.

Slave Uprising / San Domingo

From the time Girard started his own trading enterprise, the West Indies had been a regular stop on his voyages. As the trade restrictions against American vessels increased, Stephen and his brother managed to make the changes work for them. When it was profitable for them to be an American partner in San Domingo, they flew an American flag. When the local trade barriers were set up against American goods, out came the tricolors of France. When caught with the wrong flag and a prohibited cargo, Girard's captain would claim that their destination was not San Domingo at all but some other distant port. In 1790, the two brothers managed a profitable business—Stephen in Philadelphia analyzing market trends and deciding what goods to ship out and John in San Domingo buying those goods that would bring the greatest profit for the ship's return to America.

The catalyst for the slave uprising in the West Indies in 1791 could have been mitigated by the French slave owners had they not been so sure of their methods of controlling the slaves and had they not been so blinded by greed.

Conditions were terrible for the African slaves and might have continued unchanged had word of the French Revolution not given impetus to the uprising in the West Indies. San Domingo was controlled by the French and had the largest enslaved population in the Caribbean. It had a booming sugar industry that had created the world's richest colony, with half a million enslaved Africans. It produced more than 30% of the world's sugar and more than half of its coffee.

From our perspective in time, slavery is a horrible manifestation of human behavior. In the eighteenth century, however, it was still an acceptable business practice. Slavery in the West Indies was especially harsh. Enslaved Africans had to live in windowless huts and were over-worked and often underfed. Some owners put tin masks on the slaves, to keep them from chewing sugar cane in the fields which could provide them with energy. Enslaved Africans were whipped regularly and salt, pepper and even hot ashes were poured onto bleeding wounds. When the uprising began, hundreds of whites fled to the waterfront to escape the onslaught of angry slaves who indiscriminately slaughtered men, women and children—all white people. Not having a guillotine, they used their machetes to decapitate their victims. Girard had been alerted in a letter from his brother John that the slaves were beginning to rebel. The blacks stormed the city, plundering and setting fire to property and killing many whites. The governor fled for his life alongside hundreds of new penniless refugees. Much later, a Frenchman who had managed to escape wrote: "When the trouble began, we found that our own servants, who were numerous, would join forces with the brigands and set fire to our houses."

Girard's agent Jacques Aubert attempted to save the jewelry and other valuables belonging to the fleeing slave owners. Escaping with his family by ship, Aubert had taken as many refugees as possible and hidden all of the passengers' valuable possessions in barrels of coffee, to protect them if the ship should be boarded. And boarded it was by the privateer *Sally* (taken earlier by the British). The captain and his crew almost demolished the brigantine in search of valuables. They found the entire treasure and took everything. Girard's ship *Polly* was in San Domingo at the time under Captain Edger. Girard told Edger to take any refugees needing to leave.

On October 7th" the *Polly* was allowed to sail after paying heavy duties assessed by the Colonial Assembly and undergoing a rigorous inspection. "The rigorous inspection of American vessels practiced by officials on land, as well as by men-of-war, obliges them to truly declare their cargoes."

The rebellion lasted less than two months but not before more than two thousand whites had been killed. Many of the French families went to Philadelphia where Girard provided them with financial assistance and housing. Girard's slaves had always been treated humanely with care given to their health, nourishment and well-being. At the beginning of 1793, two years after the uprising, John Girard wrote pessimistically about conditions in San Domingo: "The country is in a deplorable condition. The law has no force."

Yellow Fever

Those who are acquainted with the life of Stephen Girard know that he became a great hero to the people of Philadelphia during the yellow fever epidemics by devoting his time, labor and resources to bring aid to the afflicted and by risking his life in this endeavor.

Why did Girard take on such a difficult and dangerous task? Stephen Simpson, Girard's first biographer writes: "The yellow fever epidemic of 1793 excited all the energies of his mind, and brought into full play the latent benevolence of his heart. Stephen Girard and his companions stood forward in the shape of ministering angels to provide asylum for the sick. When Girard made a proffer of his services, it was not merely to aid by his counsel or cooperate by his money, in alleviating the calamity of his fellow citizens, but was to undertake in person the most laborious and loathsome duties."

One might ask what caused the yellow fever epidemic that devastated Philadelphia in 1793. Since many refugees coming into the city had been infected, it was assumed that the fever came with them from the West Indies. Girard noted that a stevedore fell sick while unloading the *Polly*. He was immediately purged and bled but he grew worse and died. According to biographer Harry Emerson Wildes, Frenchmen living in Philadelphia often opened their homes to their compatriots coming from Santo Domingo who may have been ill.

Elbert Hubbard in his book, *Stephen Girard*, described Girard's courage during the epidemic: "When pestilence settled on the city like a shadow, and death had marked the doorposts of more than half the homes in the city with the sign of silence, Girard did not absolve himself by drawing a check and sending it to a committee by mail. Not he! He asked himself, 'What would Franklin have done under these conditions?' And he answered the question by going to the pesthouse, doing for the stricken, the dying and the dead what the pitying Christ would have done had He been on earth.'"

This sickness was sometimes referred to as "black death" because of the color of the vomit which contained large amounts of blood. The name of yellow fever came from the color of the person's skin as the sickness affected the liver, kidneys and heart. The hospital at Bush Hill was the private residence of William Hamilton who was at the time living in England and commandeered by the city for the purpose of admitting yellow fever patients. Bush Hill was considered ideal for its spaciousness and isolation from the general population.

The hospital committee held a meeting of people whose loved ones had been contaminated asking for volunteers to work for the patients. The committee was astonished and pleased when two wealthy men, among a handful of other volunteers in the crowd, raised their hands. The first to volunteer was Stephen Girard and the second was Peter Helm. The record shows a statement by a committee member, Matthew Carey, about Girard: "...sympathizing with the wretched situation of the sufferers at Bush Hill, he voluntarily and unexpectedly offered himself as a manager to superintend that hospital." The conditions at the hospital, prior to Girard's arrival, were deplorable. It was dirty, badly regulated, crowded and poorly supplied. To make matters worse, there were no experienced nurses to care for the sick; they had all fled thinking that merely being near the hospital would be fatal to them.

As acting manager, Girard took it upon himself to supervise all the matters inside the hospital. This was more dangerous. He delegated to Peter Helm the work outside the hospital, such as organizing public support and raising funds.

Among Girard's first tasks was to fire several dilettante doctors whom Girard considered incompetent. He also dismissed several prostitute nurses. Biographer Henry Arey described the risks that Girard and Helm took in caring for the patients. "These men performed the most loathsome duties ... and the only reward possible was a nameless grave upon the heights of Bush Hill."

Girard selected Dr. Jean Deveze to head up a team of serious doctors to handle the flood of patients arriving at the hospital.

For sixty days, Girard and Helm took care of all the people in their charge. Girard gave generously of his time and financial support to the afflicted. Half the population had fled the city. The others remained in their houses. Most of the churches, the Great Coffee House, and the library were closed. Of the four newspapers, only one remained open. To ward off the sickness, people smoked tobacco; others chewed garlic, or carried bags of camphor in pockets or around their necks. No one offered to shake hands.

At the height of the epidemic, Girard had a touch of the illness himself but told no one except a trusted business acquaintance. He treated himself with what he called a daily "lavage" and soon the symptoms disappeared. The disease raged on but he continued to put himself at serious risk. While many in the city with the means to escape fled the city limits for a safer environment, Girard stayed to care for the sick and dying. He wrote: "I shall accordingly be very busy for a few days and if I have the misfortune to be overcome by the fatigue of my labors I shall have the satisfaction of having performed a duty which we owe to one another." When the outbreak subsided, the City Hall of Philadelphia hailed him as a hero.

From August 1st 1793 through November 9th 1793, in a population of twenty-five thousand, (many residents were not counted because they would not return to the city until much later) there were four thousand thirty-one burials from the fever. During the height of the yellow fever epidemic, the dead had to be disposed of quickly. How was this done? Every evening a horse-drawn cart circulated around the city in the dark of night. The call was heard far and wide: "Bring out your Dead!"

Doctors were not very effective in treating this disease. They knew very little about this epidemic. Without understanding the problem, they resorted to purging and bleeding and often amputation. Doctors were often the cause of early death. It had often been said that Girard fancied himself as a sensible country doctor. He was quoted as saying: "I consider myself as competent as any (doctor) in the United States." Salt was Girard's favorite prescription for sores and cuts. He regarded most doctors as inept who killed more people than they healed. In his opinion, doctors were only good at bone setting. Girard was one of the first to speak out against bloodletting or bleeding. He criticized Dr. Benjamin Rush for weakening his patients by bleeding them. Many of them did not survive.

Looking back on his experience at Bush Hill, Girard is quoted as saying: "Would you believe it, my friend, that I have visited as many as fifteen sick people in a day? And what will surprise you much more, I have lost only one patient, an Irishman, who would drink a little. I do not flatter myself that I have cured one single person; but in my quality of Philadelphia physician, I have been very moderate, and that not one of my confreres has killed fewer than myself."

Dr. Cheesman Herrick writes: "One young man, unfortunately, had been infected with yellow fever while living in Girard's home. Girard wrote most tenderly showing his affection for the young man, Peter Seguin, and his deep distress at the illness which had overtaken him. His letters indicated that he had watched all night by the bedside of this young man and no more tender solicitude for a member of one's own family would have been possible than Girard showed to one in need, although Seguin was a comparative stranger."

The daily death toll from yellow fever at the height of the epidemic on October 11, 1793, was one hundred nineteen. The fever began to wane by the first of December. During the epidemic, President Washington visited Philadelphia on November 10th. He traveled from his home in Mount Vernon, Virginia by horseback, rode through the empty streets of the city but he determined that it was too soon to take up residence again. In December, he returned to stay.

The fever returned to Philadelphia in subsequent years. The first time it returned was in 1797, another in 1798, a third in 1802 and a fourth in 1820. In each of these new crises Stephen Girard was a leader in preventive measures and in the care of those stricken.

Danger on the High Seas

During the months of the 1793 yellow fever epidemic, trading in Philadelphia came to a standstill. In late December, the port became alive once again with activity. With the danger now past, Girard's concerns turned once again to the problems of trying to protect American ships on the high seas. During the War of Independence, the American colonies relied on the French navy to protect them from Britain. When President Washington took the advice of Alexander Hamilton to declare the United States neutral in the conflict between France and England, Frenchmen took this action as an affront. Had Washington forgotten the great sacrifice France had made to help the young nation fight off the British? Britain was convinced that without the help of General Lafayette and his troops, there would not have been a new nation. Now in the 1790s, France would not be there to help the American merchant ships. At a time when France had trouble at home with a dangerous revolution and war once again with Britain, the native country of Stephan Girard needed a good friend who unfortunately decided to remain neutral.

So angry was the Secretary of State, Thomas Jefferson at President Washington's decision that he resigned his position saying that neutrality in this case was a grave mistake. Girard showed his sadness and dissatisfaction with this policy as well when he wrote: "The war now being carried on by the European pirates is very disturbing to our commerce... Our ships are not only stopped and plundered daily but even run the risk of being taken to the ports of these despots."

In a letter to Alexander Hamilton, Girard asked that the Federal Government take steps to have his ship released from a French port. "Justice and the interests of a citizen of the United States may require."

The danger on the high seas became now twofold for Americans. Not only did they have the belligerent British to contend with, they now had a disenchanted friend who was now an angry new enemy.

From our perspective of the 21st century, we may better understand President Washington's decision for neutrality. The angry son-in-law had eloped with the King's colonies but was still an Englishman at heart eager to cause the Crown no more grief and certainly not add insult to injury by siding with France against Britain. The Americans and the British spoke the same language (apologies to George Bernard Shaw), had the same customs and, in most cases, followed similar religious practices. Few members of the Federal Government spoke French – Franklin and Jefferson were notable exceptions. Girard and his fellow French countrymen were stricken by Washington's decision. They felt betrayed that America did not fully appreciate the dedication of the French people to liberty and independence. Perhaps Girard had tried harder than most to show his adoptive country that Frenchmen could show nobility of spirit in their generosity to the needy and bravery in times of mass suffering. Perhaps Girard felt that his physical handicap and his inability to express himself fluently in English would never be fully compensated by his extraordinary intelligence, his hard work and his remarkable patriotism to the United States of America.

Girard was becoming more and more a public figure, so great was his desire to have the government take up this cause. He took to the streets and sponsored a rally in support for a change in US Foreign Policy. Focus was placed on three areas of concern: (l) better protection for US merchant ships, (2) compensation for loses due to confiscations, (3) higher tariffs on goods exported to the US from countries failing to respect US trade.

To pacify those Americans who also wanted the government to take a more progressive position in the matter of protecting US interests, a meeting was arranged between John Adams and Lord Howe. Negotiations predictably failed. Lord Howe could not recognize the independence of the King's colonies or negotiate with a legislative body, the existence of which the King had not acknowledged.

While waiting for the nation to tire of having its merchant ships taken or destroyed, Girard let his anger show. When both presidents—Washington and Adams failed to take measures to protect American merchant ships, Girard took matters into his own hands. He had guns mounted on the decks of his cargo vessels. He also sent ships out in convoys so they could protect one another. On a voyage to Cuba, his two ships carried 48 guns.

During the early months of 1794, Britain had seized two of Girard's ships and France had seized the remaining three ships. Piracy was hidden under the guise of necessary war time conditions allowing nations at war to do what they deemed necessary for their own war efforts. In a speech to a crowd of interested supporters on March 18th 1794, Girard accused Great Britain of violently seizing American ships; attempting to impose limits on American commerce; imprisoning American citizens and forcing some into the British navy; encouraging Barbary States, especially Algiers, to prey on American ships; refusing to abandon British outposts on America's western frontier; and fomenting war with Indians. The speech was very effective. Thousands in attendance started to bring pressure on President Washington and on Congress. Because of the tensions that this issue created, John Adams did not seek a second term. He had barely had a victory for his first term and because his popularity had suffered when so many American ships had been seized, he opted not to run a second time.

In addition to the dangers that British and French warships posed, American merchant ships had to fear the Spanish who kept ships in Florida and the West Indies to search for easy pickings on the open seas. To make matters worse for Girard and other merchant mariners, North Africa joined in the fray showing such brutality in their kidnapping, pillage and rape of any ship within sight of the Barbary Coast. These pirates were especially vicious in dealing with European and American interests. In 1785, the Dey of Algiers was extorting tremendous sums in exchange for prisoners his ships had taken. During the presidential administrations of Washington and Adams, the US government paid about two million dollars to Barbary pirates in extortion payments. It wasn't until 1801 that President Jefferson had a navy powerful enough to destroy the Barbary pirates. Stephen Girard's voice had at last been heard.

Girard the Banker

In viewing the life of Stephen Girard, one can see a natural progression in his personal development: 1) He desires to be; 2) He becomes; 3) He excels; 4) He moves forward.

As a boy he wanted so much to be like his father. He begged and pestered until he went aboard to help in all the duties of a pilotin. At sea he was everywhere and did all that was expected of him. Soon he exceeded expectations and learned all there was to know about sailing a ship, managing cargo, and studying prices and markets. Then he wanted to be captain of his own ship and at a very young age he realized his dream. Then perhaps he thought that better than being a captain was to be a captain of many captains. From his house at port side in Philadelphia he created a network of ships taking his trade as far as China, India and Africa. His captains were assaulted by privateers and pirates. His ships were taken or destroyed but he persisted until the seas became relatively safe and he was ready for his next step forward. Dissatisfied with how banks handled his ever-growing fortune, Girard was sure he could do better.

"Alarmed by the suggestions of war between the United States and Great Britain, and the certainty of the confiscation of his credits by the British Government in that untoward event, Girard resolved to exhaust these credits by the purchase in London of American six percent stock sand shares of the Bank of the United States. Accordingly, in 1810, he forwarded instructions to Messrs. Baring Bros. & Co. to make these purchases charging them to his account, the bank shares being then, much depreciated by reason of the state of affairs, as well as through the apprehension of the non-renewal of its charter. After much delay in London, this was finally accomplished in the following year, four hundred and twenty dollars per share, on a par value of five hundred dollars being paid for the bank stock and after an additional delay caused by his correspondents' neglect to deliver the stock when requested after he had purchased it. Girard sent a special agent to England to whom it was finally transferred and by him forwarded to America."(Henry Atlee Ingram)

"On a visit to London, Mr. Curwen found that "All acknowledged that money was as abundant in the country as ever, but that there was an inexplicable want of confidence, and what is remarkable the run was made on some of the most wealthy bankers in the city, and some who could not at a day's notice pay up all the balances in their hands were obliged to stop, although, as Mr. Baring stated, there were many of them worth twice or thrice as much as they owed. Some of them are going on again. The Bank of England did all they could to relieve them."(John Bach McMaster)

The single event that gave Girard his first step into the banking world came with the occasion of difficulties at the First Bank of the United States. It was uncertain that its charter would be renewed. Having funds in the First Bank, Girard's first impulse was to help the bank manage its problems. He worked the entire year of 1811 to help the bank survive. In November of that year, he realized that his efforts had been in vain. The US Bank was to close its doors. Faced with the problem of liquidating its assets, the bank turned to Girard for help. Girard agreed to buy the bank's entire holdings.

Then, Girard purchased most of the stock as well. With the buildings, he purchased all the furnishings. His staff was small. He began his operation with eight employees—a cashier, two tellers, two bookkeepers, a clerk, a messenger and a janitor. Girard hired George Simpson, the cashier of the First Bank, as cashier of the new bank, and opened for business on May 18, 1812. He allowed the Trustees of the First Bank of the United States to use some offices and space in the vaults to continue the process of winding down their affairs at a very nominal rent.

His own bank was variously known as "Girard's Bank," or as "Girard Bank" or also as "Stephen Girard's Bank" or even the "Bank of Stephen Girard." Girard was the sole proprietor of his bank, and thus avoided the Pennsylvania state law which prohibited an unincorporated association of persons from establishing a bank, and requiring a charter from the legislature for a banking corporation. When it was a question of legality to own an unincorporated bank, Girard wanted to be sure, because it had never been done before in Pennsylvania, so he hired two Philadelphia lawyers—Jared Ingersoll and Alexander Dallas to research the matter. But being the risk taker that he was, Girard opened his bank before his lawyers had their answer. As he anticipated, the lawyers told him it was legal. This bank was located in the same building as the First US Bank, on South Third Street.

When the charter renewal for the First US Bank was refused, Girard was determined to use the funds he had drawn from London to capitalize his bank. Girard deposited funds from checks he had drawn from other bank accounts. This amounted to $71,000. To that sum, he added $556,115 in securities he owned. On May 23rd, he notified Governor Simon Snyder of Pennsylvania of his actions. Girard was a firm believer that fortune smiles on the audacious. He had the capital, he had the property and he had the valuable services of George Simpson. Girard was curious as to how the public would react to the change in bank management. Most people never saw or knew of any change. The change-over was mostly seamless. Some professionals were against the establishment of an unchartered bank but few knew the details of the succession. The impression spread unchecked that Girard was closely affiliated with the US Treasury. This misconception gave Girard prestige and helped his business. After the first year of operation, Girard, by his own estimate, earned a reasonable profit. He was sure as his reputation grew, he would do better than 3% in subsequent years.

The banking community began to show its attitude towards a new private bank. Two weeks after Girard's opening, only the Farmers' Bank of Lancaster and the Bank of Wilmington recognized Girard's bank. The Mechanics Bank of Baltimore began relations with him a bit later. By September of 1812, two New York bank institutions recognized Girard as their Philadelphia agent. As for Philadelphia banks, it was completely different. They were far from welcoming. The four state-chartered institutions conspired to put Girard out of business. They resorted to unfair criticism telling Girard's clients that they were risking their money in a dangerous venture. Some said that upon Girard's death the money in the bank would become part of his estate. Girard reacted quickly to these lies. He immediately declared that upon his death, five trustees would immediately assume control of the bank's management and continue its operations as before. All investments and accounts would be secured.

Girard's Bank was a principal source of government credit during the War of 1812. Towards the end of the war, when the financial credit of the U.S. government was at its lowest, Girard placed nearly all of his resources at the disposal of the government and underwrote up to 95 % of the war loan issue, which enabled the United States to carry on the war. After the war, he became a large stockholder and one of the directors of the Second Bank of the United States. Girard's bank became the Girard Trust Company, and later Girard Bank. It merged with Mellon Bank in 1983, and was largely sold to Citizens Bank two decades later. Its monumental headquarters building still stands at Broad and Chestnut Streets in Philadelphia.

In 1816, Girard influenced the Government to establish the Second United States Bank. Girard was appointed a board member of the bank and bought nearly a million and a half dollars of its stock. His involvement influenced others to purchase stock. He believed his involvement was necessary for the bank to succeed, but he disliked this appointment because he thought some of the other members were corrupt or incompetent. He accepted the appointment for only two years.

Later Years, Part One

The timid but determined lad who had landed in Philadelphia just as the young nation was about to declare its independence from Great Britain grew into manhood. He was driven to express his devotion to the United States in many ways over the years. His ability to make large sums of money was not to serve any desire for self-aggrandizement but rather to turn Philadelphia into a city of splendor and accomplishment. When he donated money to several religious denominations to build churches, it was not because he necessarily shared their views but to add to the general beauty of his adoptive home.

Some detractors called his generosity capricious. It may have seemed so but in reality his decisions to give to others came from a deep sense of propriety. When a poor church leader asked Girard for a donation, Girard doubled his request. When an arrogant leader of a prosperous church asked Girard for a check and was disappointed that the sum had not been greater, he asked Girard if he could add a zero to the amount. Girard took the check and tore it up and sent the man off with nothing. This was the same Girard who risked his life daily when his city fell prey to horrible epidemics while helping the poor and the not so poor alike in their time of distress. This was the same man who would leave buckets of coal at the doorstep of homes that would have no other means of heating during the cold Philadelphia winters.

Girard was about to show once again his love and patriotism for his country. For years after the end of the War of Independence, America had to endure the arrogance and disdain of Great Britain as that nation continued to treat the United States with condescension, stealing away American ships and abusing laws against piracy. Attempts at resolving these problems peaceably came to naught. On June 18, 1812, President Madison signed an official declaration of war against Great Britain, a nation the United States had defeated three decades earlier in the War of Independence. Just as America was poorly prepared to fight the British in 1776, America was hardly capable of conducting a war in 1812. Resources and money were lacking. A developing nation such as the US had more urgent needs for money without adding war to its budget. The various embargoes of England and France during the Napoleonic wars, the general invasion of the rights of neutral powers, and the impressment of their seamen by the belligerents, led to a feeling of great resentment in the United States.

The Treasury Department under Albert Gallatin floated a bond issue of sixteen million dollars of which only six million had been sold to support the war. Gallatin then turned to Stephen Girard of Philadelphia and John Jacob Astor of New York and a few smaller financiers for the remaining funds. Girard invested a bit over eight million dollars and John Astor put in about two million. Without demanding the concessions from the government, concessions that he could readily have obtained, Girard displayed the courage and the patriotism that few others could or would. He risked his entire fortune in granting a loan to the Treasury.

The war lasted two years. The Treaty of Ghent officially ended the war in December of 1814. America once more retreated to a peace that was obtained largely because of one man. Girard displayed the confidence in his nation that others lacked. Bold and fearless, wise, and with indomitable spirit, Girard gave

America a lesson in courage and love of country that should have been recorded by historians with greater depth, certainly with a more profound passion and eloquence. Professor William Wagner, formerly an apprentice to Girard, mentioned Girard's role in supporting the US government during the War of 1812 in one of his lectures. He stated:

"During the whole of the War of 1812, Girard's bank was the very right hand of the national credit. While other banks were contracting, it was Girard who stayed the panic." When asked why David Parish did not give money to the cause, Wagner said: "David Parish made a fortune speculating in silver and land in upstate New York. Although some authors credit Parish with the Government bailout, in 1813 he owned lots of land but was nearly bankrupt." This investment was particularly risky because had the war not been won with the money of these men, the new nation might have collapsed and history might have been written in another way.

In addition to offering critical funding to the US Treasury, Girard offered to provide the US Government free use of his fleet of ships and volunteered to serve personally in the war effort without pay. Girard once again had made a daring investment which proved to be profitable as well. He summed up the results of the War of 1812 in a letter to his correspondent, Morton in 1815. Girard wrote: "The peace which has taken place between this country and England will consolidate forever our independence and insure our tranquility." Cheesman Herrick wrote in *Stephen Girard, Founder*: "Once again Girard demonstrated his true allegiance to the United States over France. Correspondence at this time indicated the high regard in which Girard held America. A letter of Joseph Bonaparte held out to him a temptation to return to France and with his large wealth create a great estate. Girard refused point-blank saying that he did not wish to figure as a great proprietor in a country to which he would never go and under a government inimical to republicans."

Later Years, Part Two

Girard remained active in banking until his death; as he aged he devoted increasingly more time to his farm. It was located in Passyunk Township, now south Philadelphia. He bought this farm and farmhouse in 1797 from George Copper who obtained it through default from Henry Seckel. Seckel had used this farm to introduce and grow Seckel pears. The farm consisted of two lots totaling

75 acres. The east wing of the farmhouse was built about 1750. Girard added the middle section in 1800 and the west wing in 1825. He hired a caretaker, increased the productivity of the orchard, added crops and cattle and marketed his products. As the years passed, he purchased nearby acreage, and when he died he had accumulated 583 acres.

With the war now behind him, Girard again turned his attention to more pleasant activities when on September 13, 1815 he learned of the death of Mary Lum Girard. She had lived happily with him during the first eight years of their marriage when she began a long sorrowful descent into insanity. For twenty-five years she lived in the Pennsylvania Hospital at 8th Street and Pine having little contact with the outside world. She was buried on the hospital grounds. Girard had been and continued to be a benefactor of the hospital which had sheltered his wife. William Wagner wrote about Girard's reaction at his wife's burial: "I shall never forget the last and closing scene. Mr. Girard stepped forward and kissed his wife and his tears moistened her cheek." Mary Lum Girard was fifty-six years old at her death.

In later years, Girard began to fail physically but his mind remained sharp and full of ideas. He began to realize that he might not have time to pursue all his interests but he would try. "Coal and the railroad became a new, exciting and profitable challenge for him as he approached the twilight of his life." McMasters continued: "Girard purchased land in upstate Pennsylvania; the value that Girard perceived in making his bold venture was to be accrued as coal mining would bring him new riches. He was then seventy-nine years old. When eighty-one, he invested in railroading, the vehicle that would carry the coal to the markets he envisioned would be there. Coal had been discovered in the Pottsville region, mines had been opened, and that coal had been transported on the Schuylkill Canal since 1825."

It would also seem possible that land speculators knowing of the coal discoveries had possibly influenced Girard's bank trustees—or at least the trustee knowing of the existence of these deeds—to withhold any action on these tracts until the last possible moment. Undoubtedly, this information convinced Girard that these lands were valuable, and he decided that his business interests would be better served if he acquired them. The trustees had held the tracts for 19 years, and shortly after the deeds were turned over to the receiver, Girard, an advertisement appeared in a Philadelphia newspaper that these tracts of land deeded to them by the First Bank would be sold at public auction at the Merchant's Coffee House on April 17, 1830. The auction was held as scheduled and Stephen Girard, being the highest bidder, purchased the 67 tracts for $30,000. Harry

Emerson Wildes wrote in his book *Lonely Midas:* "The lands were exceedingly valuable. After litigation and compromise, they had been reduced to less than nineteen thousand acres of which only about five thousand were coal-bearing. Up to the beginning of 1942, these acres produced about 119,869,794 tons of anthracite."

Death of a Great Olympian

Perhaps this last biographical chapter should be named "Death of a Colonial Olympian." Mount Olympus was the home of the twelve leaders of the ancient world. Surely, Stephen Girard would have been placed among the great leaders of young America—not only for his wisdom, courage and generosity but for his great allegiance to his adopted home. Had Girard not risked his entire fortune during the War of 1812, this country may have had quite another history—that of becoming just another cog in the machinery of the British Empire.

Girard was a hard worker and had every reason to be proud of his work ethic. He once said that death would find him at work, if he was not in bed sleeping. How many great men and women in history looked upon the frailness of their bodies as impediments, unable to continue their tasks of housing their vigorous minds? Girard with only half as much vision as the average human probably saw twice as much through his extraordinary intelligence. Girard was, however, imperfect as all humans are. He never used his enormous wealth to draw to himself the attention of the world. "*My deeds must be my life,*" he said. "*When I am dead, my actions must speak for me.*" He shunned portrait painters and any outward signs of opulence. If he had a fault and he would admit that he had many, it would be that he had little patience that others could not grasp the scope of his vision. He was quick to forgive those who spoke unkindly of him—whether it was a brother, sister, nephew or a business competitor.

In the book, *The Life and Times of Stephen Girard Merchant and Mariner,* written by John Bach McMaster, the author wrote: "At the time of his death, Girard had well passed his eighty-first year. For more than fifty-five years, he had been a resident of Philadelphia; yet such was the secluded life he led, so careful had he been to keep his affairs, both private and business, to himself, that nothing concerning his life was known. The sketches of his career, therefore, which appeared in the newspapers of the city after his death, were wanting in detail and of no value. Stephen Girard died on December 26, 1831 during an influenza epidemic in Philadelphia which had taken a high toll of the city's population.

He contracted the disease that quickly developed into pneumonia and proved to be fatal. His death came about six months after his purchase of the forty-five acre farm." After lying in a stupor, he arose from his bed. Placing his weak, thin hand on his forehead, he exclaimed: "How violent is this disorder! How very extraordinary it is!" He then died without speaking again. Girard certainly knew he would not survive his attack of influenza which brought on pneumonia. As he never exhibited any concern for his life, he now displayed no fear of death which was meeting him, as he always hoped, in the midst of active labor.

Stephen Simpson, Girard's employee and first biographer wrote: "As a citizen Mr. Girard discharged his duties with exemplary zeal fidelity and rigor. He was repeatedly elected a member of councils; and gave his time, which to him was always money, to the improvement of the city. As a director of the bank and insurance company, he always did his duty never falling short of his portion of labor and often exceeding it." The account of the Girard funeral which appeared in the *United States Gazette* relates that after the members of the family came, the following mourners arrived: the mayor, the recorder of the city, the city councils and the members of a society of which Girard was a member and citizens of Philadelphia.

On the day after his death, the will was opened in order that any directions, or wishes, regarding his funeral might be duly respected. James Parton writes:

> "The old man lay dead in his house on Water Street. While the public out of doors were curious enough to learn what he had done with his money, there was a smaller number within the house, the kindred of the deceased, in whom this curiosity raged like a mania. They invaded the cellars of the house, and, bringing up bottles of the old man's choice wine, kept up a continual carouse. Surrounding Mr. Duane, who had been present at Mr. Girard's death, and remained to direct his funeral, they demanded to know if there was a will. To silence their indecent clamor, he told them there was, and that he was one of the executors. On hearing this, their desire to learn its contents rose to fury."

No objections were found, but it then became known that large bequests had been made to Philadelphia and many charitable and benevolent institutions, and it was decided to formally invite them to be represented at the funeral. Girard was not alone at the moment of his death. His faithful slave, Hannah was at his bedside when he died. She had served Girard for more than fifty years and was generously rewarded in Girard's will.

At Stephen Girard's funeral, his long-time friend and business associate Nicholas Biddle said:

> "He has now taken his rank among the great benefactors of mankind. From this hour that name is destined to survive to the latest posterity and while letters and the arts exist he will be cited as the man who with a generous spirit and a sagacious foresight bequeathed for the improvement of his fellow men the accumulated earnings of his life."

It was Nicholas Biddle, Director of the Second Bank of the United States, and Chairman of the Building Committee who recommended that the architect include Grecian columns on the main building.

Girard's death greatly affected the people of Philadelphia. For more than forty years, Philadelphia had not seen so many people in attendance at a funeral. There were about three thousand people crowding the streets. Not since the death of Benjamin Franklin had there been such a large turnout. "There were some prejudices that Girard faced during his lifetime." Cheesman Herrick wrote. "He lived in a time when there were intense political, national, racial and religious controversies. That he was a Frenchman brought against him from some quarters a prejudice which was strong against that nation. Girard's religious independence made him the object of intolerance during his life and particularly so after his death. His identification with the pronounced republican views of the time brought much political antagonism upon him; certain it is he had a cordial dislike for the English and after the Jay Treaty he wrote terming it infamous and calling the English a 'worthless and contemptible nation.' After citing some of the indignities which England had heaped upon America at that time and America's seeming supineness he concluded: 'I must say our government deserves it.' As a Frenchman, Girard was naturally identified with the republicans in the demonstration against Jay's Treaty with England."

At Girard's death his real estate holdings were assessed. He owned prime property and buildings that generated enough revenue to allow his estate to continue growing long after his death. George Morgan's book, *The City of Firsts, A Complete History of Philadelphia*, reported that in 1926, Girard's property in the city, excluding Girard College, was assessed at $20 million.

Girard was buried in the vault he built for Baron Henri Lallemand, his nephew, in the Holy Trinity Catholic cemetery at Sixth and Spruce. Bishop Kendrick refused to permit a Catholic burial mass because the Masons in attendance would not remove their ceremonial aprons. Twenty years later, his remains were re-interred in the Founder's Hall vestibule at Girard College behind a statue sculptured by N. Gevelot, a French sculptor living in Philadelphia. Dr. Wagner said that the face was copied from a death mask taken at the direction of Dr. John Y. Clark. He continued that the artist Gevelot had never seen Girard but was obliged to formulate details from descriptions by untrained observers.

Girard had purchased the property on which Girard College would be built on June 6, 1831; he paid William Parker $35,000 for the forty-five acre farm located on Ridge Road in Penn Township, then in suburban Philadelphia. By codicil to his will he changed the location for his school to the Peel Hall farm. William Duane, his lawyer, indicated the change was made because Girard preferred that the college be built outside the congested city.

The Girardians who read these pages know as well as I the impact Stephen Girard has had on their lives. Thousands upon thousands of us, some still living, many more now dead could form an army of respect, affection and gratitude, walking a hundred abreast through the gates of Girard College, taking months for all to cross the threshold of our former home to pay homage to that lonely man who gave so much and asked so little in return. Those people who have read with interest the history of the American Colonial Period and have not known about this great Olympian, be advised: There once was a man named Stephen Girard.

Appendix 1

Stephen's Twilight Visitors

A Fictional Dramatization of Stephen Girard's Last Evening
An Excerpt
by
James J. Raciti

Scene I

Narrator: It's December in Philadelphia in the year of 1831. Stephen Girard has become ill—first with influenza and then with pneumonia. He has been bedridden for weeks and is now lying on his bed in his night gown, having kicked off his covers. (He sits up.)

Girard: The house is too warm. My home in Chartrons was never warm enough. Sometimes we had to sleep with our clothes on—never enough wood to burn. I hated winters in France. Cold air made my bad eye ache. (He sits on the edge of his bed.) I wasn't the first born in the family, although it was often thought that I was. My mother, Mlle. Anne Odette La Fargue got herself in a family way, suffered through a full-term pregnancy only to lose her little girl a few days after birth. I was next, followed by many more children. My father believed in farm animal production, like everyone else in those days and the church encouraged this, having its fingers in every phase of our lives. I was called Etienne, a popular name. It's the French name for Stephen.

(Girard's mind calls up a rural scene near his home. Young children are playing near a wooded area.)

Paul: Go home, Etienne. You're too little to play with us.

Etienne: I'm not little and I'm playing by myself not with you.

Paul: *Petite merde, fiche nous la paix.* Go home.

Etienne: I'm not bothering you.

Paul: Pain in the ass. Go home. (Paul takes his homemade bow and shoots his arrow into the air in Etienne's direction.)

Etienne: (starting to laugh) I'll catch it for you. (He runs toward the falling arrow. Etienne's scream penetrates the quiet woods.)

(Girard's bedroom. The old man leans forward and stands, holding on to the bedrail.)

Girard: I caught the arrow in my right eye. I never told my mother the truth. I said I was running through the woods and fell. A liar, I was, at four years old. I never talked much about my childhood because it was so bad. When I could understand how miserable my life was, I was already ten years old. The house was full of kids and I got the blame for everything that made my father angry. I missed the years when mother had the time to spend with me, teaching me to read and add figures. But she became so occupied with my brothers and sisters; she no longer had time for me. All the chores fell to me and my father would never think of lending a hand.

Scene II

(House on Rue Ramonet. Chartrons, France. Pierre Girard enters the kitchen shouting.)

Pierre: Etienne, I told you to sweep out the yard. Get that horseshit out of my sight. Why are the dishes still not washed? Your mother is tired and can't do everything.

Etienne: I was making your office tidy like you said.

Pierre: Don't answer me in that tone. You are the oldest and you have to do your share.

Anne Odette: Let him be, Pierre. He has been working all day. He's still a child.

(Girard's bedroom)

Girard: (Wiping a tear from his eye.) I loved my father and wanted to go with him out to sea. (Shouting with a French accent) But you're too young! I implored him to give me a small job on board one of his ships but he wanted me to stay at home. (Too weak to remain standing, Girard sits down again.) She was all worn out. My mother would never again be close to me; she was exhausted by the strain of bearing ten children in fourteen years. She died so young at thirty-six years. I would have so gladly given her some of the many years I have had on this earth. I was twelve and in charge of seven brothers and sisters.

Scene III

(House on Rue Ramonet.)

Pierre: (His hand on Etienne's neck) So, you want to learn the mysteries of merchant mariners? There is much more than raising the sails, you know. You must first learn the elementary secrets of cash books and invoices.

Stephen: Yes, father. I want to learn everything. Perhaps I can go to the school to learn the basics of mathematics and writing.

Pierre: No you must stay with the children. I will give you things to do for me. This will give you the training you need.

(Girard's bedroom)

Girard: I was never sent to school as were all the boys in my family. Not a sou was spent on my behalf for an education. I became bitter at wanting something for myself. I was not a good brother to my siblings. I began to shout at them as my father shouted at me.

Scene IV

(The bedroom becomes dark. A single light shines on the face of Stephen's mother who has been dead for six months. Young Stephen sits up in bed)

Stephen: *Maman, c'est bien toi?*

Anne Odette: *Oui, mon cheri, c'est ta mère.*

Stephen: Mommy, why did you go away and leave us. I want you to come back. We all need you here.

Anne Odette: When the good Lord calls us we must obey.

Stephen: (Weeping) But you're here now. Can't you stay?

Anne Odette: *Mon petit chou;* I have come for just a moment to dry your tears. You are a big boy now with many years before you. Help your father as best you can and when it's time to set out on your own, I know you will be honest and hardworking. May you be blessed with a long life and much happiness. (As she speaks, she slowly disappears.)

Stephen: *Non. Reste un peu.* Stay. I have much to tell you.

(Anne Odette's voice comes from afar.)

Anne Odette: Speak to me in your prayers, Etienne.

(Old Girard sits on his bed and wipes tears from his eyes)

Girard: I barely had time to know thee, Mother. (With the help of his cane, Girard stands next to his bed). Today would be a good day to see visitors.

Scene V

Girard: I was in my twenties when I saw Benjamin Franklin for the first time. He was being sent off to Paris to try to convince the advisors of King Louis XVI that the American Colonies were worth his support. It was not an easy task. George Washington had just been beaten at Germantown. Then fate seemed to smile at the efforts of the American Army at Saratoga in upstate New York. It may have been because of the American triumph under General Horatio Gates or the constant pleas from General Lafayette or the presence of Benjamin Franklin in Paris that convinced King Louis to enter the war on the side of the young nation. I was so proud of that decision and wanted to speak with my French friends in Philadelphia about it but my young wife and I had moved our lives to Mount Holly—far from the excitement. I could have learned much from Mr. Franklin. His reputation alone made me want to be like him.

(From across the room, a puff of mist settles and reveals Ben Franklin himself.)

Franklin: And what, young man, would you talk to me about?

Girard: (Still in his dressing gown and weak from his illness) Oh, Mr. Franklin what a pleasure to have you come to see me today. I suppose you can call me a young man since you are my senior by forty-five years. When you were experimenting with electricity, I was having my breakfast in my mother's lap.

Franklin: Surely your early breastfeeding is not a subject I can be of help with.

Girard: I am convinced that as I learned more about your life, I might have done things better, made more enlightened decisions of my own.

Franklin: As a role model, I fear I might fail the task. I eat too much and drink even more. I constantly spill tokens of each meal on my vest. I am an arrogant fool who passes for a man of the people. I mostly speak for my own pleasure. You, on the other hand, have always been measured in your speech, never, that I know of, fathered a child out of wedlock or fathered any child at all which I commend.

Girard: But your achievements – you are celebrated internationally for your achievements in science, philosophy, politics and journalism. You...

Franklin: I sleep late or whenever the alcohol dissipates itself and have constant difficulty getting around my stomach to buckle my shoes.

Girard: Oh, to have been in Paris in December of 1776. You could not have timed your visit better for America's cause.

Franklin: I played to the French stereotypical opinion of Yankees. As a doting seventy-year-old diplomat I gave them the backwoods version of their Voltaire. They loved it and treated me very well. Now John Adams never enjoyed any of that pomp at the French Court. He wanted to get things done quickly and return to his wife and children.

Girard: I have always admired the philosophy of Voltaire, and have read much of his voluminous works. As I grew older, however, I detected a bit of snobbery in his treatment of Rousseau.

Franklin: A bit of snobbery you say, he was a walking franchise. I remember I was once asked by the French crowd to embrace Voltaire for the public's pleasure. The impeccable Voltaire took a sniff of my vest and made the hug a short one. Yes, Rousseau was a long-suffering philosopher, capable of splendid thought especially on his philosophy of property ownership and the education of young men. I suggest you read *Emile* if you haven't already done so.

Girard: Yes, *Emile*–volumes and volumes on proper education principles. I do believe that it was Voltaire who gave Rousseau a backhanded compliment by saying he would gladly wrap a dozen pages of *Emile* in Moroccan leather. What effrontery! I have often thought that if the occasion should arise wherein you and I had enough time to discuss the great issues of our lives, I should feel fulfilled.

Franklin: Well, as for time, I have all eternity. You, however, have much less.

Girard: I am confused about your position on slavery.

Franklin: Slavery is a complex issue. Indeed, one could argue that Jefferson did more to undermine slavery during the era of the American Revolution than did I. While I was making the British a target of blame for slavery, the Virginian was urging an end to the international slave trade and gradual emancipation in Virginia and almost succeeded in eliminating the entire Northwest Territory of slave owners. When Jefferson and I were writing the original draft of the Declaration, we converged with a simultaneous indictment of slavery.

Girard: But it is true that you owned a few slaves.

Franklin: I am guilty of having evolved with age and sensitivity. I did live long enough to see my slaves run away or die in place, and for antislavery to become politically acceptable in Pennsylvania. Let's say that in theory, I believed it was a terrible practice. As time went by I took on the role of an abolitionist and took every opportunity to denounce slavery. I could hardly speak of the United States as a land of freedom while in France and not uphold the principles of freedom for all.

Girard: Were you ever a church goer? Did you believe in God?

Franklin: Maybe I'll need more than eternity to address that matter. Perhaps through my father's influence, the strict puritan that he was, I felt the presence of a great spiritual force—God, if you will. As for Jesus of Nazareth ... I think the system of morals and religion that he espoused can be a model to us all. He has been an inspiration to us all for many years.... but I have ... some doubts to his divinity; though, it is a question I do not dwell upon, having never studied dogma, and think it is needless to busy myself with it now.

Girard: If I had read that statement in a book, I'd say the narrative was classic Franklin, witty and finely focused. What would be the need for religion if it did not guide us to a more virtuous life? Jesus was a great teacher who remains for many a person to emulate but I do not believe he was immortal, even in spirit. Having been raised a Roman Catholic, I was, I'm certain a great disappointment to my father.

Franklin: And I was taught that God was almighty by my father Josiah. He was a member of Boston's Old South Church. I sat next to him and learned the purest principles of Calvinism as practiced by good people of New England. Man could not approach the supreme level because he was blemished with Original Sin. You know that story. So we both disappointed our fathers.

Girard: If you had died at the age of twenty, you would not have been a disappointment to your community, so great was you contribution. Aside from your journalistic skills and your scientific inventions, you were a member of the Second Continental Congress, a drafter and signer of the Declaration of Independence and U.S. Constitution and Commissioner to France during the Revolutionary War. What more could any country ask of its leaders? When you died, the streets of Philadelphia were overflowing with mourners. When I saw what you did in creating America's first university, I was moved to follow your lead in planning an orphanage for poor fatherless boys. The plans have been placed in my will.

Franklin: In our present political climate there are many who would use religion as do many leaders in America to further their own causes. It is curious that in a relatively small city, we have not met before. As you know, during the war, I was away in France. My flame died out just as yours was beginning to glow. Perhaps one day we will talk again. (Benjamin Franklin's form disappears.)

Scene VI

Girard: (in his bedroom) Hannah, Hannah. (His black slave of many years comes quickly into his room.)

Hannah: What is it, Mr. Girard?

Girard: Please bring some fresh water. (Hannah hurries out of the room and returns immediately with a pitcher of cold water.) Has anybody come to call this morning?

Hannah: Not a soul. You've been asleep for hours. Do you want me to tidy the room now or shall I come back later?

Girard: I'll ring when I'm ready. (Hannah leaves the room.)

Voice: I don't like to be kept waiting and for that matter I don't know why I'm here.

Girard: Unless you show yourself, I won't know who you are.

Voice: Having lots of house guests, are you?

Girard: My mind is being invaded with many thoughts, mostly unresolved concerns.

Jefferson: I'm Thomas Jefferson. (Reveals himself) This will be a short visit because you and I have no unresolved concerns.

Girard: I didn't ask you to come, but since you're here, let me say briefly that my political tendencies were for the Democratic Republican Party.

Jefferson: How nice for you.

Girard: However, when Washington was in office, I detected more zeal in your efforts for changing the grip the Federalists had on our country.

Jefferson: Come on, Girard. You are a merchant. Your only interest is to receive the maximum protection from the Federal Government while paying as little as possible in taxes.

Girard: I'd like to have that maxim engraved over the door of my office. It sounds like an honest motto for all businessmen. The maxim you should hang over your door might be: "I promised everything to everybody while campaigning, just try to make me keep my promises."

Jefferson: You sound like a bitter old man who will shortly leave this world. If there is nothing else, I'll be ...

Girard: And I liked the younger Jefferson who had fire in his belly, who was not afraid to criticize Washington for declaring neutrality for the United States, after using the armed forces of France to do his dirty work. You must have been angry as hell because you resigned your position as Secretary of State for that reason.

Jefferson: I resigned because I could not work for a Federalist government that had as its principal advisor Alexander Hamilton. Is there anything else?

Girard: Of course there is something else. You resigned because of the Hamilton thorn in your side. I have had to live in a nation that stupidly alienated France that might have protected our ships against the British and pirates until we could develop a navy of our own.

Jefferson: Your criticisms are just. I have spent much of my political life trying to resolve that problem. My focus was to build an international coalition against unconventional enemies like the Barbary Pirates of North Africa.

Girard: Before the United States became independent from Great Britain, American merchant ships and their crews were protected from the pirates of Tripoli, Morocco, Tunis and Algiers by the navy of Great Britain.

Jefferson: Yes, and as you already mentioned, during the Revolution, the ships of the United States were protected by the 1778 alliance with France, requiring France to "protect vessels and effects against all violence, insults, attacks, or depredations on the part of the Princes and States of Barbary or their subjects."

Girard: I suppose the new United States Government did not count on having to pay the pirates for ransom of ships and crews and funds for relief of prisoners.

Jefferson: Being a sovereign country meant having many new costs. As early as 1784, Congress began to follow the tradition of the other European countries and appropriated $80,000 as tribute to the Barbary States. I was a minister in Europe with John Adams at the time when we began our negotiations.

Girard: As you know my experience was on the side, that of merchant ships. Not only did we have to contend with the pirates of Barbary, we also had Great Britain seizing our ships and taking our crews. We merchants wanted to be reimbursed for our losses. Eighty thousand dollars was not going to be enough to set aside.

Jefferson: Exactly right! Trouble came in 1785. The Algerians captured two American ships. The Dey of Algiers notified us that the ships, their crews and passengers would be held for a ransom of about $60,000. As minister to France, I was opposed to the payment of tribute. I put together a plan for the following interested partners: Portugal, Naples, the two Sicilies, Venice, Malta, Denmark and Sweden. They all agreed to form an association. Because England and France were reluctant, the plan did not get started.

Girard: While these countries were trying to find a solution to piracy, ships were being taken and crews were being imprisoned.

Jefferson: I still believed that force was the only way to solve the problem. I wrote to James Monroe in Congress saying we needed to use the rod for a change. In a letter to the President of Yale College in December of 1786, I said it would be easier to raise ships and men to fight these pirates into reason, than money to bribe them.

Girard: It must have angered you that the United States ended up paying the Dey of Algiers almost a million dollars in cash to ransom a frigate and over a hundred sailors.

Jefferson: To cut this story short, it was by force that we got the attention of the Barbary States. However, it was not until 1805, when an American fleet under Commodore John Rogers and a land force raised by an American naval agent to the Barbary powers,

Captain William Eaton, threatened to capture Tripoli and install the brother of Tripoli's pasha on the throne, that a treaty brought an end to the hostilities. In fact, it was not until the second war with Algiers, in 1815, that naval victories by Commodores William Bainbridge and Stephen Decatur led to treaties ending all tribute payments by the United States. European nations continued annual payments until the 1830s. However, international piracy in Atlantic and Mediterranean waters declined during this time under pressure from the Euro-American nations, who no longer viewed pirate states as mere annoyances during peacetime and potential allies during war.

Girard: I did my part by getting the American people to understand the plight of our merchant navy. I held meetings, wrote letters to my agents abroad and to our members in Congress. I even entered politics.

Jefferson: Thank you for letting me attend this gathering. I didn't mean to stay so long or talk so much. I do wish you well in whatever life has in store for you.

Girard: Thank you for coming Mister President.

Scene VII

Girard: So many times, I've spoken to my mother in prayers and tried to be the person she wanted me to be. I would sometimes succeed but often I would fail. I remember my mother coming to my bedside to hear my prayers. When I was in my bed she would always kiss my dreadful eye and tell me how very beautiful I was. When she died she took with her almost all of the love on this planet directed toward me. I was lost and afraid. It was only after my hair turned gray with age that I reached out to my brothers and sisters and offered them the help they needed.

Voice: Yes as a family we needed your help but for years you ignored us.

Girard: That sounds like my brother Jean who would always dog my steps like a frightened puppy.

Jean: Was it so bad that I admired you and wanted to be just like my big brother?

Girard: I wonder if you will show yourself to me or just shout from the darkness.

Jean: I wasn't sure you wanted to see me. There were some harsh words between us.

Girard: Show yourself to me as you are—a ghost, a spirit or just as you were a failed business partner.

(Jean appears. He is taller that Stephen and more slender. His posture is apologetic as it has always been.)

Jean: *Me voilà. Maintenant tu me vois!*

Girard: Come give me a hug for the many years we haven't seen each other.

Jean: You have not learned, with all your wisdom and intelligence that you cannot hug vapor. For the only form that is visible to you is the combined gases and churning waves of air, that once was Jean Girard.

Girard: You died much too young, Jean. It was back in 1803, almost thirty years ago and I, your older brother, still live, and am still made of bone and flesh.

Jean: A happy moment for me to remember was the time after my studies at Sorèze that you asked the captain of the ship *Superbe* to let me replace you when you were promoted to first mate. Yes, we worked together under Captain Jean Petiteau. We used to laugh at his name "Little Water." We called him "pee-pee" behind his back. The captain promoted you to second mate for the voyage to the West Indies. This was a special honor for you being only twenty-two years old.

Girard: Although, that was an unfortunate voyage for the captain to end up in irons for smuggling contraband into a controlled port. I had almost forgotten that incident. We were separated after that trip and I lost sight of you.

Jean: And you probably also forgot the time I had become sick with yellow fever and I was so sad not having you nearby. I was in Louisiana. You remember that it was Hannah that nursed me back to health.

Girard: You were always much too sensitive for your own good. Not my kind of partner. We argued all the time because you wanted all our clients to like you and didn't have the necessary meanness to close a profitable deal. Business is tough. It's not a popularity contest.

Jean: And you have too much meanness. You were never satisfied until you extracted blood from every negotiation. I wanted to leave San Domingo and get married and live near you in Philadelphia. You wouldn't let me. I was almost killed during the revolt.

Girard: You were never in any danger but you wanted sympathy. Then you go to France and try to get our father to make you the executor in his will. That is lower than any brother should stoop. You are a back stabber.

Jean: Goodbye Stephen. (Jean disappears)

Girard: He does not mention how I paid his bills when he had no money; I took care of his children when he died.

Scene VIII

(Girard is stretched out on his bed, mumbling to himself. There is a knock at the door. Girard does not respond but a tall gentleman, elegantly dressed comes into the bedroom.)

Girard: Who are you Sir and what business do you pursue in my home?

Man: I have come without invitation to pay my respects to Monsieur Girard, Esquire.

Girard: (Now sitting up, his face is covered with perspiration. His illness has made his voice weak) Do I know you, Sir? There is something familiar about your bearing?

Man: We have never formally met but I'm sure you know of me as I know of Stephen Girard. I have had much fame but you have earned much more.

Girard: Come to the point, Man. My hours on this earth are few remaining. Are you a churchman come to ask for alms?

Man: I come for no reason at all but to ask for a few moments of your time. You came to this city while you were still a young man of twenty-five. I saw trouble written on your face from the very start but I was always going hither and yon, always to battle the very nation I once fought for.

Girard: *Mon Dieu! Le Général* George Washington! (Girard starts to rise but falls back.) But you died some thirty years ago!

Washington: Your mind is not affected by your illness. Yes, I am Washington and as I remember, I was not your favorite president.

Girard: But if you are dead and I'm speaking to you, it means that I am...

Washington: Not yet... but soon. We'll extend this evening for you as long as possible.

In paying my respects; I must first say that I have done myself no service in failing to make your acquaintance. At a time when this young country was struggling to gain its independence, you encouraged the French community to rally support of the monarch of France to come to our aid.

Girard: Yes, it was King Louis who agreed to send the Marquis de Lafayette to bring defeat to the arrogant British on land and on sea. Yes, my mind is working clearly but my body cannot keep up.

Washington: And do you remember why Frenchmen turned against me years after the war? Why you spoke out publicly against my decisions?

Girard: *Ah oui, Mon Président*. I remember that you accepted all the sacrifices of my people as though it was your due and when France needed your support against its enemies, you decided to remain neutral. The dead French soldiers on the fields of Pennsylvania cry out in outrage that you would not help their motherland.

Washington: (Moves closer to Girard and wipes the perspiration from his brow) Yes, that was my decision. Some agreed with it, others did not. Now you must not become too agitated.

Girard: Agitated? Let me at least have my anger. We were told that you wanted America to become a strong nation without enemies. You succeeded though in making France, your friend—your new enemy. Not only did Britain continue stealing or destroying your ships but France began doing the same. It was a bad decision, *Mon Président*.

Washington: Thinking about it now, I may have decided differently but we were building a nation and could not afford the luxury of going to war again.

Girard: But I knew that at heart you were an Englishman. You spoke their language, enjoyed their food, as though that were possible, laughed at their humor. France offered you friendship but we could never compete with the British who were your kind of people.

Washington: I have often wished I had done more for the French community in Philadelphia but there was always some crisis that took my energy and time. I wanted to thank you personally for coming to the aid of Philadelphia during the epidemics of yellow fever in 1793 and later. While the leaders of our government left the city in haste, you and a handful of brave men remained with the afflicted to help them survive or to bury their bodies. Why did you do it? You could have contracted the illness.

Girard: It may have been as universal as having the mentality of the immigrant who wanted to be accepted in a hostile environment by taking dangerous risks. Or maybe it was the need to reach out to help the helpless and to bring order to the chaos. I knew I had to stop that ridiculous practice of bleeding the patients who needed all their strength to fight off the sickness. Someday, a better understanding of yellow fever will prevail.

Washington: You certainly had sufficient resources to leave the city for a more hospitable environment.

Girard: Money was never an issue.

Washington: When we learned that you and that fellow Helm had volunteered to work with the diseased patients, we were all astonished. Rumors were flying that Peter Helm trusted in God to save him from the illness, but you trusted in your instincts that yellow fever was not contagious. You were severely criticized by the College of Physicians for taking unnecessary risks with the lives of the patients as well as with yourself.

Girard: When I volunteered to work at Bush Hill, I made it clear that I wanted complete authority to make decisions I felt were necessary to save lives. I received that authority and began by firing the incompetent doctors who believed that working at Bush Hill was no more important than playing tennis. They were dilettantes and needed to be sent home.

Washington: This is no criticism, mind you, but why were you against hiring American doctors?

Girard: They lacked the qualifications. None met the strict requirement of having worked with this disease before. The ones who asked to be reinstated all fell in behind Benjamin Rush and his unshakeable theory of bleeding and purging. The man I asked to join the staff, a Frenchman, had worked closely with yellow fever in the West Indies and had even contracted the disease on two occasions and cured himself as well as many of his patients. With the concurrence of the hospital committee, we brought Dr. Jean Devèze into the hospital and accepted his desire to volunteer his services.

Scene IX

Washington: In what way was Dr. Devèze different than other competent doctors?

Girard: He believed that a healthy body can fight off many diseases. He understood that a healthy environment is essential to recovery. It was his belief that bleeding and purging can seriously diminish a patient's ability to recover.

Dr. Devèze: (Enters the room) Ah! *Mon cher* Etienne. *Comment-vas tu?*

Girard: What a coincidence. We were just talking about you. (Turns to Washington) President Washington, I should like to present Doctor Devèze who is the main physician at Bush Hill. (The men shake hands.) I'm glad when you are nearby so that you can answer questions the answers for which I am not qualified to give. General Washington and I were discussing yellow fever and that it may have been infecting people since ancient times.

Dr. Devèze: That may be so but it has not been cited in any literature during ancient times. For example we know that leprosy appears in the Old Testament in the *Book of Leviticus.* The word quarantine comes from the Latin meaning forty. It was believed that forty days was the necessary time that a person had to remain apart from others. We are reasonably certain that yellow fever had its first appearance in Africa, although it was probably not called that. In the Western Hemisphere, yellow fever appeared in 1648. The Spanish called the disease "vomito negro" or black vomit. Patients in the last stages of the disease are known to vomit large quantities of digested blood.

Washington: Do all those who contract yellow fever die?

Dr. Devèze: To date, there have not been many studies as to the fatality of yellow fever patients. We do know that many recover. I would estimate more than fifty percent.

Girard: Do you believe that yellow fever is contagious, Jean?

Dr. Devèze: My experience tells me that the disease probably does not pass from person to person. (Turning to Washington) Our friend here, Stephen Girard, had a most unusual and unpleasant experience with a patient he was comforting. As he was wiping the patient's forehead, the poor man vomited into Girard's lap.

Washington: What did Girard do?

Dr. Devèze: With a calm professional air, he cleaned the man's face and garment and went off to wash his own face and hands and change his clothes. Within fifteen minutes, he had returned to the patient to ask if he needed anything.

Washington: I've heard many stories of the events at Bush Hill, but I had never heard about that. Girard, what became of the poor fellow?

Girard: He died that evening.

Dr. Devèze: The story may support the belief of many that, since Girard did not become ill with the disease, contagion was not at issue. Please forgive me, but I must leave now. I still have rounds to make and it's getting late. (Exits)

Washington: What an extraordinary fellow. We were lucky to have him. The results of the 1793 epidemic were favorable. You, Girard, and your team brought the deaths down from over one hundred a day to no deaths in about sixty days.

Girard: *Merci, Mon Président.* I must tell you that yellow fever is a hot weather illness. As the weather turned cooler, we had fewer deaths. What I have learned is that the filth of our streets with garbage and dead animals does not bode well for healthy living. People who abuse of drink have a harder time with a regime of good healthy food and drinks without spirits.

Washington: I was much concerned with the epidemic and its damage to the capital as well as the fear it sent out to bordering cities. I urged the churchmen to stop the bells from tolling at each death because public morale would suffer. I wanted my wife Martha to leave the city immediately for our home in Mount Vernon but she would not think of going alone. I then explored the possibility of moving the capital out of town. My federal employees believed that it would be possible but the matter of convening Congress remained a problem.

Girard: When was it Sir, that you left Philadelphia?

Washington: After moving the federal offices away from the city to Germantown, I left Philadelphia for Virginia on September 10th. I had put Secretary of War Henry Knox in charge of the government, giving strict instructions to send me reports on the pestilence. He, however, decided to close his house and move. He wanted to settle in Manhattan but he was not allowed to stay there.

Girard: I don't mean to criticize, Sir, but as an old sailor myself, I find it difficult to believe that any ship captain would jump into a rowboat to get away from an endangered vessel while others were still aboard.

Washington: You don't mean to criticize but you do and you have. It was a political matter. Alexander Hamilton and others in my party believed that Congress could be moved.

Girard: Others such as Jefferson and Madison did not share that belief. Clearly the matter was political. You left the capital in the hands of a person who was quick to leave as well. But you were not alone, thousands panicked and left. Even our dear Governor Mifflin stayed behind just long enough to arrange a hasty departure after reporting to his office that he was feeling poorly.

Washington: Now that we are speaking frankly, a captain who puts his vessel in harm's way has the obligation to stay behind until matters are corrected.

Girard: Are you saying what I think you are saying?

Washington: If that is what you think I am saying, then it is not the first time you've entertained the thought yourself.

Girard: I'm too ill to follow your sophist arguments.

Washington: No, you are too clever to let on you understand. Let me break it into digestible morsels. The College of Physicians declared that yellow fever was an imported disease. The college went on to say: "No instance has ever occurred of the disease called yellow fever, [as] having originated in this city, or any other parts of the United States." Are the morsels still too large for easy digestion?

Girard: No. I gather you are saying that those individuals involved in importing cargoes from other countries may be guilty of contributory negligence and responsible for bringing a foreign disease to our shores. But my good man, the reasoning is off kilter. Just because a disease has not originated in this country does not mean that it could never start anew here. Furthermore, my own brother, while living in Louisiana more than twenty years ago became ill with yellow fever in an isolated case and was quickly cured. No. I maintain that this disease is not contagious. Why would I have taken such a needless risk if I did not firmly believe that the disease spreads by other means? I may be completely wrong and proved so in the future, but I suspect that the culprit is garbage, swamp water and the mosquito.

Scene X

(As Girard is speaking to George Washington, a woman's voice calls out.)

Voice: Stephen, Stephen I have come for you my dear husband.

Girard: Is that you Mary with a voice ever so clear as it was when I first offered you fresh water from the street pump?

Mary: It is. It is. And you have taken your sweet time getting here.

Girard: I can hardly believe my ears. You are as frisky as I remember you to be when first we honeymooned aboard my boat in the harbor. Has your illness left you?

Mary: It has, as well as all those other earthbound concerns. I have so much to thank you for. The roses you left at my grave each month were a joy to me. I thank you as well for never taking another woman in marriage. I do know, however, that you did not go unattended. May I show myself to you?

Girard: I would immediately say yes but for the fear that you might be still the beautifully chaste bride who gave herself so eagerly to me. I, as you can plainly see, am not a pleasant sight in my advanced years.

Mary: You are and always will be my darling Stephen. Now, look at me. (Mary appears as the lovely young woman. It takes Girard's breath away.)

Girard: Even in my heyday, I could never deserve so beautiful or so enchanting a bride. But what are those three dark spots on your cheek?

Mary: Ah, my Stephen, with only one eye which has now grown dim, you still see more than most of us. The spots on my cheek are marks of shame. They signify the three times I was unfaithful.

Girard: For thirty-five years, while suffering with a troubled mind, you strayed only three times? You are an angel. When I pass and if I can still have you near me, you will count the spots on me like those of an African hyena. No, my dear, you have nothing to reproach yourself about.

Mary: And yet you attempted to divorce me.

Girard: On so many occasions, I was told by doctors of the hospital that your condition was irreversible. I was convinced that I would precede you in death and then you would be incapable of managing my financial legacy. I thought of divorce to protect the dream I had of founding an orphanage for poor fatherless boys.

Mary: Yes, it's astonishing how clearly I now see. But you Stephen were so blind to the fact I could truly love you. So many times you were insanely jealous of the men who only looked at me.

Girard: And the ones that kissed you when I was away.

Mary: Don't begrudge me for my pleasant appearance. It is the only attribute I had to offer a young brilliant man with so promising a future. Even your flirtatious brother was childish in my eyes. I wanted many children because I knew it would make you happy. You accused me of infertility, since all the Girards were so prone to reproduction. I'll have you know that one of my dark spots produced a child. Have you ever, with your playful mistresses, produced an heir?

Girard: My soothsayer tells me that I will be the father of many children but none will be an issue of my loin.

(A spotlight picks out the face of Washington)

Washington: Well, Girard, it seems you have forgotten your other guest, (Turning to Mary). Allow me to introduce myself. I am George Washington.

Girard: General George Washington served under le Marquis de Lafayette in the War of American Independence.

Washington: And they all said that you were humorless.

Mary: I am very pleased to meet such a distinguished friend of my soon-to-be-departed husband.

Girard: General Washington also has the distinction of being the first President of the United States of America.

Washington: And your husband, Madam, wanted to be the first French Ambassador to the United States.

Girard: How in the world did you learn of that?

Washington: But, Mrs. Girard, he decided instead to be the first millionaire of this nation. You may not know it, Madam, not once but twice he came to the rescue of America. Aside from being a hero of Philadelphia during the epidemics beginning in 1793, he also provided the American government with most of his fortune to fight the British in the War of 1812. Without his generosity, we, as a nation, might have ceased to exist.

Girard: Again, it must have been a latent need of the oppressed immigrant to survive in a hostile environment.

Washington: Or the dedication and patriotism of a man destined for greatness.

Mary: I died in 1815, many years after you, General. You seem to be much better informed than I am.

Washington: Perhaps it is the network of presidents that keeps me informed. (Stage goes dark)

Scene XI

Hannah: (Running into Girard's bedroom) Sir, did you call?

Girard: Hannah, please stay a moment. I want to talk to you.

Hannah: Yes, Sir.

Girard: Do you remember when you first came here?

Hannah: That I do, Mr. Girard. It was when your brother, Jean took us away from Santo Domingue and left us with you. It was a long travel and Rosette got sick in the stomach for three days until she felt better.

Girard: Have you been happy while living in my house and working for me?

Hannah: Not happy and not unhappy.

Girard: Can you explain that to me?

Hannah: Santo Domingue was my home. It was warm in winter and fresh fruit all the year. Many friends. Lots of laughing and music. Here it is quiet, no laughing, no friends, no music.

Girard: What else?

Hannah: You sent my baby away. Rosette was a little girl and needed her mother.

Girard: But you remember how difficult she became at a time when Mrs. Girard was ill. We had to send her away. (Pauses.) I would hear the two of you laughing in your room and singing together.

Hannah: A long time ago. Now there is nothing but more work. Always more people coming and going.

Girard: You have help with the cooking and cleaning.

Hannah: Mr. Girard, I am not complaining. You think about sending me away?

Girard: *Mais non!* I have been sick for a year and you have taken good care of me. You were patient and kind to Mrs. Girard before she went to the hospital. I have many regrets tonight. I am sorry for the thoughtless things I have done. This home would not be the same without you.

Hannah: (Her eyes filling with tears.) Can I get you something?

Girard: (Sitting up in bed.) How violent is this disorder! How very extraordinary it is! (Girard dies.)

Hannah: (Taking Girard's head into her lap and swaying back and forth, tears running down her face.) And *mon cher*, Etienne, this home will not be the same without you. I wanted you to hear that I was as happy as a slave can be and now you will never hear my voice again. (Stage goes dark)

Appendix 2

Girard On Voltaire
Voltaire and the Quakers

Voltaire's "Lettres Philosophiques," published in 1734, contains four letters about the Quakers. I have translated the extract below from the French.
It gives a wonderful picture of the religion of the time.

At the time the letters were written, Voltaire had already had two spells of imprisonment in the Bastille for his advocacy of toleration and enlightenment. The extract from the first letter (below) was published in Quaker Monthly *in January 1988. It deals with the Quaker attitude to baptism.*

Joe Latham
Glasgow Meeting, Scotland

I believed that the doctrine and the history of such extra-ordinary people were worthy of curiosity. To find out about them, I visited one the most eminent Quakers in England (Andrew Pitt) who had been in commerce for thirty years, but had decided to limit his wealth and wants, and had retired to the countryside close to London. I went to seek him out in his retreat which was a small house, well-built and clean and without ornaments.

The Quaker was a fresh-faced old man who had never been ill, because he had never known passions or intemperance. I have never seen in my life a nobler or more engaging countenance than his. He was dressed, like all those of his religion, in a plain coat without pleats in the sides or buttons on either the pockets or the sleeves. He was wearing a large hat, with turned down brim, like our clergy.

He received me with his hat on his head, and came towards me without the slightest inclination of his body, but there was more politeness in the open, humane expression on his face than in the custom of drawing one leg behind the other, and carrying the head-covering in one's hand.

***

On Voltaire (From Andrew Pitt's conversation with Voltaire):

"My dear Sir," I said to him, "are you baptized?"

No," replied the Quaker, "and neither are my brethren."

"My God!" I replied, "Then you are not Christians."

"My son," he replied in a gentle voice, "do not swear. We are Christians and try to be good Christians, but we do not think that Christianity consists of sprinkling cold water on the head."

"Good Heavens!" I replied, shocked at this impiety, "have you then forgotten that Jesus Christ was baptized by John?"

"Friend, no more swearing," said the benign Quaker. "Christ received baptism from John, but he never baptized anybody. We are not disciples of John but of Christ."

"Alas," I said, "you would surely be burned in countries of the Inquisition, you poor man. For the love of God, how I wish I could baptize you and make you a Christian."

"Were that all," he replied gravely, "we would willingly submit to baptism to comply with thy weakness. We do not condemn anyone for using the ceremony of baptism. But we believe that those who profess so holy and so spiritual a religion as that of Christ must abstain, as much as they can, from Jewish ceremonies."

"What! Baptism a Jewish ceremony!" I exclaimed.

"Yes, my son," he continued "and so Jewish that several Jews today still use the baptism of John. Consult antiquity. It will teach thee that John only revived this practice, which was in use a long time earlier amongst the Hebrews, in the same way as the pilgrimage to Mecca by Muslims is copied from the Ishmaelites.

"Jesus was willing to receive the baptism of John, in the same way that he submitted to circumcision. But circumcision and the washing with water must both be superseded by the baptism of Christ, this baptism of the Spirit, this washing of the soul, which is the salvation of mankind. Thus the fore-runner, John, said:

'I baptize you to the truth with water, but another will come after me, mightier than me, whose shoes I am not worthy to carry. He will baptize you with fire and the Holy Ghost.'

"Likewise, the great apostle to the gentiles, Paul, wrote in Corinthians: 'Christ has not sent me to baptize, but to preach the Gospel.'

"Indeed, this same Paul only baptized two people with water, and this was in spite of his inclination. He circumcised his disciple, Timothy. The other apostles also circumcised all who wanted it. Art thou circumcised?" he added. I replied that I did not have that honour.

"Ah well," he said, "Friend thou are a Christian without being circumcised, and I am a Christian without being baptized."

* * *

The following statement about Friends' attitude toward war is also from Andrew Pitt's conversation with Voltaire:

"We never go to war. This is not because we fear death. On the contrary, we bless the moment that unites us with the Being of Beings. It is because we are neither wolves, tigers nor mastiffs, but Christian men.

"Our God, who has commanded us to love our enemies and to suffer without complaining, would not permit us to cross the seas to slaughter our brothers, just because murderers clothed in scarlet, wearing caps two feet high, enlist citizens by making a noise with two little sticks beating on a stretched ass's skin.

"When after a victory, all London is lit up with illuminations, and the sky is ablaze with fireworks, and the noise of thanksgiving is heard from bells, organs and cannons, then we groan in silence about the murders which caused the public rejoicing."

Appendix 3

Girard On *Polly*

The following is an excerpt from a study made by David S. Miller titled *The Polly: A Perspective on Merchant Stephen Girard* telling of the activities of one of Girard's vessels between the years 1789 and 1794. The entire study covers the eighteen voyages and offers insight into the life of her remarkable owner, gives a peek through the historical porthole into Philadelphia's merchant community, provides analysis of West Indies trading in the infant United States, and uncovers a fascinating adventure story.

In April 1789 Girard entered into a relationship that he would describe to his brother in more endearing terms than his own marriage. "Jean," he wrote, "I have decided to buy a charming little brigantine the figure of a woman is the figure head." And with parental pride he added: "I have ordered the captain to announce himself, by attaching a broad blue pennant to the fore-top mast." Girard had reason to be excited. He could sense that American merchants were entering into a new era of prosperity. Previously, America's international trading pattern had been directed by English rules, taxed by restrictive levies, and subject to the risks of a hundred years of Anglo-French and Anglo-Spanish wars. Now, with the British evicted and a failed harvest in France, demand for American food and staples rose in both Europe and the West Indies. In 1789 Philadelphia merchant John Lewis observed with relief: "Philadelphia seems to enjoy a better trade at present than it has done for some time past." When he bought the *Polly*, Girard saw these opportunities. "As regards this venture," he wrote, "I am entering it in the firm conviction that the ports of the French Islands will be open to Americans for the introduction of flour."

The *Polly* was a brigantine, the trading ship of choice for West Indian and European trade, with two or more square sails on the foremast and a fore and aft sail on the main mast. This English design held the advantage of increased tonnage over both coasting sloops and schooners, averaging from "half again to more than double the tonnage" of these older ships. Although slower and less maneuverable than the smaller trading ships, the *Polly* offered affordability and large holding capacity.

To command his new ship, Girard enlisted William Edger, a captain familiar with the West Indies. Rather than contract for a commission on each voyage, Girard offered a straight salary of 7 pounds, 10 shillings a month. Here he broke with colonial tradition. Previously, the captains of trading ships held "a virtually discretionary power over their destination among the islands," would travel "odysseys" in search of suitable markets, and had "much latitude in the prices at which they might sell their cargo." But Girard, having a brother in the French sugar colony of St. Domingue acting as his agent, did not want his captains to scurry from island to island looking for high prices. Jean and Stephen kept regular contact: Jean would advise or forecast the market and Stephen would acquire and send the cargo with explicit instructions for the return lading. Thus, Girard did not have to rely upon the customary international "network" of merchants who traded on potentially inaccurate market prices.

This method offered Girard other significant advantages. First, by restricting Edger's authority to the management of the ship and Jean's to the sale of the cargo, he maximized the usefulness of each. Second, by instructing Edger to travel directly to St. Domingue, he reduced the length of time of individual journeys, allowing more trips per year. Third, since Jean owned a warehouse in St. Domingue, were the *Polly* to arrive when markets were depressed, its cargo could be stored until prices rose. The first Girard venture was launched with both Stephen Girard and Captain Edger rushing into their respective duties in the third week of April 1789, just nine days after Girard had marked the ship as his. Edger hired a carpenter, a block and pump maker, and a blacksmith to prepare the *Polly* for its first "Adventure," as Girard grew fond of calling the trips. Edger also bought varnish, canvas, twine, and provisions. Girard was equally busy, purchasing 114 terces and 19 halves of rice, 304 barrels of flour, and 109 kegs of lard. By the late 1780s, foodstuff exporters in Philadelphia had so specialized and expanded that Girard could purchase large shipments of flour and rice. With his brother's warehouse and West Indian connections ,he was virtually assured of a market for his cargo.

Equally important was the acquisition of insurance. For this voyage Girard used Wharton and Lewis, one of the standard carriers in Philadelphia. He insured the ship for its purchase price of £700, and the cargo for £1,300. The price of the policy was 9 percent or £63.5 for the ship, and 5 percent or £65.5 for the goods. This covered the vessel for a single round-trip voyage to St. Domingue, assuming the trip was completed within six months. After that period the penalty was 1.5 percent per month. The policy was underwritten by a large number of speculators, each of whom signed the document.

As April turned to May and final repairs and provisions were secured, Girard wrote letters of instruction to his brother and Captain Edger. To Jean he specified that the return cargo should be molasses, coffee, and cocoa. If there were any delay in getting these items, the *Polly* was to be sent back in ballast. Exporting flour rapidly, Stephen felt, would be the profit-making leg of the adventure. Any importation would merely add a bonus. To Captain Edger, he provided even more explicit instructions. As the importation of flour was prohibited in St. Domingue (thus making Girard a smuggler), Girard had to prepare for the possibility that the vessel would be stopped and searched. If the *Polly* were to meet a "guarda costa or others," he wrote Edger, and the crew were asked what the cargo contained, say "flour, rice and lard," but add that "you are bound for St. Thomas ,but having the misfortune of falling to the lower of your port, together with your vessel being deep loading you did propose to sell your rice at Cap Francois." Otherwise, Edger was simply to meet Jean Girard at the wharf and hand him his sealed instructions, remaining under Jean's command while in port.

On May 11, 1789, the *Polly* left Philadelphia, was piloted down the Delaware to Cape Henlopen at the mouth of the river, and sailed to the West Indies, arriving eighteen days later (May 29) at Cap Francois. To Captain Edger's pleasant surprise, the port was open to flour, and Jean sold the cargo for seven to ten dollars a barrel (Girard's buying price was a little more than five). The rice (bought at $2.69) he sold between $3.50 and $4.00 a quintal. The sales grossed almost £1,900. After deducting for all shipping expenses, Girard realized a net profit of £200 to £300 on the *Polly's* first outward journey. He would entirely pay off the cost of the vessel in three such one-way trips.

Even with this proud rate of return, Jean wrote back a pessimistic letter. "It is unfortunate," he bemoaned, "that your brig arrived three days late as that made a difference in the sales of from eight to ten thousand livres." He sent back forty thousand livres in specie, a small shipment of molasses, and the good news that the governor general of St. Domingue had extended the time during which flour might be legally imported until the first of October. The first adventure was completed rapidly. Edger set sail from Cap Francois just a few days after the ship's arrival, and within three weeks the *Polly* was back in Philadelphia. Girard was already preparing for the second trip.

Girard had hoped to get his ship back to St. Domingue by July 1, but when the first week in June passed and the ship had not yet arrived, this hope deflated. Armed with the news of continued legal shipment of flour, coupled with the high selling prices, Girard bought more this time: 547 barrels, as well as Indian meal, rice, lard, and ham. Edger rehired his seven-man crew, which included a first mate, cook, four sailors, and Sam, a black slave. He used day laborers and the crew to recondition the ship rapidly for another voyage. He bought sails, rope, a yawl (or ship's boat), and provisions including two barrels of beef and some white beans. The entire overhaul took less than three days, and on June 22, just a month and eleven days after the first embarkation, the *Polly* was piloted out of Philadelphia's harbor.

This adventure was even more successful than the first. "The brig arrived in just 19 days," Edger bragged, "and there is a good market for the cargo of flour and rice." Stephen Girard had bought his cargo for about £1,472; Jean sold it for over £2,200. Allowing for sailing costs and insurance, Girard netted over £500 from this trip. The *Polly*, in two months' time and as many voyages, had paid for itself entirely. All additional trips were profit.

Edger advanced the crew a month's pay while at Cap Francois, and this practice represented another departure from mercantile customs. Other traders usually paid their sailors a combination of wage and "privilege," "the right to load so many barrels or hogsheads on the outward and homeward voyage on the sailors' own account." This practice "was nearly universal, and it looks as though the privilege was considered more important than the money wage." Presumably, Girard did not want his men more concerned with their own ladings than with his. He paid them a straight salary to perform their specific duties. In mid-July 1789, Edger started the return voyage. Jean had loaded it this time with a larger return cargo: 56 casks of molasses, 11 barrels of sugar, and 53 barrels and 84 bags of coffee. On July 30, the *Polly* landed at Philadelphia.

For the third adventure, Stephen Girard decided to load his ship entirely with flour; he bought 659 barrels and 163 half-barrels. Again, such a practice was practically unheard of; it would have been entirely too risky for most merchants to load a ship with only one commodity. Edger hired an entirely new crew, keeping on Sam alone. Perhaps because of the unique salary arrangements, or because of the rapidity with which the *Polly* performed, sailors usually did not stay in Edger's employ for more than a single voyage. But maritime labor was plentiful in early Philadelphia, and Girard apparently had no problem manning vessels at his rate of pay. After the two quick trips, the *Polly* needed a more complete overhaul. The vessel was scraped and oil painted. A blacksmith, a carpenter, a joiner, and a block maker were all hired, and laborers were paid by the half-day. The old anchor was traded in for a new one, and rigging leather was purchased. Finally, Edger bought the provisions: two barrels each of pork and beef, some white beans, a box of candles, some cheese and rum. On August 21, the *Polly* took to sea.

This adventure was a slight disappointment when compared with the first two. Jean wrote that flour prices were low on account of "political changes in France" that were affecting the market. When all was sold, Stephen probably made only £100 profit on the leg. In the middle of October, 1789, Edger arrived back in Philadelphia. He brought a letter from Jean, informing Stephen that "flour will be a prohibited article [again] after December 1." Jean hinted about the possibility of smuggling it through: "I will then advise how it may be brought in."

By the time Edger arrived with the note, Stephen had already purchased flour for the *Polly*'s fourth trip. He quickly added an assortment of sundries to this load: the wine, liquor, and silver requested by agents in St. Domingue for their own use. Edger docked for only three days and was off again on October 25. He arrived in St. Domingue to find another disappointing market. Flour prices had dipped again; the Girards probably took a small loss on this trip when all expenses were counted. Because of the setback, Jean held the *Polly* in port for two weeks while he waited to close negotiations for a full return cargo. Prices on exports as well as imports were down, and he thought he could arrange for cheap coffee and sugar. Evidently, he was successful. The *Polly* left the West Indies with 58 barrels and 108 bags of coffee, and 61 hogsheads of molasses. As was now standard practice, Edger manipulated figures on the bills of lading from St. Domingue, reducing his apparent cargo and paying less tax.

When Edger returned the ship to Philadelphia in the middle of December, Stephen faced the fact that further shipments of flour to St. Domingue were now prohibited. Additionally, the latest letter from Jean forecasted political trouble at Le Cap. "The young people," he wrote impassionedly, "are greatly excited, and gather at public places and at theatres." The Negroes were growing restive, and the people were "clamoring for local self-government." Other independent reports confirmed the warning Jean sent his brother: "The government is helpless," he wrote, "and civil war is impending."

Since Jean did not foresee any improvement for politics or profits in the West Indies, Stephen decided that he would transfer Edger and the *Polly* to the "Marseilles route" already sailed by another of his ships, *Les Deux Freres*. Unfortunately, he was sending his ship from one trouble spot to another. In France, the Old Regime was beginning to collapse.

* * *

The following is an excerpt from John Bach McMaster's book, *The Life and Times of Stephen Girard*, Volume I, Chapter V, "La Virginie Sold. Good Friends Embargoed."

The arrival of the Polly at la Cap soon after the three dreadful days of plundering, burning and murder, and her return to Philadelphia with eight and thirty refugees gave rise to a story concerning Girard, which one of his biographer, Mr. Henry Atlee Ingram, thought necessary to tell and refute.

"The year 1793 witnessed the horrible uprising of the slaves in the island of Santo Domingo, and many foreign merchants narrowly escaped sharing in the general massacre by taking refuge on one of Girard's vessels, commanded by Captain Cochran, then in port at Cap Francais. Some of these refugees barely escaped with the clothing upon their persons, but others, more successful, saved large quantities of wearing apparel, household furniture, and silver, with which the vessel set sail for Philadelphia, where she arrived safely, loaded with valuables. It has been said that Girard's fortune was largely increased by the subsequent failure of owners to claim many of these articles, but no reliable evidence has been adduced, while both Captain Cochran and Mr. Roberjot, one of the refugee merchants, who succeeded in saving nothing but a valise of valuable papers, vouched personally that all for whom articles could be found had been returned."

Appendix 4

Girard On Amusement

His letters to Judge Bry afford occasional glimpses of his life on the farm.

"At my age the sole amusement which I enjoy, is to be in the country constantly busy, in attending to the work of the farm generally, also to my fruit trees, several of which, say about three hundred, I have imported from France and I hope will be useful to our country. In addition to that I have two extensive gardens, the whole of which I direct throughout. In consequence of not having a good overseer nor gardeners, all my valuable fruit trees are uniformly planted or trained by me. On the subject of gardening, if you want some good cabbage, lettuce, celery, onions, carrots, beets, turnips, parsnips, and other vegetable seed please to let me know it. I raise it myself, from seed which I received from time to time from different places in Europe, consequently it is pretty good, and I will send you what you want for your own use. I have taken much pain with grape vines. Our severe winters are a great obstacle to their progress. For this few years past I lay them down and cover them with earth in the fall, and take them up in April. They appear to do a little better. The last season, I had some good fruit. I have about 250 of the best sort imported from France, and Spain, except one vine which is pretty large, and raised from the seed of a grape imported in a jar from Malaga. Out of that vine I had last season several fine large grapes in full maturity."

Appendix 5

Girard On Family

The following comes from the Girard Papers as gathered by John Bach McMaster in his book *The Life and Times of Stephen Girard Merchant and Mariner.*

While Girard was worrying over the fate of his bills on Barclay & Co. ships from abroad brought letters informing him of the death of his brother Jean, his sister Victoire and of the financial distress of his aunt Lafargue. Since the death of his father and his purchase of the house in Rue Ramonet, the house in which he (Girard) believed he was born, had been occupied by the aunt and sister. The greater part was rented to a lodger who paid two hundred francs a year rent, and on this and a pittance of fifty francs a month allowed each of them by Girard, the two women managed to subsist. By 1802, rise in prices made necessary an appeal for a more generous allowance. "Although I have been forbidden to write to you I feel compelled to let you know our pitiable condition both Victoire's and mine. We lack the necessaries of life and we are living miserably on what we can borrow from other people around here without being able to avoid it. I have never relaxed my economy, but the extortionate prices asked for everything make it impossible to satisfy our creditors who furnish us the bare necessities. The baker, the butcher, the wine merchant and the wood merchant charge more than we get from you alone. Victoire needs a very delicate diet on account of her illness; and her washing, although very moderate, is costly nowadays because everything is high in price, even more so for us because we cannot lay in stock. They absolutely refuse to give us more than fifty francs every month and when we receive those fifty francs we owe more than' 60; there are always bills. That is what I call having on borrowed money without being able to lay in any provisions, so that I pay too much for everything such as soap, oil, coffee, moist sugar, etc. I pay more for everything because I take it in small quantities and Victoire's tobacco has to go very far. The cheapest wine is worth 20 sous a pint. Three-fourths of the year Victoire eats her bread dry as I cannot even let her have what she needs. Victoire is very much in need of linen; she is without handkerchiefs and other very necessary articles. She spends all her time alone in the little room in the back of the house because of the noise of the wagons in the street. She stays at the back of the house and all she needs is a little garden to get the air. She fumes against Mombrun (Jean Girard) and Sophie. In short, my dear Citizen, we implore your protection. If you will only do a little to help us I shall pray for the preservation of your health and be most grateful. Since Mombrun has quarreled with us I have written you three letters without getting any answer, and I implore you once more to write to us, sending your letters to la Rue Ramonet No.1. I do not believe they give us the letters you write us. We should not be so badly off if you were well informed of our sad condition." The allowance was doubled and writing to Strobel & Martini he said: "I have an aunt and a sister in Bordeaux to whom I give twelve hundred livres tournois per annum payable quarterly. The name of the former is Anne Lafargue and of the latter Victoire Girard, they live in Rue Ramonet au Chartron, Messrs. Hourquebie Brothers were in the habit to pay them that annuity on my account but, as have taken my business out of their hands I beg that you will pay on my account to said Anne Lafargue and Victoire Girard Three Hundred livres tournois every three months."

The sister, Victoire, died in 1803 and before the year ended his brother Jean died in the Island of St. Vincent. From Bordeaux the firm of John A. Morton reported the death of Ann Lafargue at the age of ninety years. "All that Miss Lafargue left in the shape of a testament is represented by a few livres, written and signed by herself, in which she declares that she leaves all her furniture and clothing to her housekeeper. Dame Gauduchon. But the said articles are of very little value and by no means sufficient to compensate the latter for her constant care of Miss Lafargue. Indeed she nursed her with a constancy worthy of the highest praise just as a good daughter would in a similar case have nursed her mother. I believe it is only right to recommend her to your generosity. (On learning of his Aunt's death, Girard wrote: "This news has deeply affected me, but we must submit to the wish of Providence, especially after passing the age of 90 years. "As to the will of my said aunt in favor of dame Gauduchon, nee Moussac, I hope it has been executed. Although I am willing to make compensation for the care which the latter gave the deceased, I am not well enough informed to judge of the value of the services rendered. Nevertheless, I beg you to pay for my account to the said dame Gauduchon, nee Moussac, five hundred francs, and if you and Mrs. Morton think this too small, kindly communicate me your opinion on this subject."

The last years of Jean's life was spent sailing about the world in his own ship, trading now at Lisbon, now at St. Sebastian, now at Hamburg or Bordeaux and filling his letters with complaints of ill luck, unasked advice, offers of service, and reproaches that his brother who had no confidence in his business ability, gave commissions to strangers and none to him. Early in 1803 he was in Bordeaux with his brig Lucie " about to leave for Senegal," on his way to Sierra Leone, "to find out what has become of the cocoa taken by my brig Mentor." On the way thither his brig Lucie, was captured by a British sloop of war and ordered to the Barbados, but went to St. Vincent, where in November he died. When Girard heard of this he wrote Hourquebie: "On the 2d of November last my brother wrote me a letter to ask me to obtain from our custom house some documents that he says are necessary before he can proceed. By the same mail I received a letter from Messrs. Solomon L Stowe & Co in which they announce to me the cruel news of the sudden death of my brother. This news afflicted me so much the more on account of this unfortunate man leaving behind him four children to the care of a mother who does not deserve the name. She left here about two months ago to go to Charleston on the pretense of regaining health. Her residence seems to be a secret. She intends to return next spring. "Since the departure of my brother from here I have been supplying the needs of his family. As far as I can see he has no means here. He is even my debtor for about 2600 dollars a sum daily increased by the maintenance of the children, house, rent, etc.

"From this you will understand how important it is to preserve, as far as possible, the remaining fortune of the father of these unfortunate children. I therefore beg you very earnestly to let me know how you stood with my brother, to send me your account current, and keep in your hand the balance that may be due his estate, until further notice from me. As to the brigantine Lucy from what my brother wrote me in regard to the crew, who testified against him, I very much fear this vessel will be condemned to the profit of the captors. If this is the case I hope she is insured in your city by good underwriters against all risks. Kindly tell me how this matter stands, also as to that of his brig Mentor Captain Jacobs." To the widow, who, just at this time, ignorant of the death of her husband, wrote from Charleston for money, he replied: "Nothing less than the death of my brother, John Girard, induces me to write to you. He departed this life in the Island of St. Vincent, on the 5th of last month after having been brought in there with his brig *Lucy* by a British Cruiser. While I lament and regret the loss of that unfortunate brother I meet with some consolation in thinking that he is relieved forever from his daily difficulties and dissatisfaction particularly when I represent myself with the death stroke which he should have received by hearing at his return to this city, of your precipitate departure for South Carolina." I do not wish you to believe that the intention of this letter is to convey any reproach. I leave that to your conscience and will confine myself to what I conceive to be my duty, therefore as brother to the deceased I will relate you the steps which I have taken."1st. Immediately after hearing of the death of my brother I have wrote to several persons with whom I supposed him in habit of doing business and have requested them to send me their accounts and to remit me the balance thereof." 2nd. have taken letters of administration and have proceeded to the house of the deceased accompanied with Mr. George Hunter and Mr. Roberjot with the intention to examine if the furniture in the house did correspond with the Inventory which you have left with Mrs. Philips. Finding that lady in the house and everything therein appearing to be in its place, we have opened two closets in what is called the tea room where we found in one next to the front window sundry printed Books, the other contained plate. Linen and other articles, of this we have taken an Inventory sent the plate to my house with a small cane, put the remainder of the effects in same closet. We have also opened a bureau containing principally papers which we did not examine and have sealed up every draw as also the doors of the two closets. "Presuming that there was no necessity to examine any further and wishing to take no steps which will create any uneasiness I have left the whole furniture together with the children under the care of Mrs. Philips until your return, consequently I entreat you to come back home immediately so some arrangements may take place respecting these fatherless children." She came and for a while supported herself and children by pledging plate and furniture and borrowing small sums from such neighbors as would lend. When no more could be borrowed Girard was appealed to and sent a hundred dollars to redeem the pieces of plate and furniture, and a hundred and fifty dollars to pay the debts, and offered sixty dollars a month for support of the family provided the pledging and borrowing ceased. The offer was accepted, but the pittance proved too small and one day in July 1805, the three children, Antoinette aged nine, Caroline aged seven and Henriette aged five, scantily and shabbily clad, " almost naked," says Girard, came to his house in search of a home. Great was his indignation and astonishment; but the children were received, put under the care of his housekeeper, and the two eldest promptly sent to a boarding school in Bethlehem. When the boy William, who was at school Sorèze, became sick and died in 1808, Girard paid the bill for board, clothing and tuition for the last five years. Towards Mrs. Jean Girard he had always shown an intense dislike, had never allowed her to enter his house, and now suffered her to shift for herself.

Appendix 6

Girard On Life

Education: Girard believed that male children should go to school to prepare them for business or trade. Girls should be kept at home to learn the skills of home keeping and raising children. Girard received no formal education or financial help from his father; yet, he was generous to a fault to his brothers and sisters and their children in providing school learning.

Religion: An adult should be able to follow the religion of his choice or follow none at all. Under no circumstances should young children be indoctrinated into a specific doctrine by church people. Girard was raised a Roman Catholic but did not adhere to its tenants.

Work: Labor of the mind and the body is essential to being a balanced adult. Girard took great pleasure working which brought him peace and satisfaction. He liked to dig his hands into the rich soil of his farm land and experiment with various kinds of vegetables and fruit.

Charity: Give to those who cannot provide for themselves. Give what you want but do not expect gratitude or recognition.

Readings: Learn from the great philosophers. Put into practice the teachings of those you most admire. Girard spent his life with the teachings of Voltaire as well as Montesquieu, and Jean-Jacques Rousseau.

Romance: Girard had little time for romantic notions or discussions about love. He was happy with his wife for eight years until she became mentally disturbed. He knew he had great feelings for her and wept when she died. His mistresses filled a need in his life–a well-functioning home, sensible conversation and peace.

Conversation: Girard was not a talker. He spoke when he had something worthwhile to say. He rarely spoke about himself and could not bear idle chatter.

Lifestyle: Girard wore sensible clothing made of good broad cloth and good shoes. Never did he draw attention to himself or show the wealth he had acquired. He admired the life of the community of Friends. He believed that the simple lifestyle of the Quakers was much closer to his basic beliefs than any dogmas he had learned about.

Role Models: Aside from the French philosophers, Girard admired Benjamin Franklin, Thomas Paine and Thomas Jefferson.

Pet Peeves: Girard could not tolerate pompous people. He thought doctors were mostly ineffective and members of organized religions were unbearable. He couldn't suffer fools from any walk of life.

Government: Girard once mentioned that he could not return to live in France because that country was not friendly to business. All his concerns about the US government over the years were related to having the government make the climate one of collaboration between the leaders of government and the various businesses that paid taxes to support government.

Intelligence: Girard had a great opinion of his own mental capacities. He understood relationships between events and opposing forces in business and trading markets. He felt that he was as capable of healing the sick as any trained doctor. His success in earning huge profits from his trading came from his ability to predict future movements in investments and needs of his clients. Often there was a great disparity between the intelligence of people around him and his own thought processes.

Humor: Very often those making jokes in his presence felt that Girard had not understood the humor. He did smile at times when his mistress Polly would attempt to amuse him. His life was one of serious dedication and hard work. There were not many moments for levity.

Music: There is no evidence that Girard had any time to understand or appreciate music although his mathematical skills would seem to be appropriate for it.

Inhibitions: Although he suffered a good deal as a child from the fact that his right eye was blind and he was constantly hurt by the teasing school boys, Girard managed to come to terms with this handicap. It might even be said that his desire to help others and serve his community may be the continued need to be accepted by those around him. His spoken English was never very good and his physical appearance not very pleasing. His clothing, although of good quality, would often hang unflatteringly on his stocky frame. The few social settings he found himself in over the years were awkward for him. He was a Frenchman in an Anglo-Saxon world. Perhaps his amassing a great fortune was his way of equalizing his stature in this environment.

Frustration: Perhaps the fact that Girard had never had children of his own was his greatest disappointment. He was, however, warm and loving to the children of his family. Had Mary Lum been able to give him a family and a long life of happy matrimony, perhaps he might have been less driven. This might have been a great loss to the people of Philadelphia and to the people of the United States and to the thousands of children who gathered around his spirit over the years.

Notes

(Websites and references current at time of the publication of this book.)

Chapter 1

1. Harry Emerson Wildes, Lonely Midas; The Story of Stephen Girard, (New York: Farrar and Rinehart, 1943), 3.
2. John Bach McMaster, The Life and Times of Stephen Girard, Mariner and Merchant, vol. 1, (Philadelphia; London: J. B. Lippincott, 1918; Internet Archive, 2007), www.archive.org/stream/lifetimesofsteph01mcmauoft#page/n0/mode/2up.
3. Wildes, Lonely Midas, 10.
4. Stephen Simpson, Biography of Stephen Girard, with his Will Affixed Comprising an Account of his Private Life, Habits and Manners (Philadelphia, 1832), 16. Simpson is both a primary and secondary source. As an employee of Girard's bank for the last fifteen years of Girard's life, Simpson observed Girard on a regular basis. Simpson's father, George Simpson worked for Girard as cashier for ten years.
5. Henry Atlee Ingram, The Life and Character of Stephen Girard, (E. Stanley Hart, Philadelphia 1885), 20. "Girard's description of the thick yellow cataract descending over his eye leads modern oculists to believe that the ailment was in fact no cataract but in reality a scarred shrunken globe which was the belated effects of a wound in early childhood." See Wildes, Lonely Midas, 350.
6. Wildes, Lonely Midas, 362.
7. Ibid.
8. Elbert Hubbard, Stephen Girard, (East Aurora: NY: Roycrofters, 1909), 43.
9. Wildes, Lonely Midas, 137.
10. Ibid, 43.
11. McMaster, Life and Times, 27.
12. Ingram, Life and Character, 23.
13. Wildes, Lonely Midas, 6.
14. Ingram, Life and Character, 26.
15. Mike DiMeo, "Stephen Girard: Merchant, Mariner, Banker, Humanitarian, Patriot," Independence Hall Association [website owner], "UShistory.org," www.ushistory.org/people/girard.htm. DiMeo uses an alternative form of his name, Michael D. Mayo as the author of The Stone Cocoon, Warminster, PA: Neibauer Press, 1997.
16. Wildes, Lonely Midas, 9.
17. Cheesman A. Herrick, Stephen Girard, Founder, 5th ed. (Philadelphia, Girard College, 1945), 16.
18. Wildes, Lonely Midas, 20.

Chapter 2

1. Simpson, Biography of Stephen Girard, 19.
2. McMaster, Life and Times, 122.
3. Ingram, Life and Character, 27.
4. McMaster Life and Times, vi.
5. Letter to Stephen Girard, 1792. Girard, Stephen. The Papers of Stephen Girard, Philadelphia, Girard College.
6. Wildes, Lonely Midas, 115.
7. Ibid., 80.
8. DiMeo, "Stephen Girard: Merchant, Mariner."
9. Simpson, Biography, 7.
10. McMaster, Life and Times, 6.

Chapter 3

1. Wildes, Lonely Midas, 34.
2. McMaster, Life and Times, 8.
3. DiMeo, "Stephen Girard: Merchant, Mariner."
4, Wildes, Lonely Midas, 324.The belief that Girard was a member of Lodge No. 3 in Philadelphia came from confusion regarding the acceptance of a Captain Girard on September 3, 1778. According to a book titled, *History of Brother Stephen Girard's Fraternal Connection with the R. W. Grand Lodge F&AM of Pennsylvania*, Barratt and Sache, New Era Printing Co. Lancaster Pa., that Captain Girard was an officer in the revolutionary army and not Stephen Girard.
5. Simpson, Biography, 34.

Chapter 4

1. Wildes, Lonely Midas, 22-24.
2. Ibid., 25.

Chapter 5

1. Ingram, Life and Character, 35.
2. McMaster, Life and Times, 11.
3. Herrick, Stephen Girard, Founder, 18.
4. Ibid.
5. Steel & Garnet, December 1963, 12.
6. Wildes, Lonely Midas, 62.
7. Ibid., 33.
8. Herrick, Stephen Girard, Founder, 115.
9. Simpson, Biography, 32.
10. Wildes, Lonely Midas, 33.

11. George Wilson, Stephen Girard, America's First Tycoon, (Conshohocken, PA: Combined Books, 1995), 83.Wilson quotes [a letter] Stephen Girard to Pierre Girard, circa February 1779 cited in The Papers of Stephen Girard.

12. Ibid., 84.

13. Ibid.

14. Ibid., 38.

15. Herrick, Stephen Girard, Founder, 128.

16. McMaster, Life and Times, 18.

17. Ibid., 20.

18. Ibid.

19. Ibid.

20. Wildes, Lonely Midas, 35.

21. Wilson, Stephen Girard, 89.

Chapter 6

1. Wilson, Stephen Girard, 89.

2. Ingram, Life and Character, 35.

3. Wildes, Lonely Midas, 73.

4. Herrick, Stephen Girard, Founder, 23.

5. Thomas G. Morton, The History of the Pennsylvania Hospital, 1751–1895, (New York: Arno Press), 1973, 138.

6. Herrick, Stephen Girard, Founder, 138.

7. Ingram, Life and Character, 85. Ingram was a great-grandson of John Girard, Stephen's brother. Part of the research for this book on Girard was made up of interviews with William Wagner who worked for Stephen Girard for twenty-one years and three nieces of Stephen Girard who lived with him for many years while they were growing up. One of the nieces was Ingram's grandmother.

8. William G. Malin, ex steward, Pennsylvania Hospital.

9. McMaster, Life and Times, 49.

10. Ibid., 58.

11. Wildes, Lonely Midas, 13.

12. Ibid., 49.

13. Herrick, Stephen Girard, Founder, 9.

14. McMaster, Life and Times, 53.

15. Ibid., 56.

16. Wildes, Lonely Midas, 13.

Chapter 7

1. Wildes, Lonely Midas, 13.

2. Ibid., 14.

3. McMaster, Life and Times, vii.

4. Ibid., 36.

5. Ibid., 38.
6. Ibid.
7. Ibid., 39.
8. Wilson, Stephen Girard, 137.
9. Ibid., 134.

Chapter 8

1. Wildes, Lonely Midas, 39.
2. Ibid., 40.
3. Ibid., 37.
4. Wilson, Stephen Girard, 184.
5. Hubbard, Stephen Girard, 24.
6. Wilson, Stephen Girard, 185.

Chapter 9

1. Wildes, Lonely Midas, 76-83.
2. Ibid., 83.
3. Ibid., 228-229.
4. Ibid.
5. Ibid., 324.
6. Ibid., 228.
7. Wilson, Stephen Girard, 98.
8. John's letter to Stephen, 1789. Girard, Stephen. The Papers of Stephen Girard.
9. McMaster, Life and Times, 326.
10. Wildes, Lonely Midas, 135.
11. Ibid., 192.
12. Wilson, Stephen Girard, 114.
13. Richard G. Miller, "The Federal City, 1783–1800" in Philadelphia: A Three Hundred Year History, Russell Frank Weigley, Nicholas B. Wainwright, and Edwin Wolf, contributors. (New York: Norton, 1983), 188.
14. Hubbard, Stephen Girard, 56.
15. James Parton, "Stephen Girard and His College," in Famous Americans of Recent Times, (1867, Project Gutenberg, 2004), www.gutenberg.org/cache/epub/12971/pg12771.html.
16. Ibid., 56.

Chapter 10

1. Wilson, Stephen Girard, 119.
2. Herrick, Stephen Girard, Founder, 47.
3. Louise Stockton, The Continent, An Illustrated Weekly Magazine, (Philadelphia: Our Continent Publishing Company), 1883.
4. Powell, Bring Out Your Dead, 11.

5. Herrick, Stephen Girard, 40.

6. J.H. Powell, Bring Out Your Dead; The Great Plague of Yellow Fever in Philadelphia in 1793, (Philadelphia: University of Pennsylvania Press, 1949), 11.

7. Herrick, Stephen Girard, Founder, 40.

8. Powell, Bring out Your Dead, 146.

9. Wildes, Lonely Midas, 279.

10. Stephen Girard letter to Bentalou, Oct. 1793, Girard, The Papers of Stephen Girard.

11. Herrick, Stephen Girard, Founder, 32.

12. Ibid., 48.

13. McMaster, Life and Times, 221.

14. Thomas J. DiFilippo, "Girard, A Man to Remember," in Stephen Girard, The Man, His College and Estate, 2nd ed. (1999), 1-22. www.girardweb.com/girard/download.htm.

15. Ibid.

16. Ibid.

17. Ibid.

18. Ibid.

19. McMaster, Life and Times, 239.

20. William Wagner, "Life and Times of Stephen Girard, Lecture 5," (Philadelphia: Wagner Free Institute of Science, n.d.).

21. Henry W Arey, The Girard College and its Founder: Containing the Biography of Mr. Girard, the History of the Institution, Its Organization and Plan of Discipline, with the Course of Education, Forms of Admission of Pupils, Description of the Buildings, &c. &c. and the Will of Mr. Girard, (Philadelphia, C. Sherman, 1856), 19-20. Arey was secretary of Girard College when he wrote this biography, published twenty-one years after Girard's death. Arey is a primary source for matters on the founding, the development and history of Girard College.

22. Simpson, Biography of Stephen Girard, 110.

Chapter 11

1. Herrick, Stephen Girard, Founder, 117.

2. Ibid., 116.

3. Ibid.

4. Wildes, Lonely Midas, 242-243.

5. Simpson, Biography, 71.

6. Ibid., 73.

7. DiFilippo, "The Will, No Longer Sacred," in Stephen Girard, 23-32.

8. Herrick, Stephen Girard, Founder, 72.

9. Ibid., 98.

10. Ibid., 99.

11. Osgood E. Fuller, "Stephen Girard: The Napoleon of Merchants—His Life Successful and Yet a Failure," in Brave Men and Women Their Struggles, Failures and Triumphs, (1884, Project Gutenberg, 2004), www.gutenberg.org/files/13942/13942-h/13942-h.htm#XXIII.

12. Simpson, Biography, 98.

13. Herrick, Stephen Girard, Founder, 8.

14. Wildes, Lonely Midas, 242.

15. Simpson, Biography, 74.

16. Herrick, Stephen Girard, Founder, 10.

17. Simpson, Biography, 31.

18. Ibid., 74.

19. Ibid., 241.

20. Ibid., 87.

21. Herrick, Stephen Girard, Founder, 12.

22. Wildes, Lonely Midas, 136.

23. Ibid., 142.

24. Ibid., 124.

25. Ibid., 177.

26. Ibid., 146.

27. Arey, Girard College, 5.

28. Ingram, Life and Character, 53.

29. Wildes, Lonely Midas, 133.

30. Stephen Girard letter to Bonnaffe Frères et Fils, 6 January 1794, Girard, The Papers of Stephen Girard.

31. Girard letter to Alexander Hamilton, 26 Feb. 1794, Girard, Stephen. The Papers of Stephen Girard.

32. Wilson, Stephen Girard, 195.

33. Ibid.

34. Ibid., 196.

35. Ibid., 146.

36. Herrick, Stephen Girard, Founder, 106.

37. Parton, Famous Americans of Recent Times.

38. Herrick, Stephen Girard, Founder, 102.

39. Ibid., 10.

Chapter 12

1. Ingram, Life and Character, 127.

2. Herrick, Stephen Girard, Founder, 12.

3. Ibid., 105.

4. Ibid.

5. Ibid., 106.

6. Wilson, Stephen Girard, 147.

7. DiMeo, "Stephen Girard Merchant, Mariner."

8. Herrick, Stephen Girard, Founder, 84.

9. Ibid.

10. Ibid., 114.

11. Ibid., 27.

12. Louise Stockton, The Continent, An Illustrated Weekly Magazine, (Philadelphia: Our Continent Publishing), June 20, 1883.

13. Herrick, Stephen Girard, Founder, 27.

14. Ibid., 34.

15. Wildes, Lonely Midas, 228-229.

16. Ibid., 179.

17. Mayo, Michael R, The Stone Cocoon. Warminster, PA: Neibauer Press, 1997.

18. Wildes, Lonely Midas, 180.

19. Ibid., 184.

20. Ibid.

21. Fuller, Brave Men and Women, 200.

22. Ibid.

23. Wilson, Stephen Girard, 219.

24. Ibid., 224.

25. Ibid.

26. Herrick, Stephen Girard, Founder, 73.

27. Ibid., 14.

28. Simpson, Biography, 152.

29. Ibid., 163.

30. Ibid., 168.

31. Herrick, Stephen Girard, Founder, 24.

32. Simpson, Biography, 168.

Chapter 13

1. Wildes, Lonely Midas, 220.

2. Wilson, Stephen Girard, 280.

3. Herrick, Stephen Girard, Founder, 76.

4. Columbia County [Bloomsbury, PA] Deed Book E, 407.

5. Wildes, Lonely Midas, 353.

6. DiFilippo, "Girard, A Man to Remember," in Stephen Girard, 1-22.

7. Wildes, Lonely Midas, 290.

8. Wagner, "Life and Times of Stephen Girard," Lecture 2," (Philadelphia: Wagner Free Institute of Science, n.d.).

9. Wilson, Stephen Girard, 339.

10. Simpson, Biography, 109.

11. Herrick, Stephen Girard, Founder, 9.

12. Wildes, Lonely Midas, 288.

13, Simpson, Biography, 184.

14, McMaster, Life and Times, 444.

15. Simpson, Biography, 183.

16. Herrick, Stephen Girard, Founder, 112.

17. Ibid., 110.

18. McMaster, Life and Times, 445.

19. Herrick, Stephen Girard, Founder, 127.

20. Thomas J. DiFilippo, "The Collage Construction and Opening," in Stephen Girard, The Man, His College and Estate, 33-40.

21. Wildes, Lonely Midas, 267.

22. DiFillipo, "The College Construction and Opening," in Stephen Girard, 33-40.

Chapter 14

1. Simpson, Biography, 112.

2. Ibid, 360.

3. Simpson, Biography 152.

4. Wildes, Lonely Midas, 204.

5. Ibid., 356.

6. Herrick, Stephen Girard, Founder, 15.

Chapter 15

1. Kenneth L. Brown, "Book Review: Lonely Midas: The Story of Stephen Girard," Pennsylvania Magazine of History and Biography 68, no.2, 217-218.

2. Herrick, Stephen Girard, Founder, 81.

3. Simpson, Biography, 122.

4. Herrick, Stephen Girard, Founder, 109.

5. Ibid., 108.

6. Herrick, Stephen Girard, Founder, 109.

7. Wildes, Lonely Midas, 288.

8. Herrick, Stephen Girard, Founder, 108.

9. Mayo, Michael R, The Stone Cocoon. Warminster, PA: Neibauer Press, 1997.

10. Herrick, Stephen Girard, Founder, 102.

11. Simpson, Biography, 18.

12. Ingram, Life and Character, 104.

Chapter 16

1. DiFilippo, "The College Construction and Opening," in Stephen Girard, 33-40.

2. Ibid.

3. Ibid.

4. Herrick, Stephen Girard, Founder, 84.

5. Wilson, Stephen Girard, 343-369.

6. DiFilippo, "Trying Times" in Stephen Girard, 97-102.

7. Clark v. City of Philadelphia, Oct. 1850.

8. DiFilippo, "Trying Times" in Stephen Girard, 97-102.

Chapter 17

1. DiFilippo, "The College, Fulfillment of Stephen Girard's Dreams," in Stephen Girard, The

Man, His College and Estate, 41-56.

2. Ibid.

3. Vidal v. Girard's Executors, 127 1844.

4. Girard v. Philadelphia, 74 U.S.1 1869.

5. Philadelphia v. Heirs of Stephen Girard, 45 Pa 9 1863.

6. Girard's Appel, Penn 347 1880.

7. Mayo, The Stone Cocoon.

Chapter 18

1. DiFilippo, "Girard, A Man to Remember," in Stephen Girard, 1-22.

2. Herrick, Stephen Girard, Founder, 7.

3. Hubbard, Stephen Girard.

4. DiFilippo, "A New President, A New Era," in Stephen Girard, 57-72.

5. Ibid.

6. Herrick, Stephen Girard, Founder, 74.

7. DiFilippo, "Girard, A Man to Remember," in Stephen Girard, 1-22.

8. Ibid.

9. Herrick, Stephen Girard, Founder, 5.

10. William E. Zeil, Stephen Girard, Girard College Committee on Stephen Girard Papers and Effects, American Philosophical Society, A Catalogue of the Personal Library of Stephen Girard, 1750-1831, (Philadelphia: Girard College and the American Philosophical Society), 1990.

11. Herrick, Stephen Girard, Founder, 7.

12. Simpson, Biography, 46.

13. Herrick, Stephen Girard, Founder, 2.

14. DiFilippo, "The College, Fulfillment of Stephen Girard's Dreams," in Stephen Girard, 41-56.

15. DiFilippo, "A World War II Changes the College and Society," in Stephen Girard, 73-83.

16. Ibid.

17. Martha Woodall, "A 'Berlin Wall' Crumbles In His Will, Stephen Girard Provided for Orphaned White Boys. The 14th Amendment, Though, Guarantees Equal Protection. The Question Arose: Was Girard College Public Or Private?" Philadelphia Inquirer, May 1, 1991.

18. DiFilippo, "Trying Times," in Stephen Girard, 97-102.

19. DiFilippo, "Turn Around Then Stability," in Stephen Girard, 97-102.

Bibliography

Adams, Donald R., Jr. *Finance and Enterprise in Early America: A Study of Stephen Girard's Bank, 1812–1831.* Philadelphia: University of Pennsylvania Press, 1978.

Arey, Henry W. *The Girard College and Its Founder: Containing the Biography of Mr. Girard, the History of the Institution, Its Organization and Plan of Discipline, With the Course of Education, Forms of Admission of Pupils, Description of the Buildings, Etc., and the Will of Mr. Girard.* Philadelphia: C. Sherman, 1852; reprinted 1866.

Bartlett, Richard A. *The New Country: A Social History of the American Frontier, 1776–1890.* New York: Oxford University Press, 1974.

Beard, John R. *The Life of Toussaint L'Ouverture, the Negro Patriot of Hayti: Compressing an Account of the Struggle for Liberty in the Island, and a Sketch of its History to the Present Period.* 1853. Reprint, Westport, CT: Negro Universities Press, 1970.

Beck, James M. *Stephen Girard, Merchant and Mariner: An Oration Delivered at the Unveiling of a Statue to Stephen Girard on the West Side Plaza of the City Hall, Philadelphia, on May 20, 1897.* Philadelphia: J. B. Lippincott, 1897.

Biddle, Nicholas. *The Correspondence of Nicholas Biddle Dealing with National Affairs, 1807–1844.* Edited by Reginald C. McGrane. Boston: Canner, 1966.

Binzen, Peter H. "Philadelphia's Negroes Challenge a Will," *The Reporter,* October 21, 1965, 43-45. www.unz.org/Pub/Reporter-1965oct21-00043.

Bridenbaugh, Carl and Jessica Bridenbaugh. *Rebels and Gentlemen: Philadelphia in the Age of Franklin.* New York: Reynal and Hitchcock, 1942.

Burt, Maxwell Struthers. *Philadelphia, Holy Experiment.* Garden City, NY: Doubleday, Doran, 1945.

Chandler, Charles Lyon, Marion V. Brewington, and Edgar P. Richardson. *Philadelphia, Port of History, 1609–1837.* Philadelphia: Philadelphia Maritime Museum, 1976.

Cope, Thomas P. *Philadelphia Merchant: The Diary of Thomas P. Cope, 1850–1851.* Edited by Eliza Coe Harrison. South Bend, Indiana: Gateway Editions, 1978.

Cowen, David J. *The Origins and Economic Impact of the First Bank of the United States, 1791–1787.* New York: Garland, 2000.

Cunningham, Ernest. *Memories of Girard College.* Philadelphia: Girard College, 1942.

Diemand, John A. *Stephen Girard (1750–1831), A Proposal for Posthumous Award; a 200th Anniversary Address.* NY: Newcomen Society in North America, 1950.

DiFilippo, Thomas J. *Stephen Girard, The Man, His College and Estate,* 2nd ed. 1999. www.girardweb.com/girard/download.htm.

DiMeo, Mike. "Stephen Girard: Merchant, Mariner, Banker, Humanitarian, Patriot," Philadelphia, PA: Independence Hall Association (website owner). "UShistory.org," www.ushistory.org/people/girard.htm.

Doerflinger, Thomas. *A Vigorous Spirit of Enterprise: Merchants and Economic Development in Revolutionary Philadelphia.* Chapel Hill: University of North Carolina Press, 1986.

Dunaway, Wayland F. *A History of Pennsylvania.* New York: Prentice-Hall, 1935.

Eaton, Reed Russell. *The Public Life of Stephen Girard.* Ann Arbor, Michigan: University Microfilms, 1971.

Evans, Owen D. and Raymond I. Haskell. *Proceedings of the Girard College Centennial.* Philadelphia: Girard College Print Shop, 1948.

Fisher, Sydney George. *Men, Women and Manners in Colonial Times.* New York: J. B. Lippincott, 1897; reprinted, 2 vols., Detroit: Singing Tree Press, 1969.

Fuller, Osgood E. *Brave Men and Women Their Struggles, Failures and Triumphs,* 1884. Project Gutenberg, 2004. www.gutenberg.org/files/13942/13942-h/13942-h.htm#XXIII.

Gallatin, Albert. *The Writings of Albert Gallatin.* Edited by Henry Adams. 3 vols. Philadelphia: J. B. Lippincott, 1879.

Gates, Albert. "Stephen Girard West Indian Trade 1789-1812," *The Pennsylvania Magazine of History and Biography,* 72, no. 4, (October 1948), 311-342.

Girard College. *Presidents Report and Catalogue of Pupils.* Philadelphia, Girard College.

Girard, Stephen. The Papers of Stephen Girard, the Stephen Collection, and the Personal Library of Stephen Girard. Founders Hall, Girard College, Philadelphia. The Papers of Stephen Girard also may be seen on microfilm in the Library of the American Philosophical Society, Philadelphia. www.amphilsoc.org/mole/view?docId=ead/Mss.xxxx-ead.xml.

Goldstein, Jonathan, *Philadelphia and the China Trade, 1682-1846: Commercial, Cultural, and Attitudinal Effects.* University Park: Pennsylvania State University Press, 1978.

Herrick, Cheesman A. *Stephen Girard, Founder.* 5th ed. Philadelphia: Girard College, 1945.

——.*Girard College Worthies.* Scranton, PA: Haddon Craftsmen, 1948.

——. *History of Girard College.* Philadelphia: Girard College, 1927.

Hickey, Donald R. *The War of 1812: A Forgotten Conflict.* Urbana: University of Illinois Press, 1989.

Hoffman, John N. *Girard Estate Coal Lands in Pennsylvania, 1801–1884.* Washington: Smithsonian Institution Press, 1972.

Hubbard, Elbert. *Stephen Girard.* East Aurora, NY: Roycrofters, 1909.

Ingram, Henry Atlee. *The Life and Character of Stephen Girard.* Philadelphia: E. Stanley Hart, 1885.

_____. *The Life and Character of Stephen Girard of the City of Philadelphia, in the Commonwealth of Pennsylvania, Mariner and Merchant with an Appendix Descriptive of Girard College.* Seventh Edition Revised. Philadelphia:[s.n.], 1896. Internet Archive, 2011. archive.org/details/lifecharacterofs01ingr.

Jackson, John W. *The Delaware Bay and River Defenses of Philadelphia, 1775–1777.* Philadelphia: Philadelphia Maritime Museum, 1977.

James, C.L.R. *The Black Jacobins; Toussaint L'Ouverture and the San Domingo Revolution.* New York: Vintage Books, 1963.

Kemp, Peter. *The History of Ships.* Stamford, CT: Longmeadow Press, 1988.

Kennedy, Roger G. *Architecture, Men, Women, and Money in America, 1600–1860.* New York: Random House, 1985.

Kennedy, Roger G., *Orders From France: the Americans and the French in a Revolutionary World, 1780–1820.* New York: Alfred A. Knopf, 1989.

Klamkin, Marian. *The Return of Lafayette. 1824–1825,* New York: Scribner, 1975.

Leach, Josiah G. *The History of the Girard National Bank of Philadelphia, 1832–1902*. Philadelphia: J. B. Lippincott, 1902.

Mayo, Michael R. *The Stone Cocoon*. Warminster, PA: Neibauer Press, 1997.

McCabe, James D.,Jr. *Great Fortunes and How They Were Made; or, The Struggles and Triumphs of Our Self-Made Men*. Philadelphia, New York: George McLean, 1871. Gutenberg Project, www. gutenberg.org/files/15161/15161-h/15161-h.htm

McCullough, David. *1776*. New York: Simon & Schuster, 2005.

McMaster, John B. *The Life and Times of Stephen Girard, Mariner and Merchant*, 2 vols. Philadelphia: J. B. Lippincott, 1918. Internet Archive, 2007. Volume One: archive.org/details/ cu31924092517014. Volume Two: archive.org/details/cu31924092517022

Meese, James. *The Picture of Philadelphia*. B. and T. Kite, 1811; reprinted, New York: Arno Press and the New York Times, 1970.

Merchant of Philadelphia. *Memoirs and Auto-biography of Some of the Wealthy Citizens of Philadelphia with a Fair Estimate of their Estates, Founded upon a Knowledge of Facts; with an Appendix Containing Particular Accounts of the Lives of Stephen Girard, Jacob Ridgway, and Obed Coleman, Obtained from Authentic Sources*. Philadelphia: The Booksellers, 1846.

Miller, David S. "The Polly: A Perspective on Merchant Stephen Girard."*The Pennsylvania Magazine of History and Biography*, 112, no. 2, (April 1988), 189-208.

Minnigerode, Meade. *Certain Rich Men: Stephen Girard-John Jacob Astor-Jay Cooke-Daniel Drew-Cornelius Vanderbilt-Jay Gould-Jim Fisk*. Freeport, NY: Putnam, 1927.

Morgan, George. *The City of First, Being a Complete History of the City of Philadelphia From Its Founding, in 1682, to the Present Time*. Philadelphia: Historical Publication Society, 1927.

Morton, Thomas G. *The History of the Pennsylvania Hospital, 1751–1895*. New York: Arno Press, 1973.

Murphy, Jim. *An American Plague: The True and Terrifying Story of the Yellow Fever Epidemic of 1793*. New York: Clarion Books, 2003.

Odgers, Merle M. *Alexander Dallas Bache: Scientist and Educator, 1806–1867*. Philadelphia: University of Pennsylvania Press, 1947.

——. *Brothers of Girard*. Philadelphia: Girard College, 1944.

Outlines of a Plan for the Administration of the Girard Trust, Agreeably to the Will of the Testator, and for Reducing the City Debts and Taxes; Shewing the Violation of Stephen Girard's Will by the Present Councils, in their Plan for a College and the Consequent Forfeiture of the Whole Estate. Philadelphia, ca 1833.

Pares, Richard. *Yankees and Creoles: The Trade Between North America and the West Indies Before the American Revolution*. Cambridge: Harvard University Press, 1956.

Parton, James. *Famous Americans of Recent Times, 1867*. Project Gutenberg, 2004. www. gutenberg.org/cache/epub/12971/pg12771.html.

Perkins, Samuel G. *Reminiscences of the Insurrection in St. Domingo*. Cambridge, MA: Wilson and Son, University Press, 1886.

Philadelphia (Pa.) Board of Directors of the City of Trusts. *First Annual Report of the Directors of City Trusts for the Year 1870*. Philadelphia: (Printed by) King & Baird, 1871.

Philadelphia (Pa.) Board of Directors of City Trusts. *Annual Report of the Board of Directors of City Trusts*. Philadelphia: [The Board], 1871–1958.

Pierce, John R. and Jim Writer. *Yellow Jack: How Yellow Fever Ravaged America and Walter Read Discovered Its Deadly Secrets.* Hoboken, NJ: Wiley, 2005.

Powell, J.H. *Bring Out Your Dead: The Great Plague of Yellow Fever in Philadelphia in 1793.* Philadelphia: University of Pennsylvania Press, 1949.

Pennsylvania. Inspector of Mines and Pennsylvania Governor (1873-1879: Hartranft). *Reports of the Inspectors of Mines of the Anthracite Coal Regions of Pennsylvania, for the Year 1877.* Harrisburg: Lane S. Hart, State Printer, 1878.

Rhoades, Lillian Ione. *The Story of Philadelphia.* New York: American Book Co., 1900.

Rosenberg, Charles E. *The Care of Strangers: The Rise of America's Hospital System.* New York: Basic Books, 1987.

Rupp, George P. ed. *Semi-Centennial of Girard College, 1848-1898.* Philadelphia: J. B Lippincott, 1898.

Scherman, Katharine. *The Slave Who Freed Haiti: The Story of Toussaint L'Ouverture.* New York: Random House, 1954.

Semi-Centennial of Girard College. *Biographical Sketch of Stephen Girard, His Will, and Other Papers Relating to the College and its Development and Government. Account of the Exercises on the Occasion of the Celebration of the Opening of the College, January 3, 1898.* Philadelphia: Girard College, 1898.

Shepherd, Jack. *The Adams Chronicles, 1750-1900.* Boston: Little, Brown, 1975.

Simpson, Stephen. *Biography of Stephen Girard, with his Will Affixed Comprising an Account of his Private Life, Habits and Manners.* Philadelphia, 1832.

Smith, E. Alfred. *Stephen Girard and His Will.* Philadelphia: Girard College Alumni Association, n.d.

Stacton, David. *The Bonapartes.* New York: Simon and Schuster, 1966.

Wainwright, Nicholas B. *A Philadelphia Perspective; The Diary of Sidney George Fisher Covering the Years, 1834-1841.* Philadelphia: Historical Society of Pennsylvania, 1967.

Weigley, Russell Frank, Nicholas B. Wainwright, and Edwin Wolf, contributors, *Philadelphia: A Three Hundred Year History.* New York: Norton, 1983.

Wildes, Harry Emerson. *Lonely Midas; The Story of Stephen Girard.* New York: Farrar & Rinehart. 1943.

——. *William Penn.* New York: Macmillan 1974.

Wilson, George. *Stephen Girard, America's First Tycoon.* Conshohocken, PA: Combined Books, 1995.

——. *Yesterday's Philadelphia.* Miami. E.A. Seemann, 1975.

Wright, Robert E. *The First Wall Street: Chestnut Street, Philadelphia and the Birth of American Finance.* Chicago: University of Chicago Press, 2006.

—— and David J. Cowen. *Financial Founding Fathers: The Men Who Made America Rich.* Chicago: University of Chicago Press, 2006.

Zeil, William E., Stephen Girard, Girard College Committee on Stephen Girard Papers and Effects, and American Philosophical Society, *A Catalogue of the Personal Library of Stephen Girard, 1750-1831.* Philadelphia: Girard College and the American Philosophical Society, 1990.

——, ed. *The Diary of Peter Sequin: A Young House Guest of Stephen Girard.* Philadelphia: Girard College, 1984.

Index

CPSIA information can be obtained at www.ICGtesting.com
Printed in the USA
LVOW08s1449170716

496677LV00003B/106/P